FIREFOX AND THUNDERBIRD GARAGE

# The Garage Series

## Street-smart books about technology

Each author **presents** a unique take on solving problems, using a format designed to replicate the **experience** of Web searching.

Technology presented and **organized** by useful topic—not in a linear tutorial style.

Books that cover **whatever** needs to be covered to get the project done. Period.

**Eben Hewitt,** *Java Garage.* ISBN: 0321246233.
**Tara Calishain,** *Web Search Garage.* ISBN: 0131471481.
**Kirk McElhearn,** *iPod & iTunes Garage.* ISBN: 0131486454.
**Marc Campbell,** *Web Design Garage.* ISBN: 0131481991.
**Don Jones,** *PHP-Nuke Garage.* ISBN: 0131855166.
**Dan Livingston,** *ActionScript 2.0 Garage.* ISBN: 0131484753.

```
          <a garage is where you work.
  in a garage, you do your  work, not somebody else's.
  it's where you experiment and listen to the old ball
                          game. make music.
                                 get away.
                                  tinker.
  it's where you do projects for passion, make your own
                                rules, and
              plot like an evil genius./>
```

( Irreverent. **Culturally rooted.** )

Edgy and fun. Lively writing.
(The impersonal voice of an
omniscient narrator is not
allowed!)

[ · **Eben Hewitt, series editor** ]

Check out the series at  www.phptr.com/garageseries

# FIREFOX AND THUNDERBIRD GARAGE

## Chris Hofmann
## Marcia Knous
## John Hedtke

Prentice Hall Professional Technical Reference
Upper Saddle River, NJ • Boston • Indianapolis • San Francisco
New York • Toronto • Montreal • London • Munich • Paris • Madrid
Capetown • Sydney • Tokyo • Singapore • Mexico City

The publisher offers excellent discounts on this book when ordered in quantity for bulk purchases or special sales, which may include electronic versions and/or custom covers and content particular to your business, training goals, marketing focus, and branding interests.
For more information, please contact:

    U. S. Corporate and Government Sales
    (800) 382-3419
    corpsales@pearsontechgroup.com

For sales outside the U. S., please contact:

    International Sales
    international@pearsoned.com

Visit us on the Web: www.phptr.com

Library of Congress Catalog Number: 2005922661

Pearson Education, Inc.
Rights and Contracts Department
One Lake Street
PRENTICE
HALL   Upper Saddle River, NJ 07458
PTR

ISBN 0-13-187004-1

Text printed in the United States on recycled paper at Edwards Brothers in Ann Arbor Michigan.
First printing, April 2005

To Sweetlou, Rachel, and Sam, who are the inspiration for my life; and to Sparky, the Eddie Haskell of the dog world and ringleader at the Mozilla Foundation office. —Chris

To all of my friends and family for putting up with me, but most especially to MZJ, who makes seeking the gold of time look like it's actually within reach. —Marcia

To Brian and Fong Chinn and their son, Raymond Chinn. —John

# Contents

# About the Authors

**Chris Hofmann** is Director of Engineering at the Mozilla Foundation. For eight years, he worked at Netscape and was involved in every Netscape and Mozilla Browser release since Netscape 3.01. In August 2003 he was hired as the first employee at the Mozilla Foundation and spent the first 18 months in startup mode, working with the small team that has been successful in getting the Mozilla Foundation off the ground and running as an independent and self-sustaining organization and continuing to organize the work of thousands of open source contributors to make great Internet software. In 2004, he contributed a wide variety of management efforts that led to the worldwide release of Firefox 1.0 in November, and is helping to fulfill the Mozilla Foundation's goal of continuing to support open web standards and provide innovation and choice for Internet client software.

**M**arcia **Knous** is a Project Manager at the Mozilla Foundation and has been working with the Mozilla Project for five years. She is involved with both the Firefox and Thunderbird projects. In the freelance realm, she is a frequent contributor to a number of online websites, including www.fanstop.com, where she writes a weekly NFL column called *Monday Night Musings*. In addition, she has written dozens of online articles about the historical contributions women have made to the world of sports. Marcia has a Masters in Cinema-Television and enjoys working on films in her spare time. She recently wrapped up cinematography on the documentary *Common Hours*. Born and raised in the splendid confines of New England, Marcia now resides in the Bay Area.

**J**ohn **Hedtke** has written 24 books, close to 100 magazine articles, and hundreds of manuals and online help systems for all kinds of technical and non-technical documentation for all levels of readers. John owns and operates a company that provides writing, consulting, and training services to private and government clients in all fields. He also speaks to professional groups all over the world on subjects such as career planning, time management, and writing books and magazine articles. John is a Fellow of the Society for Technical Communication. In his spare time, John writes buttons for a button company in California, donates blood, and sings and plays banjo and guitar (something he's been doing since 1971). He says he gets a lot of requests when he plays the banjo, but he goes ahead and plays it anyhow. A long-time resident of Seattle, John now lives in Eugene, OR, with his amazingly patient wife, Marilyn, where they share four cats. He can be reached through his website, www.hedtke.com.

# Foreword

The Internet has become central to our lives—it's how we communicate, find, and share information with colleagues, friends, and family. It has permeated the fabric of our lives to the point where its enticements can now be found on prominent display on television, print media, movies, and any other form of advertising you care to think of. The Internet has grown so rapidly and taken such a hold, not just because of its fundamental utility, but also because of the ease of which people are able to make use of it. In the 1980s, for the first time computer software evolved to a point where it was possible for ordinary people to transmit and receive information through networks. The early 1990s followed with the development of the World Wide Web and software designed to navigate it—web browsers. The rich nature of the web with its graphics, flexible presentation options, and open construction made it easy for people to connect, contribute, and benefit. Throughout the 1990s and early 2000s, software vendors have focused on making connecting to the Internet as simple as possible. They have had a large degree of success. In 2002, the CIA's *The World Factbook* estimated 159 million Internet users in the United States alone.

With so many people using the Internet and the technology behind computers still being something of a mystery to most of us, in the past few years, Internet users came under attack. Computers began to slow down and crash. Data was lost or, even worse, stolen. The web experience began to degrade as more and more sites began showing popup windows with advertising. Junk email was on the rise. It became harder and harder to get value out of the Internet when much of people's time was spent dealing with this new generation of digital annoyances. The situation was in part due to the open design of the underlying systems—Microsoft Internet Explorer and Outlook/Outlook Express were never intended to be exploited in such ways, in part due to tricks of social engineering and in part due to flaws in the Internet software most people used. Microsoft had won market dominance after several years of fiercely competitive battle with Netscape Communications Corporation and ended up distributing its software to every user of Microsoft Windows, in effect becoming the portal to the Internet for most people.

Microsoft designed Internet Explorer to be a developer's paradise, an extensive programming API that allowed for rich content and add-ons to be effortlessly deployed to thousands of users. With the flexibility came a price, however—it was not long before individuals sought to capitalize on users' lack of understanding to foist "spyware" software onto their machines: key loggers, data grabbers, popup ad generators, viruses, and other deviants. Microsoft Outlook suffered a similar set of problems whereby users could inadvertently run malicious programs attached to unsolicited email.

One of Netscape's last great acts was to open its client development process with the creation of mozilla.org in 1998—the source code of its web browser and email reader would be opened for all to read, understand, and contribute to. Two and a half years after the source release in November of 2000, Netscape released Netscape 6.0 based on the results of this effort to date. The product was exceptionally buggy, slow, and laden with misguided attempts to make a quick buck from browser users. It was a product marketing disaster, and much of the remaining user base abandoned Netscape for Internet Explorer. But the core was solid, and Netscape and the open source community continued to develop the browser over the following years, improving the performance, stability, and features. Security was always important to Netscape and its customers, so the software was designed with a more restrictive view of how content should be handled.

Eventually, a group of us who had worked for Netscape during the 6.0 development cycle and some others from the Mozilla community decided that the secret to better success in the marketplace was better presentation—more of a focus on relating to the user, more focus on simplicity of purpose, and then selling the resulting software on those strengths first to a technically adept set of early adopters and then to the world as a whole. It was this set of ideals that led to the formation of the Firefox browser project, initially known as Phoenix and Firebird and the Thunderbird Email project.

By staying true to these principles, the relentless pursuit of perfection in the details of user conversion, and optimizing common tasks such as searching for and managing information while staying true to some of the original design philosophies of Mozilla and Netscape software, we have created a useful tool that is also remarkably successful at keeping much of today's Internet nastiness at bay.

That said, no software is perfect, and, as I have said, many exploits are cunning tricks of social engineering. What is really called for is an increased awareness from people as to what's going on when they browse the web. We've tried to make increased awareness easier in Firefox and Thunderbird, and we will continue to develop them to better alert you when we think you might be going down an undesirable path. But fundamentally, the more you know about the way your software and the Internet works, the safer you'll be from exploitation.

This book should give you a better understanding of what makes Firefox and Thunderbird tick, how to get the most out of them so that you get the most out of the Internet, and how to stay safe when you're online. I hope you enjoy your Internet experience with Mozilla software. Stay safe out there.

**—Ben Goodger, Lead Engineer, Firefox Project**

# Acknowledgments

**E**very book is a collaboration by literally dozens of people. The following is a list that acknowledges in an all-too-inadequate way the contributions of many people without whom this book would not be what it is now.

First, our special thanks to series editor, Eben Hewitt, technical reviewers Asa Dotzler, Eric Hamiter, Els van Bloois, and Matthew Whitworth, and Ben Goodger for providing the Foreword to the book as well as a number of helpful review comments.

Thanks go out to all of the members of the Mozilla Foundation staff as well as the mozilla.org staff. They are a dedicated group of individuals deeply committed to the project and to preserving choice on the Internet. We would also like to acknowledge anyone who has ever checked in code to Firefox, Thunderbird, and Mozilla, anyone who has taken the time and effort to file a bug in Bugzilla, and anyone who has taken the time and effort to chase down a regression window. We would like to tip our hats to all of our open source contributors and extension and theme developers. Your contributions are essential to keeping Firefox and Thunderbird at the top of their game.

We would be remiss if we did not acknowledge all of the people who keep our Mozilla Foundation infrastructure up and running—our hats off to the sysadmins, including the folks over at OSL who have been helping us out with hosting. Without their efforts, end users would not have easy download access to all of the Mozilla products as well as extensions and themes.

Finally, where would our products be without documentation? Special thanks to David Tenser for all his work on Firefox and Thunderbird help documentation.

Additional thanks to MozillaZine, for providing web forums and the Knowledge Base so that all users of Firefox and Thunderd have a place to go when they need help.

The staff at Prentice Hall:

- Karen Gettman, editor-in-chief
- Jill Harry, acquisitions editor
- Jennifer Blackwell, development editor
- Marty Rabinowitz, director of operations
- Robin O'Brien, marketing manager
- Gina Kanouse, managing editor
- Michael Thurston, project editor
- Elise Walter, copy editor
- Cheryl Lenser, senior indexer
- Jake McFarland, compositor
- Gayle Johnson, proofreader

In addition, we want to make the following personal acknowledgements:

**Chris:** To John and Marcia, whose dedication and perspiration were the keys to making this book happen.

**Marcia:** Mitchell Baker, Chris Beard, Asa Dotzler, Ben Goodger, Chris Hofmann, Elaine King, Sarah Liberman, Scott MacGregor, Myk Melez, Tracy Walker, and Cathleen Wang.

**John:** First and most importantly, I want to acknowledge my beloved wife, Marilyn, for being herself: Thank you, sweetheart; life wouldn't be half as fun without you in it. Kudos to Laura Lewin, dazzling agent, and the rest of the wonderful folks at Studio B, for great work. Thanks to Eric Smith and Nick Chase, for providing me with email accounts to test Mozilla Thunderbird with. I also want to acknowledge the gracious contributions of Kathi Graue, Elisabeth Knottingham, Daniel Lemin, Art Menius, B. Townes, Mason Williams, and Kelly Wright, for permission to include some of the websites featured in this book. And last but not least, a special thanks to Yvonne Stam for her "timely" contribution to the list of websites.

# Introduction

Welcome to *Firefox and Thunderbird Garage*. This book will introduce you to the exciting world of safe and secure browsing and email using two great products: the Firefox browser and the Thunderbird email program.

## Why This Book Is for You

This book is for you for a number of reasons. It might be that you are seeking an alternative browser or email program that will give you features that you can't get with another program. You might be looking to switch from your current browser or email program because you have concerns about security. Perhaps you are an existing Firefox or Thunderbird user who is looking for ways to get more out of the programs. Or, you just might be ready for a change from what you're using now. This book will show you what sets Firefox and Thunderbird apart from their competitors and the ways you can use both products to increase your organization and productivity. Here are some of the things that will be covered in the book:

**Proactive software = more secure software.** Firefox and Thunderbird are designed with built-in features that protect your security and privacy. Taking the "better to be safe than sorry" approach, Firefox and Thunderbird are engineered to let you know when bad things might be on the horizon. Features like remote image blocking and preventing scripts from running by default are examples of ways these products prevent potential trouble before it unfolds.

**Flexible software.** We all use browsers and email programs differently. Firefox and Thunderbird provide you with a wide variety of ways to customize the look and feel of the user interface with themes. Extensions—small programs and feature sets—can be added to Firefox and Thunderbird to enhance and extend both products' capabilities. For example, you can install an extension in Firefox that blocks advertisements, or a calendar program that runs from the Thunderbird menu. Other extensions add a bevy of additional features that will satisfy even the most discriminating user.

Both products offer many performance features. Firefox has built-in Bookmarks and Download Managers that give you extensive control for tracking your favorite websites and the files and applications you've downloaded. Similarly, Thunderbird offers you many features that let you organize your mail in different fashions, with features such as Grouped by Sort and Saved Searches.

**Dynamic software development.** There is something that sets Firefox and Thunderbird apart from commercial products. Mozilla, the organization that brings you Firefox and Thunderbird, doesn't have any interest in selling you a software product (after all, they're free) and then locking you into paying for upgrades when they're released. Firefox and Thunderbird rely on a vibrant open source community to provide input and feedback as new versions of the products are being developed. This means the software is always fresh and is continually undergoing scrutiny by the eagle eyes of open source contributors all over the world.

Finally, this book is for you because you are interested in exploring alternatives to what you already have and in learning as much as you can about harnessing the power of these programs. After reading this book, you'll have a better appreciation of open source software development and the many advantages it offers. You'll also have learned about two great programs that can make your computing life safer and more fun. Hop aboard—you're in for a fascinating ride!

## About This Book

This book is meant to be an introduction to the many features of Firefox and Thunderbird. You first learn about the open source concept and how it provides strong, secure software. You are then introduced to Firefox: what makes it unique and how to install it on your system, whether it's Windows, Linux, or Mac. As part of the installation process, you'll see how to import your settings and bookmarks from other browsers to make the process as seamless as possible. This book continues with information on security and privacy: how to surf the web and be safe while doing so. Along the way, you'll learn about making the trip less annoying by cutting out popups and advertisements.

From there, this book continues with information on the many ways in which you can search the web from within Firefox to find just the thing you're looking for. When you've found the right website, you need to keep track of it, so the book discusses bookmarks and history. Next, you'll learn about one of the most popular features of Firefox: tabbed browsing, which allows most Internet users to multi-task in a whole new way. If you're still looking for ways to enhance Firefox, you'll see how to download and install extensions, plug-ins, and themes to customize the way Firefox does things to better suit your needs. The Firefox portion of the book concludes with information about downloading and customizing toolbars.

The Thunderbird section of this book picks up with information on installing and configuring Thunderbird. You'll learn how to navigate Thunderbird and you'll also see how to get help with the product. This book continues with information on setting up your mail accounts, with a particular eye toward migrating from an existing email program to minimize the time and effort you need to spend. You'll next see how to avoid spam—the bane of email everywhere!—and avoid viruses and trojan horses that may come in via email. There's extensive information on setting up mail folders and filtering your mail to them automatically. Finally, you'll see how to customize Thunderbird using extensions and themes, similar to what you saw earlier for Firefox. Specific technical information is contained in a variety of appendices.

**TOOL KIT**

**To Linux and Mac Users**

There are some necessary differences in the Firefox and Thunderbird keyboard commands and menu options between the Windows, Linux, and Mac versions. For example, where Windows keyboard commands frequently incorporate the Ctrl key, Mac commands use the Cmd key. And while Windows and Linux keyboard commands and menu options are usually the same (or very similar), it's not always true... and Mac menus can be different from both. In some cases, we've added the Linux and Mac commands to the text, but not always, simply because it would've complicated some otherwise straightforward procedures too much to no good effect. The book tends to use Windows commands only because the majority of our readers are likely to be using Firefox and Thunderbird on Windows and not because we're trying to express a personal preference for one operating system over another. The appendices have a comprehensive list of keyboard commands, mouse commands, and menu options for Windows, Linux, and Mac versions. If you're using a Linux or Mac system, you'll quickly pick up the few differences, and you'll be zipping along before you know it.

# How This Book Is Organized

This book is divided into 13 chapters. Each chapter discusses one or two aspects of Firefox or Thunderbird and how to apply these programs to your specific browsing and email needs. Chapters and concepts are organized in the order you are most likely to need them.

Chapter 1, "Getting Started," introduces you to the open source model of software development and why Firefox is so cool. You learn what you need in the way of hardware and software to install Firefox on your computer. You'll also see how to get around in Firefox, how to transfer your settings and bookmarks from other browsers, and how to get help from a variety of sources.

In Chapter 2, "Protecting Your Security and Privacy," you see how Firefox protects you from several serious security risks. The chapter first describes spyware, one of the biggest security and privacy problems on the web, and shows you how to avoid it. You then see how to use the Firefox Password Manager to maintain a comprehensive list of passwords. You also learn how to clean out your cache and your history to prevent someone from snooping on your computer and seeing what you've been doing on the Internet.

Chapter 3, "Ridding Yourself of the Annoyances of the Web," is a short but snappy exposition on how to stop popups and banner ads from throwing sand in the gears. You'll see how to suppress popup windows and how to avoid obnoxious graphics, either wholesale or selectively.

Chapter 4, "Searching the Web," tells you how to use Firefox's built-in searching features. You first learn about the Search bar and how to augment it. The chapter then shows you how to use the Find features to search for information within a web page. The chapter concludes with information about Smart Keywords, quick (and customizable) keywords to get you to a variety of websites for quick information.

Chapter 5, "Bookmarks and History," describes how to save and view information about the websites you've been to. You first see how to create bookmarks of various kinds, including live bookmarks that update automatically. You learn how to organize bookmarks into folders and to sort them, both on the bookmark list and through the Bookmarks Manager. The chapter also shows you how to import and export bookmarks. In addition, you see how to use bookmarklets, very small single-purpose applications that look like bookmarks. The chapter concludes with information on how to use the sidebar to display your bookmarks as well as the history of the websites you've been to already.

Chapter 6, "Harnessing the Power of Tabbed Browsing," teaches you how to use one of Firefox's most popular features: tabs. You learn what tabs are, how to create them, and how to open web pages in them. You also see how to open entire folders in tabs on-the-fly.

Chapter 7, "Customizing Firefox with Third-Party Extensions and Themes," introduces extensions and themes. The chapter opens with a description of where to look for extensions and how to download and install them. The chapter then takes you on a cook's tour of the types of extensions available for Firefox and some of the best extensions out there. You next learn about themes and how to change the look and feel of Firefox with a theme. You also see a few themes that you might want to try yourself.

In Chapter 8, "Other Interesting Features," you learn about downloading files using the Download Manager. You see how to pause and resume downloads and clear your download history. You also learn about such diverse topics as printing, customizing toolbars, and zooming in and out on a website's text.

Chapter 9, "Getting Started with Mozilla Thunderbird," introduces you to Thunderbird, the email client. You learn what you need in the way of hardware and software and you see how to install it on your computer. After a brief discussion of the basic screen elements, the chapter concludes with information on where to find·online help.

Chapter 10, "Setting Up Your Mail, RSS, and Newsgroup Accounts Using Mozilla Thunderbird," shows you how to migrate your settings and email information from other email programs that you have been using. The chapter shows you how to set up and configure your email accounts in Thunderbird, including how to set up RSS (news) accounts. You also see how to send and receive messages, use the address book, and maintain multiple email accounts in the same program.

Chapter 11, "Protecting Your Privacy and Blocking Spam," gives you tips on how to avoid spam and what to do with it when it does show up. The chapter teaches you about junk mail and how to filter it automatically. You also see how to use passwords and privacy options to make sure you're as secure as possible.

Chapter 12, "Organizing Your Email Topics," presents information about filtering email and using folders to organize your email so you can find it easily in the future. You'll also learn about sorting, doing quick searches, and using mail views and mail labels.

In Chapter 13, "Customizing the Look and Feel of Mozilla Thunderbird," you learn about extensions and themes for Thunderbird (similar to what you saw earlier in Chapter 7). You also learn how to customize the toolbars in Thunderbird for maximum efficiency.

In addition to the chapters, there are six appendices:

Appendix A, "Keyboard and Mouse Shortcuts for Firefox," lists the keyboard and mouse shortcuts that are available to you in Firefox for Windows, Linux, and Mac. You also see how these compare to the keyboard and mouse shortcuts in several other browsers, so your conversion process from another browser to Firefox is made that much easier.

Appendix B, "Keyboard and Mouse Shortcuts for Mozilla Thunderbird," does much the same as Appendix A did for Firefox.

Appendix C, "Menu Commands for Firefox," and Appendix D, "Menu Commands for Mozilla Thunderbird," list the menus and commands for both programs and gives a description of what each menu command and option does.

Appendix E, "Hacking Configuration Files," gives the technically minded some background on how you can get into the code for the product configuration files and make programmatic changes to what happens.

Appendix F, "Security, Certificates, and Validation" tells you how to set some additional security options and how to work with digital certificates.

# PART 1:

## Firefox

**C**ongratulations! You have the premiere book on Firefox and Thunderbird, the new stars of open source software. The first part of this book deals with Firefox, the Internet browser. The chapters show you how to install it, how to use its many security features and prevent web annoyances, how to find the websites you need and bookmark them for future reference, how to enhance Firefox with extensions and themes, and how to download files, print web pages, and customize toolbars.

This part doesn't have to be read in order, although it's probably best if you read Chapter 1, "Getting Started," first to learn the vocabulary of Firefox concepts. But you can dip into the book wherever you like and spread out from there. Already have Firefox on your computer and want to learn how to use Smart Keywords to make your life easier? Jump to Chapter 4, "Searching the Web." Need to find out how to take advantage of Firefox's many security features? Go straight to Chapter 2, "Protecting Your Security and Privacy." You can even open the book at random and see what you can learn in the way of tips, techniques, web games, and popover recipes.

This book as a whole doesn't have to be read in order, either. If you're more interested in Thunderbird, the Mozilla email program, you can skip the Firefox part entirely and start with Chapter 9, "Getting Started with Mozilla Thunderbird," and then go from there. But when you're done with that part of the book, be sure to come back here; Firefox is way too cool a program not to learn more about. And you really do need to try the popover recipe.

# Getting Started

## What Is Firefox?

Firefox is a powerful new Internet browser from the Mozilla Foundation that runs on Windows, Mac OS X, and Linux. It has an incredible array of features that help you browse faster, safer, and more effectively, including a built-in popup blocker, text zooming, tabbed browsing, built-in search tools, and live bookmarks.

Possibly the best reason to use Firefox is its many enhanced security features. A comprehensive set of privacy tools keeps your online activity your business. You can also install a wide range of themes and extensions to customize the browser's appearance and enhance its capabilities to suit the way you surf the web. It's all free!

Millions of people are trying Firefox. You should, too!

**DO OR DIE:**

>> Firefox 101

>> Open source. It's a good thing.

>> Mozilla, not Godzilla

>> Finding your way around

>> Getting help, both local and remote

## What Is Open Source?

Firefox is one of many *open source* products, along with the Linux operating system, the Apache web server, and the OpenOffice Suite. Open source products are products for which the source code is available for users to examine and, if they wish, to modify. This model promotes software reliability and quality via a worldwide community of developers who can submit their own improvements to the code or simply patch it for their specific needs. The open source model differs radically from the "closed source" or "proprietary" model used by Microsoft, Adobe, and most other software manufacturers, who will do almost anything to prevent outsiders from viewing their products' source code.

Open source software is not freeware (although most open source products, including Firefox, are free), nor does it just mean that users can have access to the source code. The license for a true open source product must provide for such things as

- Free redistribution
- Modified and derivative works (all of which can also be distributed under the same terms as the original product)
- No discrimination against persons, groups, or fields of endeavor
- No restrictions on other software
- Software that's not predicated on a specific technology or style of interface (such as Microsoft's .NET technology or a requirement that the product looks like a Macintosh product)

Open source products are often released under the General Public License (GNU) or other similar licenses. Firefox is released under the Mozilla Public License, but if you're interested in finding out more, you can find a selection of open source licenses at the Open Source Initiative website (www.opensource.org).

Most open source products have a devoted community of hundreds and even thousands of developers who are deeply interested in making the products stronger and better. As a result, open source software tends to be more robust: as soon as bugs or security holes are found (all software has bugs), the community of programmers usually discusses the problem, and typically several people will develop and release patches to the source code.

According to the Open Source Initiative, open source is good for consumers and businesses because it lets everyone review, distribute, and modify the code for software, which results in a faster evolutionary cycle. You don't have to wait for [insert the name of any large software company here] to identify problems and issue patches or updates for a product; you can usually get a programmer to develop a custom correction or modification right away. In addition, because the source code is available, you're never held hostage by a company's pricing, its desire to release new versions, or its continued existence. The people who use the products can adapt, patch, or even enhance them to meet their own requirements.

**Are there other open source products?**

Open source doesn't apply just to software. Creative Commons is open source-style licensing for all kinds of intellectual property: audio, images, video, text—even curricula of all kinds (http://creativecommons.org). The licenses let you release intellectual property for general distribution without losing all rights by putting it into the public domain. You can share the things you create while still having some license protection against outright expropriation of your work.

There's even open source beer: a delightful beer called "Vores Øl" ("our beer") is brewed by a group of students at the IT-University in Copenhagen under a Creative Commons License. The beer is deep golden-red with an aromatic hops bouquet. You can't buy the beer—at least, not yet—but the recipe is published on their website (http://www.voresoel.dk/main.php?id=70), so you can brew it yourself. You can also use their recipe to create your own beers, even commercial brews, provided that you publish any derivative recipes under the same License.

# A Brief History of Firefox

Firefox is the result of many different efforts that grew together. Many of these were the outgrowth of innovative efforts to develop software in new ways and using open source communities of volunteers in the development and promotion of the software. In many ways, Firefox is a response to years of development of browsing software and reflects a passion to improve the software most often used by millions of people each day.

## The Start of Mozilla

Firefox is a direct outgrowth of the Mozilla project, started in 1998 by Netscape to engage a volunteer engineering development community that could help Netscape with continued development of the Netscape browser and associated Internet software technology. As part of this effort, Netscape released the source for the Netscape browser under a combination of open source licenses. Later that year, efforts began to rewrite much of the Netscape code to make it easier to understand and to facilitate future development. (This was the result of substantial pressure put on Netscape by the new community that sprang up around Mozilla.) A key element was the rewrite of the Netscape browser layout engine and the creation of a cross-platform application development platform that would allow developers to create a single application for Windows, Macintosh, and Linux.

**FRIDGE**

Not familiar with the "early days" of the Internet? If you only started on the Internet in the last few years and aren't familiar with Netscape and things that happened before the turn of the calendar, you may want to check out two documentaries: "Code Rush" (2000) and "Nerds 2.0.1: A Brief History of the Internet" (1998). "Code Rush" focuses on a year in the life of Netscape and the days leading up to the release of the Netscape source code. "Nerds 2.0.1" is a collection of interviews with many of the players who made the Internet what it is today.

Although most of the rewrite was initially done by Netscape engineers, an engineering community composed of professors, grad students, undergrads, and even high school students began to get involved in research, code development, and testing. Between 1998 and 2003, several of the most visible and active volunteer contributors were hired by Netscape as full-time contributors and summer interns as Netscape and AOL funded a large percentage of the development work. Companies such as IBM, Sun Microsystems, Oracle, Red Hat, and Novell joined with scores of small Silicon Valley startups such as Monta Vista, OEOne, Active State, and many others to participate in the development of the code.

The early years of the project were focused not only on designing the Mozilla Suite—a combined web browser, email and newsgroup client, IRC chat client, and HTML editor—and creating the core technology, but also in trying to figure out how to develop software using this revolutionary model as well as building the development and testing communities.

As the project continued, daily test releases of the Mozilla Suite spurred the development of a community of thousands of Mozilla developers and testers. Bugs are reported in the project's open bug database, Bugzilla (https://bugzilla.mozilla.org). This daily testing and monitoring of feedback from testers and users has helped keep the application stable, even as new features are added.

Mozilla 1.0 was released on June 5, 2002. Mozilla 1.0 included many new features, such as popup blocking, that attracted many people interested in using the newest technology. While Mozilla 1.0 was originally intended to be a test platform for technology and features that would in turn be incorporated into Netscape Navigator and was the foundation of the Netscape 7.0 browser, and Mozilla started getting publicity in its own right.

A new community of localization experts and translators began to form around creating international releases of Mozilla. About 15 language versions were produced for Mozilla 1.0 and. Since then, the Mozilla Suite has been translated into over 100 languages.

## Beyond the Mozilla Suite

Many of the engineers working on the Mozilla Suite knew there was room for substantial improvement. Because Mozilla originally was a test platform for Netscape, it had become a kitchen sink for a long list of features and had a user interface that was hard for many users to understand and operate. If a Mozilla browser was ever going to make it into the general user population, a new, streamlined application was needed.

Blake Ross and Dave Hyatt, Netscape employees at the time, with input from a few friends and colleagues, began work on some of these ideas to create a new Mozilla browser in early 2002. The goals for the project were simple: start from scratch at the user interface level and create a very small, fast, easy-to-use browser that had only the features most commonly used by the majority of users. This new Mozilla browser would also provide an extension mechanism that would let users customize the browser for particular individual needs and would provide a framework for continued experimentation and innovation. The project involved building a new user interface from scratch that would use the solid and well-tested "Gecko" core technology that shipped with the Mozilla Suite.

That summer, a small community of engineers, including Blake Ross, Ben Goodger, Asa Dotzler, Dave Hyatt, Pierre Chanial, Joe Hewitt, Brian Ryner, Ian Hickson, and several Netscape summer interns, began working to create a browser application that would eventually become Firefox. Although Hyatt left for Apple to work on the Safari browser in early 2003, Blake continued to work on the Mozilla browser.

There were a number of promising developments early in the project. The engineers found ways to drastically reduce the application's size and improve its performance. Team members also watched the browsing habits of many users to determine the most efficient ways of doing things. The team also examined hundreds of ideas and suggestions for improving the browser, resulting in a reduced number of keystrokes or mouse clicks to perform frequent browsing tasks. Ideas that had been built up over a decade of browser development and use began to be incorporated.

In 2003, AOL announced the shutdown of the Netscape Development team and a $2 million grant and support for the creation of an independent "Mozilla Foundation." Many engineers who had been working on Netscape releases and the underlying Mozilla technology were reassigned to other projects within AOL. With $2 million from AOL, and funding sponsorships from IBM, Sun, and Mitch Kapor (of Lotus 1-2-3 fame), the Mozilla Foundation was launched with an initial management team of Mitchell Baker, Brendan Eich, Chris Hofmann, and Bart Decrem.

**Note**

Using the same goals of making simple, small, fast standalone applications built from the Mozilla technology core, Seth Spitzer and Scott MacGregor started to develop a standalone email application that would eventually become Thunderbird and be a companion to the Firefox browser. Other projects were also started to develop a standalone HTML editor and a calendar application based on the components of the core Mozilla platform.

## Firefox 1.0

One of the first things the Mozilla Foundation did was to hire a few key engineers for the Firefox and Thunderbird projects, as well as for Gecko (the browser engine), build management, tools and infrastructure, and QA, testing, and releases. The Mozilla Foundation also continued to build communities and secure funding for long-term survival of the Mozilla technology. Shortly after they set up an office in Mountain View, CA, there was a release of Mozilla Suite 1.5 and experimental versions of Firefox and Thunderbird. About 120 primary developers and thousands of QA volunteers and testers contributed to those releases.

**FRIDGE**

For a complete list of contributors to the Mozilla project, go to the Firefox address bar, enter "about:credits," and click Go. For everyone who's contributed to Firefox, go to Help | About Mozilla Firefox and click Credits to see a scrolling list of contributors.

Early in 2004, the blogging community picked up on what was happening. Word-of-mouth praise for Firefox spread quickly. Most of the early users were attracted by the simple design of Firefox and the significant improvements in usability over other browsers. Users were also excited by Firefox's adaptability: if the browser didn't do what you wanted it to do, you could create or install a simple extension to customize the browser to suit your needs. New extensions were appearing at the rate of three to five a week, and by May 2004, over 200 extensions for Firefox and Thunderbird were available.

Interest in Firefox continued to increase dramatically. In June 2004, the top websites started seeing a significant number of Firefox users, the first sign of Firefox's reaching beyond the technical community and into the mainstream browser population. The following month, the U.S. government's Computer Emergency Readiness Team (US-CERT) warned web surfers to stop using Microsoft's Internet Explorer (IE) browser and use alternative browsers because of "significant vulnerabilities" in technologies embedded in IE. (This warning came on the heels of a sophisticated attack by malicious software (or *malware*) that targeted a known IE flaw.) The warning called out many security problems specific to the IE browser.

Traffic to the Mozilla website and downloads of Mozilla software began to grow dramatically with the CERT announcement, with up to 200,000 downloads a day. With Firefox still in prerelease versions, many users began trying it out as the alternative to IE. Because Firefox was being developed on top of a highly stable core browser technology developed from years of testing and use, and most of its streamlined and advanced user interface was completed, it appeared to many as a polished application not reflective of its "prerelease" version number. With its protections against the problems specified in the CERT warning, the number of people trying Firefox and sticking with it began to grow quickly.

In early August 2004, the Firefox development team began to brainstorm about how to leverage the new interest in browsers and create a grassroots effort to spread the word. Two groups working in parallel—Mike Homer, a former Netscape executive, and Bart Decrem, Blake Ross, and Asa Dotzler—worked out ways to build another Mozilla community around marketing and spreading the word about Firefox. Working with Bart Decrem, Chris Messina, and Daryl Houston, Spreadfirefox.com was launched. It played a key role in evangelizing the Firefox Preview Release and the 1.0 release. It also became another important promotional idea and fund-raising venue for the project: the Spreadfirefox team raised over $250,000 from 10,000 Firefox devotees in just 10 days to pay for a two-page ad in the *New York Times* and cover other expenses to promote the Firefox 1.0 release.

Market share of the Firefox browser started with very small numbers but grew dramatically over the second half of 2004. Over 8 million people downloaded the final prerelease version of Firefox. Within 100 days after the release of Firefox 1.0 on November 9, 2004, there were 25 million downloads and counting. (Similarly, over three million copies of Thunderbird 1.0 were downloaded in the first two months of its release in early December.) According to WebSideStory.com and OneStat.com in January 2005, IE usage had dropped by 5 to 7 percent in the preceding six months, with Firefox gaining almost the entire lost market share of IE.

## What Makes Firefox Unique?

Firefox has an exceptional collection of features:

- **Popup blocking**—Firefox's built-in popup blocker is very effective at stopping most popup ads completely.

- **Tabbed browsing**—Tabbed browsing lets you view multiple web pages in a single instance of the browser. You can also use this feature to open links in the background: while a link is loading in one window, you can continue working in another window.

- **Privacy and security**—Firefox has been designed with privacy and security in mind. Not only does Firefox not load potentially harmful ActiveX controls, but it also has a comprehensive set of tools to keep your online activity private.

- **Search features**—Google Search is built into the browser. Firefox also has Smart Keywords that let you customize quick searches with your favorite websites so you can just type a short keyword, add the information you want to look up, and there you are! Another great search feature is the Firefox Find bar, which finds text as you type without covering up anything on the screen.

Your system will now use IE as the default browser. You'll also need to change the file association settings so that Windows knows to open HTML (and other) files with IE instead of Firefox, too:

1. Open the Windows Explorer.
2. Right-click a file that you want IE to open, and select Open With from the context menu.
3. You may be able to select IE directly from the list of programs on the submenu; if not, select Choose Program and then select IE on the Open With screen.

Windows will now open all files of that type with IE. You'll need to do this with each type of file that you want IE to open. For example, Windows thinks of a file with an extension of .htm as different from one with an extension of .html.

### Will Firefox work on an older PC running Windows 98?

Yes. See the system requirements information immediately following this section for more information.

### Is Firefox supported for Mac OS 8/9.x?

No. Firefox is supported only for Mac OS X at this time.

### Is Firefox a replacement for MSN, AOL, or other online services?

These services provide both connectivity to the Internet and software for browsing. You can continue to use the connectivity parts of these services and use Firefox for browsing after you have connected to the Internet from any online service.

### Is Firefox available in my native language?

Chances are very good that it is. Firefox 1.0 was released with about a dozen different translated versions, and more translations (the count is close to 30 right now) are added all the time. See http://www.mozilla.org/products/firefox/all.html for the current list of translations available.

### Does Firefox have 128-bit encryption for secure transactions and banking on the Internet?

Yes, Firefox (and Thunderbird) supports encryption up to 256 bits and is suitable for secure transactions on the Internet. You can use Firefox with your bank or any other financial institution that requires strong encryption to protect your personal data. Firefox can also be customized to give you an alert when you access or leave a secure page.

### I'm very concerned about downloading files from the Internet. How do I know that I have a "safe" copy of Firefox (one that was produced by the Mozilla Foundation and not by some imposter)?

Magyarkuti Barna has a guide that explains how to make sure you have a Mozilla-approved download. You can find it at
http://bmagyarkuti.blogspot.com/2004/12/validating-your-firefox-installer-file.html.

# What Do You Need to Run Firefox?

If your computer is capable of getting on the web, chances are very good that there's a version of Firefox you can install on your computer. Firefox runs on Windows, Linux, and Macintosh computers. Here's what you need to run Firefox on each type of system.

## Windows

Firefox runs on virtually all versions of Windows currently in popular usage: Windows 98, 98SE, Me, NT 4.0, 2000, XP (recommended), and Windows Server 2003.

You also need the following minimum hardware requirements:

- Pentium 233 MHz (a Pentium 500 MHz or greater is recommended)
- 64 MB RAM (128 MB RAM or greater is recommended)
- 52 MB of hard drive space

## Linux

For Linux, you need the Linux kernel 2.2.14 with at least the following libraries or packages:

- glibc 2.3.2
- XFree86-3.3.6
- gtk+2.0
- fontconfig (also known as xft)
- libstdc++5

Firefox has been tested on Red Hat Linux 8.0 and later. You also need the following minimum hardware requirements:

- Intel Pentium II or AMD K6-III+ 233 MHz CPU (a Pentium 500 MHz or greater is recommended)
- 64 MB RAM (128 MB RAM or greater is recommended)
- 52 MB of hard drive space

**Note**

Linux distributors may provide packages for your distribution that have different requirements.

## Macintosh

Firefox runs on Mac OS X 10.1.x and later versions.

You also need the following minimum hardware requirements:

- PowerPC 604e 266 MHz (a PowerPC G4 667 MHz or greater is recommended)
- G3, G4, 64 MB RAM (256 MB RAM or greater is recommended)
- 72 MB of hard drive space

In other words, you can install Firefox on almost any computer that you can run almost any browser on.

**Note**

Users have reported that they have successfully installed and used Firefox 1.0 on computers with significantly less horsepower than the requirements listed here. Feel free to try it if you're feeling adventurous, and then drop the folks at Mozilla a line on how it all worked out. But don't be surprised if there are problems with speed or missing features.

**Why not use Mozilla?**

Because Mozilla's been around longer, you might think it'd be better to use Mozilla than Firefox. Actually, Mozilla (also known as the Mozilla Application Suite or Mozilla 1.x) is an all-in-one Internet solution that includes a browser, email client, HTML editor, and IRC chat client, as well as an array of development tools. However, Mozilla doesn't have many of the advantages of Firefox, such as customizable toolbars. Firefox is also small and fast, which makes it a better choice for browsing. In addition, although Thunderbird is a wonderful email program, there's no reason to download the entire Mozilla suite if you want to use only the browser. You can even add IRC capabilities to Firefox with an extension. (You can get more information on selecting the right products for you at http://www.mozilla.org/products/choosing-products.html.)

# Installing Firefox

One of many things I find appealing about Firefox is that it's readily available and easy to install, regardless of your operating system. To install Firefox, first get a copy at http://www.mozilla.org or at http://www.firefox.com.

> **Note**
>
> You can order a Firefox CD from the Mozilla Store at http://www.mozillastore.com if you like, but it's probably easier and faster to download the software and then burn it to a CD yourself if you need to carry it around.

After the software is downloaded, follow the instructions in one of the next sections, depending on your computer.

## On a Windows Computer

Double-click the Firefox Setup 1.0.exe installer file. The installation procedure walks you through the installation process. If you want to pick a destination directory and install options such as DOM Inspector instead of using the defaults, you should use the custom installation. On the other hand, if you're willing to trust Firefox's choices—a reasonable idea!—just go for the standard installation selection.

> **Note**
>
> In the unlikely event that you're installing Firefox on a Windows 98 computer, be aware that the Firefox icon may appear as a Windows icon. You can change this back to the normal Firefox icon if you like.

## On a Linux Computer

After you extract the tarball, enter the following commands to start the installation:

```
tar -xzvf firefox-1.0.installer.tar.gz
cd firefox-installer
./firefox-installer
```

If Nautilus is configured on your system to run executable text files, you can skip the previous commands and just double-click firefox-installer to start the installation.

> **Note**
>
> If you install Firefox to a location that has spaces in the path, Firefox may have a problem setting itself as the default browser. If this happens, Firefox will prompt you each time you start it to make it the default browser. You can fix this by installing Firefox into a path without spaces.

## On a Mac OS X Computer

Decompress and mount the Firefox 1.0.dmg.dz Disk Image by double-clicking it. (Depending on how you downloaded the Firefox installation file, this may have been done automatically.) Next, double-click the Firefox Disk Image to open it in the Macintosh Finder, and then drag Firefox to your hard disk. You can drag Firefox to your Application folder if you prefer. Unlike the Windows and Linux versions, the Mac version installs everything in the Firefox installation package. (You probably won't notice a difference, but you should know about it.)

**What else can I load Firefox on?**

The Minimo (Mini Mozilla) project is aimed at reducing Firefox's size and memory requirements so that you can load Firefox, or a smaller version thereof, on a number of handheld devices. The Minimo version will look pretty much like the version of Firefox you're used to seeing on your desktop or laptop computer, but it'll still do most of the same things.

Early test versions of Minimo are already available for Windows CE and a few other small devices. For the latest information, check out http://www.mozilla.org/projects/minimo.

# Importing Settings from Other Browsers

It's usually a major effort to switch from one application to another. Not only do you usually have to learn a whole new set of finger habits, but you also have to configure the new application to make it work the way you want it to. Firefox makes transitioning from another browser fairly simple by importing configuration information from other browsers as part of the installation process. Firefox can import your settings, preferences, and favorites from IE, Netscape, Mozilla Suite, Safari, Opera, OmniWeb, or iCab.

When you install Firefox for the first time on your computer, the Firefox Import Wizard starts automatically so that you can import settings (as shown in Figure 1-1).

All the browsers from which you can import settings and information appear on the screen. Select the browser from which you want to import settings, and click Next. (You can also choose not to import anything at this time by selecting **Don't import anything.**) Firefox imports the following types of information:

- **Internet options:** Firefox imports the browser's general settings and configures itself to match them as closely as possible.

- **Cookies:** Many websites save information about you and how you used the website—such as login information or basic website preferences—on your com-

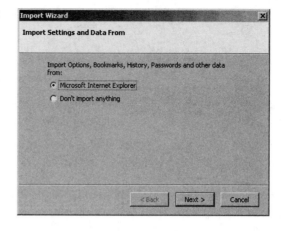

Figure 1-1

*The Import Wizard main screen.*

puter in a small file known as a *cookie* so that the next time you go to the website, the website is configured automatically for you. Firefox imports any cookies it can find from the browser so that you don't have to re-enter your login and preferences for each website you normally visit.

- **Browsing history:** Firefox imports the history of the websites you have visited to the Firefox history list.

- **Saved form history:** Firefox imports the information you enter in website forms. The next time you go to the website, Firefox can enter the information in the form's fields.

- **Saved passwords:** Firefox imports your saved passwords into the Password Manager. The next time you go to a website for which you have a saved password, Firefox can enter the password information in the login fields.

- **Favorites:** Firefox imports the favorites (also known as *bookmarks*, depending on which browser you're importing from) from the selected browser, including the folders and the order they appear in.

> **Note**
>
> A few bookmarks come with Firefox. Any imported bookmarks appear in addition to these. You're not stuck with any of these, of course; you'll learn how to add, modify, and delete bookmarks in Chapter 5, "Bookmarks and History."

**18**

**Figure 1-2**

*The Importing
screen of
the Import
Wizard.*

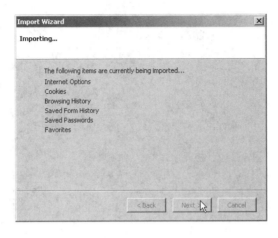

While Firefox is importing information from the selected browser, it displays a screen like the one shown in Figure 1-2.

When Firefox is done importing—the whole process should take only a minute or two—it briefly displays a screen that basically says, "All done!" You can click Finish or just ignore it; the screen disappears in a moment in any case.

## Opera Bookmarks

**TOOL KIT**

While Firefox is generally guaranteed not to rip, run, rag, bag, wheeze, sneeze, fall out at the knees, or smell bad in hot weather, it doesn't always import everything directly. If you're using Opera as your browser and you want to import your bookmarks into Firefox, you must use a third-party conversion tool to first convert the Opera bookmarks into an HTML file that you can then import through the Bookmarks Manager into Firefox (a process that's described in Chapter 5).

One of the best of these tools for Windows computers is Bookmark Converter (catchy name), available at www.magnusbrading.com/bmc. Many other utilities convert your bookmarks/favorites to an HTML file, too; check www.shareware.com for similar tools for your browser or operating system.

If you have several browsers from which you want to import settings, you can import the settings from one browser initially and then import selected items from other browsers at any time. Start the Import Wizard by selecting File | Import, and then select the browser you want to import settings from. The Items to Import screen (shown in Figure 1-3) appears.

You can select individual items to import. Check the boxes for the items you want to import, and click Next. Again, the import process is fast and painless.

**Figure 1-3**

*The Items to
Import screen
of the Import
Wizard.*

> **Caution**
>
> Favorites/bookmarks are added to the current list of bookmarks without overwriting, but importing the Internet options reconfigures the look and feel of Firefox to match the new settings as closely as possible (depending on which options are available in the other browser and what you choose to import). If you import Internet options from several browsers, Firefox has the look and feel of the most recent set of Internet options.

## Learning Your Way Around Firefox

After you've got Firefox installed, you need to take a quick tour of the Firefox screen and learn your way around. Figure 1-4 shows the Firefox screen.

**Figure 1-4**
*The Firefox screen.*

1. Title bar
2. Menu bar
3. Navigation bar
4. Bookmarks toolbar
5. Tab bar
6. Window (also known as "display window")
7. Find bar
8. Status bar
9. Live Bookmark (RSS) indicator icon
10. Location field (also known as "address field," "address bar," or "URL field")
11. Search bar

As you can see in Figure 1-4, Firefox is refreshingly clear and simple. You won't, however, have to get used to a completely new screen design. In fact, many of the menu commands and keyboard shortcuts are similar to those you're probably already used to. See Appendix A, "Keyboard and Mouse Shortcuts for Firefox," and Appendix C, "Menu Commands for Firefox," for more information.

## Setting Firefox Options

Although the Import Wizard sets up Firefox to act as much like your previous browser did as possible, you may still want to set additional options to further customize Firefox for your needs.

To set options, start by going to Tools | Options | General. The Options screen with the General options appears, as shown in Figure 1-5.

You can set the following options on this screen:

**Tip**

If you have several pages displayed using tabs, and you click Use Current Page, Firefox sets all the pages as home pages. The next time you start Firefox or click the Home icon, all the pages will be displayed. (You'll learn how to use tabs in Chapter 6.)

- **Home Page:** To set a home page, enter the location in the Location(s) field. You can use the page currently displayed by clicking Use Current Page. You can also select an existing bookmark and use that for your home page. If you prefer to have no home page at all—just a blank screen—click Use Blank Page.

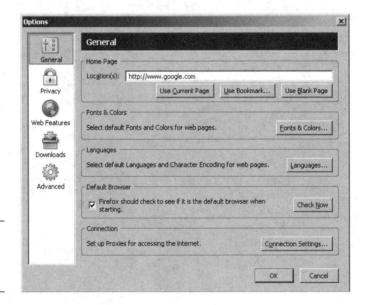

**Figure 1-5**

*The Options screen with the General options displayed.*

- **Fonts & Colors:** Click Fonts & Colors to display a standard font and color selection screen. You can select the default font, size, and display characteristics to use for displaying standard text, as well as the default text, link, and background colors. You can also override the fonts and colors specified in a web page with your own settings.

- **Languages:** Click the Languages button to specify the languages and character sets in which you prefer to see web pages.

- **Default Browser:** Check the box to set Firefox as the default browser on your computer. If you're not sure if Firefox is the default browser, click Check Now to see.

- **Connection:** Click Connection Settings to enter proxy information for your Internet connection. (If you don't know what this is, don't mess with it.)

When you are satisfied with your entries, click Advanced on the left of the screen. (Privacy options are covered in Chapter 2, "Protecting Your Security and Privacy," web feature options are covered in Chapter 3, "Ridding Yourself of the Annoyances of the Web," and download options are covered in Chapter 8, "Other Interesting Features.") The Advanced options screen appears, as shown in Figure 1-6.

You need to set only a few of the options on this screen for now. (The remainder of the options on this screen are dealt with later in this book.)

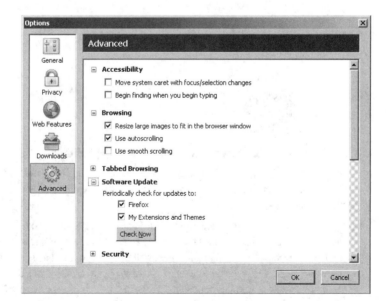

**Figure 1-6**

*The Options screen with the advanced options displayed.*

- **Move system caret with focus/selection changes:** Check this box if you're using an accessibility aid such as a screen magnifier or a screen reader that uses the system caret as the focus for what to magnify or read; otherwise, leave it unchecked.

- **Begin finding when you begin typing:** Check this box if you want Firefox to find information on the current web page as you type it into the Find toolbar. (Finding information in web pages is covered in Chapter 4, "Searching the Web.")

- **Resize large images to fit in the browser window:** Check this box to automatically resize images that are too large to fit into the Firefox window. You can click the image to display it again at its full size.

- **Use autoscrolling:** Check this box to be able to scroll web pages by holding down the middle mouse button or scroll wheel and moving the mouse up or down.

- **Use smooth scrolling:** Check this box to scroll web pages when you press Page Down or Space. If the box is unchecked, pages jump to the next screen. This feature is purely a religious preference: some folks like the screen to move smoothly, and others like it to jump to the next location. It takes the same amount of time either way, so try both options when you're reading a really long web page, and see what you prefer.

- **Software Update:** Check the boxes to have Firefox automatically look for updates to the Firefox software itself and to any extensions or themes you may have installed.

When you are satisfied with your entries, click OK.

**FAQ**

**Can I remove IE after I'm happy with Firefox?**

Although you may feel like you'll never need IE again after using Firefox for a very short time—I sure did!—there are actually some good reasons for keeping IE on your computer even if it will just gather dust.

- Many websites are programmed using ActiveX and other IE features and simply don't work with Firefox. For example, I've seen a few online accounting systems and a couple of web game sites that don't work well with Firefox; one popular weight-watching website actively blocks people not using IE or a recent version of Netscape or Safari. For these websites, you'll need to use IE.
- Both Norton and McAfee anti-virus software need IE to run automatic updates. Again, you may be able to download and manually install virus updates, but it's a lot more work.

■ For Windows users, removing IE from your computer is tricky because it's deeply integrated with the operating system. Worse, removing IE may have effects on your Internet connection as well as breaking Internet-enabled features in program plug-ins and other applications.

The bottom line is that it's probably easiest and safest to leave IE on your system. Set the security level to "High," download every security patch available, and use it only when you need it. While you can remove it if you really want to, you may destabilize many parts of your Windows system unnecessarily.

# Firefox Help

You've gotten Firefox installed on your computer, and you've seen how to configure some of the basic options. The last thing you need to know before I throw you into deeper water in the next chapter (it's only up to your knees, so don't worry) is a few ways to get help.

## Accessing Firefox Help

As with any other program, the very first place to look for information is the program help files themselves. Go to Help | Help Contents. The main Firefox help screen (shown in Figure 1-7) appears.

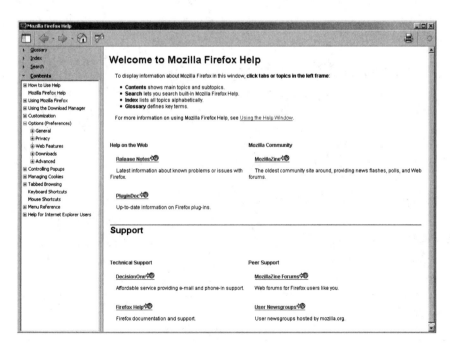

Figure 1-7

*The main Firefox help screen.*

The online help files contain pretty good help for using Firefox and understanding the features. You can use the help's table of contents (shown in Figure 1-7), search for a specific term or phrase throughout the help files, look up items in the help index, or check terms in the glossary (a sample of which is shown in Figure 1-8).

**Figure 1-8**

*Firefox help's glossary.*

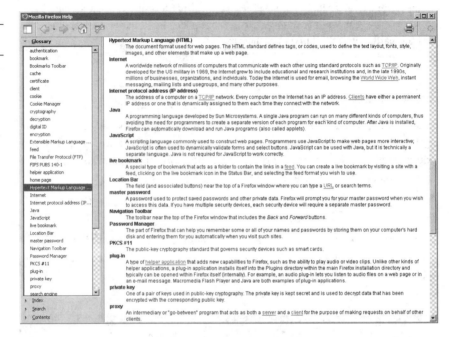

## When You Need More Detailed Help

The basic online help included with Firefox probably will give you the answers you need about three-fourths of the time, but sooner or later you'll have a complex question that needs a more detailed answer than you can get locally. Fortunately, there are a lot of places you can go for more detailed information and even expert assistance.

## Websites and Web Forums

The first place to check for more help is, obviously, the web. In addition to the documentation, release notes, and breaking-news releases about Firefox available through the Mozilla website (http://www.mozilla.org) and the online Firefox support wing (http://www.mozilla.org/support/firefox), there are a number of great places to find information about Firefox. If you're interested in a development group, look at
http://www.mozilla.org/community/developer-forums.html.

One of the best websites for Firefox information is the MozillaZine forum (use the hot link on the main page of the online help to get there, or go to http://www.mozillazine.org or http://forums.mozillazine.org). There are online forums discussing every possible aspect of Firefox. You can loft a question and frequently get an answer from half a dozen people within hours. The forums are also searchable, so you can check to see if someone else has already run into the same situation as you have (probably) and see what kinds of suggestions were made. Figure 1-9 shows part of a typical conversation thread on a Firefox question.

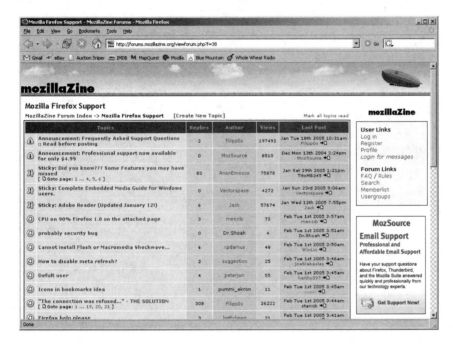

**Figure 1-9**

The MozillaZine Firefox forums.

## Newsgroups

Although most people tend to think of the Internet as being just websites and email, there are other ways of getting information, such as *newsgroups*. Newsgroups (also known as *Usenet groups*) are a bit like large cork bulletin boards on a wall on which you can post messages (known in newsgroup parlance as *articles*, or *posts*), ask questions, and get files, including the latest versions of software, documents, HTML files, and other information.

Newsgroups provide an enormous amount of information on virtually any subject you can imagine (and many you probably can't), with new newsgroups being created all the time. Currently, several dozen newsgroups focus specifically on Firefox and Thunderbird. To explore newsgroups, you need a

**FAQ**

**What do I do if I don't want to use a newsreader?**

If you don't already have a newsreader and you don't want to download and learn to use one, you can access newsgroups through Google. Go to www.google.com and select "groups." You'll have the advantage of using Firefox and Google to access the newsgroups you're interested in.

*newsreader,* a program that lets you read newsgroups and post articles to them. The newsreader displays the newsgroups in one window and the articles within the selected newsgroup in another. The content of the selected article appears in a third window. Most newsreaders have features that let you search and sort newsgroups and individual articles.

If you don't already have a newsreader that can handle newsgroups, start by checking for Firefox extensions that let you read newsgroups directly. (Extensions are discussed in Chapter 7, "Customizing Firefox with Third-Party Extensions and Themes." Plenty of free and shareware newsreaders are available, such as Free Agent for Windows (www.forteinc.com), Simon Fraser's MT-NewsWatcher for the Mac (www.smfr.org), and tin for Linux (www.tin.org).

Here's a list of newsgroups you can look in for help:

alt.fan.mozilla

netscape.public.mozilla.browser

netscape.public.mozilla.documentation

netscape.public.mozilla.general

netscape.public.mozilla.mac

netscape.public.mozilla.mail-news

netscape.public.mozilla.plugins

netscape.public.mozilla.prefs

netscape.public.mozilla.unix

netscape.public.mozilla.webtools

netscape.public.mozilla.win32

In addition to the newsgroups listed here, dozens more newsgroups of a much more technical nature will probably bore the shoes off you unless you're really into the nuts and bolts of programming or XML or things like that. Newsgroups are added all the time, so be sure to check periodically for new newsgroups that have words like "mozilla," "firefox," and "thunderbird" in the group's name. You can also look for "open source," "browser," and "email client," but the pickings are slimmer for information specific to Firefox and Thunderbird. If you're not sure which groups might be the most helpful, start with the most general groups and work your way in.

As with the MozillaZine forums, you can frequently get responses to your questions within hours.

## IRC

If you want to interact directly with people, you can try out IRC (Internet Relay Chat) and talk to real, live people and get an answer in as little as a few minutes.

To access IRC channels, you need an IRC client. There are a couple of good IRC extensions for Firefox, my favorite of which is ChatZilla. (ChatZilla is described in Chapter 7.) If you prefer a standalone application, you can also use mIRC or some other third-party production.

When you have an IRC client set up, connect to the irc.mozilla.org domain and join the #mozillazine channel as your first stop. You'll find a lot of people who are passionate about Firefox and Thunderbird. For a more developer-centric group, try #firefox. There are certainly other channels that focus on Firefox and/or Thunderbird; as with newsgroups, be sure to look for channels in other domains that have words like "mozilla," "firefox," and "thunderbird" in the group's name.

## Third-Party Support Options

Still not satisfied with the options for getting help? If you just cannot wait for information and want a guaranteed answer, there are a few companies that provide third-party support for Firefox and Thunderbird for a fee. DecisionOne (http://www.decisiononecorporate.com) and MozSource Support (http://support.mozsource.com) both offer extensive support options for a relatively small amount of money per incident.

---

So now you know a bit about Firefox and how it evolved from Netscape and Mozilla. You can even install Firefox on your computer and do some basic configuration. If you're feeling adventurous, you could romp off on your own at this point and use Firefox... but you'd miss out on how to take advantage of a lot of the really dazzling features that make Firefox so cool.

Are you ready to learn ways to protect your security and privacy on the web? Great! Then move on to the next chapter, where you'll see ways to avoid spyware, how to use Firefox's built-in password manager, and how to manage web cookies. You'll also learn how to use web form information and how to manage your cache for complete web-surfing privacy.

# Protecting Your Security and Privacy

## How Firefox Protects Your Security

**DO OR DIE:**

>> "Button up your overcoat..."

>> Maintaining your privacy

>> Passwords and master passwords

>> Have a cookie or not, as you wish

It used to be that the Internet was like a park in a small, friendly town. You could go there most any time of the day or night and have a good time without worrying about security or privacy. Now the Internet is still like a park, but it's a park in a big urban area and it's not always so friendly. There are some serious security threats out there: spyware, viruses, Trojan horses. If you'll be doing any serious surfing at all—and you are, or you wouldn't be reading this—you need to learn about ways to make things a little safer.

One of the biggest advantages that Firefox—and all other Mozilla-based products, for that matter—offers is that it's more secure than Internet Explorer. (Don't take my word for it; check out the U.S. government's Computer Emergency Readiness Team [US-CERT] warnings at http://www.kb.cert.org/vuls/id/713878. Their findings point out that there are "a number of significant vulnerabilities" with IE. Among other things, the report recommends using a different web browser.)

Here are some of the reasons that Firefox is more secure:

- Firefox is not integrated with Windows, so even if Firefox is compromised, viruses and trojan horses do not gain automatic access to many parts of Windows. The reverse is also true: if Windows is compromised, the attacking program does not necessarily gain access to Firefox.
- Firefox does not support VBScript and ActiveX, which are frequently used to exploit security holes in IE.
- Visiting a website with Firefox doesn't allow spyware or adware to be automatically installed.
- Firefox gives you complete control over web cookies.

These and many other reasons add up to a really great reason to use Firefox: you'll be safer.

# Protecting Yourself on the Web

There are a number of problems to look out for on the web:

- **Viruses**, which are programs or scripts that get into your computer and cause damage in a myriad of ways
- **Worms**, which are like viruses that replicate independently over a network without any human intervention
- **Trojan horses**, which are programs that appear to be innocuous but that cause damage to your system when you run them

There's some overlap between these definitions. A worm may not have been designed to do harm but, owing to the number of instances on your computer, it could clog up your file system or damage your email files, which might classify it as a virus. Is a program that releases a worm but that doesn't cause damage to your system a worm or a trojan horse? While the distinctions are sometimes blurry, all of these are Bad Things from Bad People. You don't want them on your computer. Using a good anti-virus program (with up-to-date virus definitions) is essential. The biggest vector for viruses is any email program that automatically loads and runs scripts. Thunderbird, described later in this book, is much safer because, among other things, it doesn't load and run scripts unless you actively tell it to.

One of the most recent computer plagues is *spyware*. Spyware is programs or scripts that are installed without your explicit permission that sit quietly in the background and do things to your system that you don't want to be done. What kinds of things? Here are some of the basic types of spyware:

- **Adware** (also known as "popupware") is certainly the most common type of spyware. When you go online, the adware displays ads in popup windows (aka "popups") about all kinds of products: hair loss remedies, herbal Viagra substitutes, cheap car rentals, you name it. Adware usually also transmits information about your web surfing habits and preferences to someone collecting information about you, who then sells it to spammers and marketers so that you get hit with targeted spam and probably more popups. (This process is known as "data mining," and there are pieces of adware that are just data miners.)

**Note**

Popups and how to suppress them are discussed in Chapter 3, aptly titled "Ridding Yourself of the Annoyances of the Web."

- **Search hijackers** (also known as "browser hijackers" or just "hijackers") change your browser's home page and your preferred search engine to something you didn't plan on (usually porn sites or some cheesy web scam). Search hijackers are also frequently data miners, just like many versions of adware.

- **Keystroke loggers** are particularly nasty. While all the other types of spyware are busy trying to sell you stuff—stuff you really don't want, but still—or gather information about you so that other people can try to sell you stuff, keystroke loggers are tracking the actual keystrokes you enter on the computer. Anytime you log in to your email account to pay websites you patronize or (worst of all!) to your credit card site to make a payment, the keystroke logger records *everything* and then sends it to someone.

There are a few other classes of spyware—dialers that look for a phone line via a modem and then dial long distance 900 numbers to rack up bills on your account, for instance, or programs that look for Quicken on your computer and then have Quicken transfer money to someone else's bank account (as demonstrated by Germany's Computer Chaos Club in 1997)—but the bottom line is that spyware and the people who create or use it have no reason for continued existence on any planet that's discovered penicillin.

Fortunately, you can do a number of things to detect and remove spyware and to avoid it in the future. Some of the best detection tools for Windows are free: Ad-Aware SE Personal Edition from Lavasoft (www.lavasoftusa.com) and Spybot Search & Destroy (http://www.safer-networking.org) are my personal favorites. I use both of them, because each tends to catch some things that the other doesn't. I also use ZoneAlarm (www.zonealarm.com) as a software firewall so that I can see if something on my computer is trying to send information elsewhere. It's also free and cheap at twice the price.

Spyware is primarily a problem for Windows computers, but Mac users may want to try a product like MacScan (http://macscan.securemac.com). You might also want to look at general Mac security sites, such as MacSecurity.org (http://www.macsecurity.org) and SecureMac (http://www.securemac.com), for information on how best to protect your Mac. Linux users have nothing to fear: spyware is not an issue for Linux computers at this time.

To avoid getting spyware in the future, first use Firefox (you knew that was coming, didn't you?). Here's why: Microsoft's approach to designing Internet Explorer was an optimistic view of security. Internet Explorer provided the maxiumum amount of capability with the hope of providing mechanisms that could and would be used to avoid risks. Unfortunately, it didn't quite work that way: ActiveX lets people silently access the operating system, the browser itself, and applications, and the Security Zone Model can allow the silent downloading, installation, and execution of programs without your knowledge. Powerful stuff that you can use to do great things? Sure!

> **Warning**
>
> Some spyware detection and removal programs actually don't do much of anything. Some of them are even loaded with spyware themselves. Before you install just any old spyware checker on your system, look around and see what people are saying about its effectiveness.

But sadly, it doesn't have enough safeguards, and as a result, ActiveX and the Security Zone model are used together as the primary mechanism to deploy spyware.

To be fair, Microsoft has recently addressed some of the issues in SP2 for Windows XP, but only a couple years after the dangers of Internet Explorer and its architecture were discussed in an article entitled "The Most Dangerous Software Ever Written" (www.networkmagazine.com/article/NMG20020701S0007). Worse, because Microsoft is focusing on Windows XP, over 200 million users of Windows 95, Windows 98, and Windows 2000 are being left out in the cold.

In contrast, Firefox takes a pessimistic, Murphyistic view of vulnerability: "Anything that can go wrong, will go wrong." Firefox attempts to create a firewall around the browser and remote content and other applications that might be available on the PC. In every case where potentially dangerous actions can happen, Firefox attempts to warn users about the risk. Furthermore, because Firefox doesn't support ActiveX and the security zone architecture, Firefox doesn't allow websites to install software automatically. Without the ability for websites to silently download and install spyware, Firefox has some immediate security advantages over Internet Explorer.

For further safety, don't put yourself in harm's way. Avoid software and websites that are likely to be infested with spyware. As you might expect, websites focusing on warez, porn, illicit mp3s, and file sharing are all likely to have spyware (you all look like nice people and would never go to places like these, but you need to know). Unfortunately, lots of sites that even a nice person like you might go to that also have spyware: online games, dating sites, contests, free software, and even some major companies' websites can all try to download spyware on your computer. The trick is to be cautious, use Firefox to filter out a lot of the spyware, use Ad-Aware and Spybot to check for spyware regularly (daily's not too often to check if you surf a lot), and use ZoneAlarm to watch what's trying to talk from your computer to elsewhere without your knowledge.

**FRIDGE**

Spyware can be bundled as part of another program so that the spyware installs when you install the program, but it's most commonly downloaded from websites. But just to be on the safe side, consider checking your system by running Spybot or Ad-Aware immediately after installing a new program. You should routinely check the Add/Remove applet in the Control Panel as well as checking your system's Pogram Files directory for things you don't recollect. (This is sort of like walking through your house and saying, "Where'd that vase come from?")

**TOOL KIT**

**Dealing with the Windows Registry**

If you're using Windows, you should also use a registry cleaner periodically to check for spyware as well as to clean up stray registry entries. Several good registry cleaners are available, the Norton Utilities version being one of the best-known, but you can find a variety of shareware registry cleaners through www.shareware.com. If you're really technically savvy, you may want to take a tour through your registry every so often using RegEdit. This is a really tedious job and it's not for the faint of heart, but it can help you find traces of buried spyware. Be sure to back up your registry before you touch anything in it.

# Setting Privacy Options in Firefox

Now that you have learned how to set some of the basic Firefox options (refer to Chapter 1, "Getting Started," if necessary), you are ready to see how to set privacy options in Firefox.

To set privacy options, start by going to Tools | Options | Privacy. The Options screen with the Privacy options appears, as shown in Figure 2-1.

**Figure 2-1**

*The Options
screen with
the Privacy
options
displayed.*

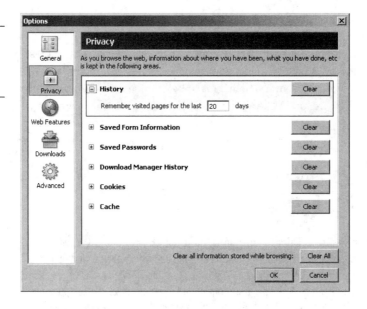

As you browse the web, information on where you have been, what pages you have visited, and so on, is stored in Firefox. The privacy options in Firefox give you control over what's stored and for how long. In addition, you can set controls to exclude specific websites from doing potentially intrusive or insecure things on your computer.

The following sections show you how to set the security and privacy options on this screen. To display a specific option, expand a section by clicking the small + button to the left of the option.

## History

Firefox, like every other browser, tracks the pages you've visited and displays them in the History sidebar. You can set the number of days you want Firefox to remember your history (there's no practical upper limit of days). Clicking Clear clears all your surfing history up to the current page. If the button's grayed out, the history is already clear. (You'll read more about how the History sidebar works in Chapter 5, "Bookmarks and History.")

Before you get frisky and clear your history, keep in mind that Firefox changes the color of the links of web pages you've visited, but if you clear the history, all the links will look like you've never clicked them. If you're working through a large page of links, you may end up losing your place and revisiting websites because you have no point of reference for where you left off. Similarly, a Google search on a topic you look up frequently will no longer show what you've already looked at. The autocomplete information when you enter the first few characters of a web address is also cleared. If you can't remember the exact site address, Firefox won't be able to help you by suggesting all the different addresses you've entered that start the same way.

## Saved Form Information

The Saved Form Information option (displayed in Figure 2-2) automatically saves information from web forms and the Firefox search bar. With this option on, common types of information such as your name, email address, address, and the like all show up on dropdown lists when you start entering information in a similar field—very convenient for quick form entry. In the same fashion, Firefox saves the things you enter in the search field. Just type the first few characters of a search entry you entered previously, and Firefox will proffer a list of search criteria that start with the same characters. If you don't want Firefox to save information, uncheck the box. Click **Clear** to wipe all the form information and search criteria you entered since the last time this was cleared.

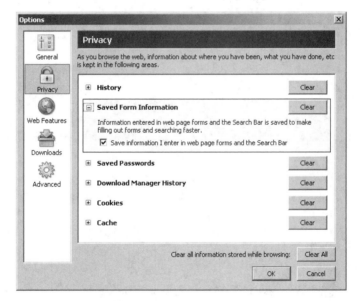

**Figure 2-2**

*The Options screen with the Saved Forms Information option expanded.*

## Saving Passwords

If you're like me, you probably have one or two email accounts, online bill paying with your bank and a couple of credit card websites, an online game account, logins to a few job websites, a few web forums or listservs for professional and personal interests, and at least three or four other miscellaneous things. That's a lot of user IDs and passwords! It's a really bad idea to use the same password for everything—if someone cracks your password once, he'll have access to everything you do—but it's also a bad idea to write your passwords down somewhere—again, if someone finds your list, he'll have access to everything. But remember that having a dozen or more user ID/password combinations is a real pest. Better to have Firefox do the remembering for you.

The Saved Passwords option (shown in Figure 2-3), which is turned on by default, actually saves user IDs and passwords.

**Figure 2-3**

*The Options screen with the Saved Passwords option expanded.*

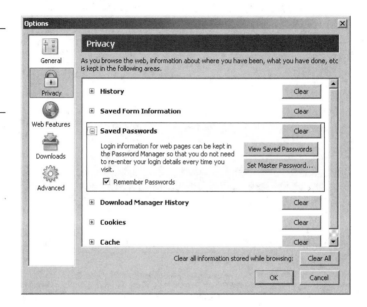

When you log in to a website, Firefox displays a dialog box (shown in Figure 2-4) and asks if you want to save the logon information. You can click **Yes** to save it, **No** to skip it this time, or **Never** for this site to disallow password saving for this site. As with previous options, you can click Clear to clear all the passwords in Firefox.

**Figure 2-4**

*The Confirm dialog box for saved logon information.*

You can examine and edit individual user IDs and passwords by clicking **View Saved Passwords**, which displays the Password Manager screen (shown in Figure 2-5). You can see the sites that have been saved and edit the list by highlighting the site(s) you want to delete and then clicking **Remove**. Clicking **Remove All** flushes all the saved sites and passwords, which is handy if you're cleaning traces from the computer.

**Figure 2-5**

*The Pass-words Saved tab of Password Manager.*

The default is for the Password Manager to show just the site and the user ID. You can also show the associated passwords by clicking **Show Passwords**, as shown in Figure 2-6. Hide the passwords again by clicking **Hide Passwords**.

You can also edit the sites you've designated to never save logon information for by clicking the **Passwords Never Saved** tab (shown in Figure 2-7). You can remove some or all of the websites by clicking **Remove** or **Remove All**, as you did before. When you are satisfied with your entries, click **Close**.

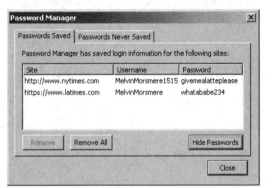

**Figure 2-6**

*The Pass-words Saved tab with the passwords displayed.*

Having your logon information set up in Firefox is really handy. However, anyone who has access to your computer can get into the Password

**Figure 2-7**

*The Pass-words Never Saved tab.*

Manager and look up your account usernames and passwords. To prevent this, you can set a master password that locks the information in the Password Manager itself so that someone can't casually extract your logon information. To set a master password, click **Set Master Password** on the Options screen shown earlier in Figure 2-3 to display the Change Master Password screen, shown in Figure 2-8.

Figure 2-8

*The Change
Master
Password
screen.*

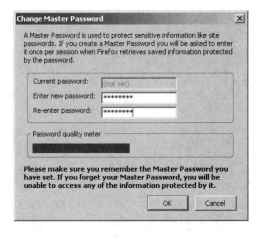

Figure 2-8

*The Change
Master
Password
screen.*

The Change Master Password screen is much like any other password screen. The first time you set up a master password, you don't need to enter the current password. You do need to enter the password (which is case-sensitive, by the way) in both the new password fields. As usual, the characters are replaced with asterisks as you type. When the passwords match, the OK button is activated. Without the master password, the passwords aren't displayed in the Passwords Saved tab of the Password Manager, and you can't add or change any passwords.

One really slicko feature of the Change Master Password screen that I've never seen anywhere else is the password quality meter. Everyone's familiar with the idea of not using names of partners, children, or pets, birthdates, or common words like "secret," "keepout," or "spiderman." The password quality meter actually rates the value of your password on criteria such as mixing capital and lowercase letters, adding numbers and characters, and uncommon groupings.

## TOOL KIT. What to Do If You Forget Your Master Password

If, despite everything, you've forgotten your password (hey, it happens—I've even forgotten passwords an *hour* after I set them up!), things aren't hopeless. With a little hacking, you can reset the master password on your computer.

Start by closing Firefox, and then go to where your key3.db file is stored on your computer. The key3.db file is where the master password information is stored.

- On Windows, this is in C:\Documents and Settings\<useraccountname>\ Application Data\Mozilla\Firefox\Profiles\default.<3-character ID>\key3.db
- On Linux, this is in ~/.mozilla/firefox/default.gdd/key3.db
- On a Mac, this is in users\<useraccountname>\Library\Application support\ Firefox\Profiles\xxxxxxxx.default\key3.db

Now rename the key3.db file to !key3.db.save so that Firefox doesn't know where to read the old master password information. Restart Firefox and go to Tools | Options | Privacy | Saved Passwords | Set Master Password to display the Change Master Password screen. (On Linux and Mac computers, go to Edit | Preferences | Advanced... instead.) The current master password field on the Change Master Password screen will now be empty, and you'll be able to set a new master password as if you'd never set one at all.

This isn't particularly secure when you think about it—the master password can be reset and even set back to where it was without an audit trail—but it's enough to keep casual users from getting into your passwords.

## Download Manager History

The Download Manager is discussed in detail in Chapter 8, "Other Interesting Features," but take a moment now to look at how to set the privacy option for it (shown in Figure 2-9). As part of its job, the Download Manager logs the files you download. You may not want everything you've downloaded to show up for the world to see, so you can set a few options for removing files from the Download Manager. You can use the dropdown list to set the Download Manager so that you can remove the download history manually one file at a time (the default), upon a successful download, or whenever you exit Firefox. To clear the Download Manager of everything all at once, click **Clear**, and poof! All traces of download history are removed.

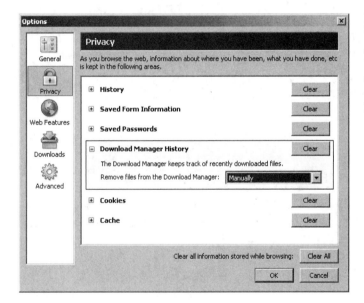

**Figure 2-9**

*The Options screen with the Download Manager History option expanded.*

## Cookies

Cookies are small information files saved on your computer by websites. Most cookies are pretty innocuous—they let Firefox remember your logon information or your website preferences—but some can be a potential security breach because they contain logon info or because they're actually cookies left by adware. The Cookies option (shown in Figure 2-10) lets you manage cookies in several different ways.

**Figure 2-10**

*The Options screen with the Cookies option expanded.*

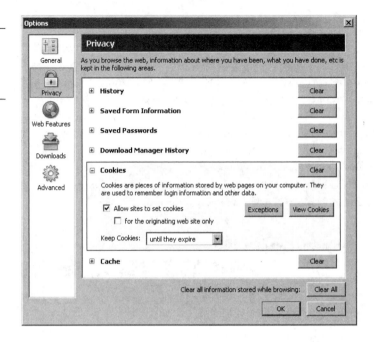

The default cookie option is to allow websites to set cookies. This is generally a good idea; cookies are just too useful to disable completely without some consideration. You can, however, restrict this so that only the originating websites can save cookies by checking that box. This means that you can log on to a site like www.squidlips.org and have cookies for your logon information for that website, but the website can't set cookies for any advertisers who also have links on the website.

The Keep Cookies dropdown list defaults to keeping cookies until they expire (many websites set their cookies to expire by a certain date or by some period after the last time they've been used), but you can make this a good deal more draconian if you wish. You can have cookies be session-temporary: as soon as you exit Firefox, the cookies are erased. You can be even more strict about the settings and specify that Firefox should ask you every time a website wants to set a cookie. When Firefox is set to manage cookies this way, every time a website wants to set a cookie, you see a dialog box like the one shown in Figure 2-11.

**Figure 2-11**

*The Confirm setting cookie dialog box.*

The Confirm setting cookie dialog box tells you that the website wants to set (or sometimes just modify) a cookie. If you have several cookies from this website already, it shows how many cookies are already stored in Firefox for this website (two cookies in this example). You can click **Allow** to allow the website to set a cookie, **Allow for Session** to set a cookie that will be erased when you close Firefox, or **Deny** to prevent the website from setting a cookie at all. If

you need more information, click **Show Details**. The information displayed is rather technical (as shown in Figure 2-12), but some people like knowing that sort of thing. One thing that's worth noting is the cookie's expiration date at the bottom of the screen.

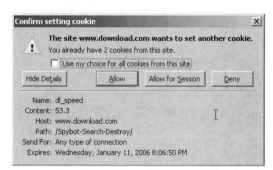

**Figure 2-12**
*The Confirm setting cookie dialog box with the cookie information displayed.*

If you're going to romp around a website for a while, it may well try to set several cookies. The second time the Confirm setting cookie dialog box appears, you may want to check the box so that Firefox automatically allows, allows for this session, or denies cookies for this website.

Everyone should try setting their cookie options so that Firefox asks them if they want to save each and every cookie, and then surf the web with that option on for as long as they can stand it (probably about five minutes) before going to one of the other two cookie options. It's a valuable lesson in just how many cookies are being set and by whom.

In addition to the general cookie options, you can tell Firefox to always ignore or always permit specific websites. Click **Exceptions** to display the Exceptions screen (shown in Figure 2-13). Enter a website in the Address of website field, and then select the appropriate permission level—Block, Allow for Session, or Allow—to add the website to the list below. You can remove websites already in the list by highlighting the websites (hold down the Ctrl key and click to select multiple sites or hold down the Ctrl key and the

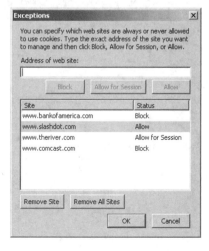

**Figure 2-13**
*The Exceptions dialog box.*

Shift key and click to select a range of websites) and then clicking **Remove Site**. You can wipe the slate clean by clicking **Remove All Sites**. When you are satisfied with your entries, click OK.

If you want to maintain really tight control over your cookies, it's a good idea to periodically review the cookies stored on your computer. Click **View Cookies** to display the Stored Cookies screen (shown in Figure 2-14). You can review the cookies and, if you wish, remove some or all of them. Like the Confirm setting cookie dialog box, the details of the highlighted cookie are displayed at the bottom of the screen. It's worth noting that, in this example, the cookie will expire in 2014, which may make the "keep cookies until they expire" setting a little silly. (I've even seen cookies that were set to expire in 2032. If you have any idea what kind of computer you'll be using in 2032, or which version of Firefox, please let me know.)

**Figure 2-14**

*The Stored Cookies screen.*

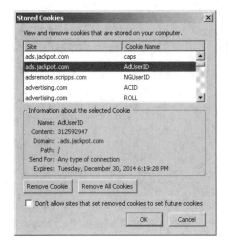

## Cache

As with every other browser, Firefox stores a copy of the web pages—HTML, images, scripts, and so on—you've visited in a *cache* so that they can be displayed quickly the next time you go to the URL. Web pages are stored in the cache until you reach the preset limit (the default is 50 MB of disk space, as shown in Figure 2-15), after which Firefox starts deleting web pages on a first-in, first-out basis. Again, if you're security-conscious, you should clear your cache periodically by clicking **Clear** for this option.

**Figure 2-15**

*The Options screen with the Cache option expanded.*

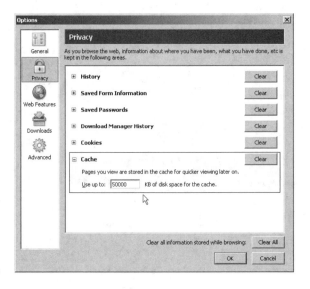

### Getting Rid of Everything at Once

If you want to clear everything all at once—history, passwords, cache, and so on—click **Clear All** at the bottom of the screen and then confirm the deletion. Think of this option as a kind of security panic button. Pretty much everything you've been doing on the web will vanish in a puff of bits.

# Limiting Web Access

For the record, I don't think much of parental controls. It's not that I disagree with the idea that kids should not be exposed to a lot of the seamier stuff on the web—they shouldn't, and parents should be the ones who set boundaries on what they consider acceptable. But parental controls aren't particularly effective if a child is really persistent.

Nevertheless, parental controls have some value that at least makes them worth considering. The first major parental control product to support Firefox was CyberPatrol (www.cyberpatrol.com). It's not bad; in fact, you can do a heckuva lot worse.

Another way to consider limiting web access is to set up a *whitelist*. A whitelist explicitly identifies the websites you can surf to. This probably won't be particularly helpful as a parental control, because there are probably lots of different sites that you'd like your kids to be able to go to, and coming up with even a partial list is likely to be impractical, but you can use the whitelist technique in any situation where you want to provide web access to a limited number of sites. For example, you may want to point a computer to an online catalog, a directory, or a single informational website.

To limit browser access, start by going to Tools | Options | General. The Options screen with the General options appears, as shown in Figure 2-16.

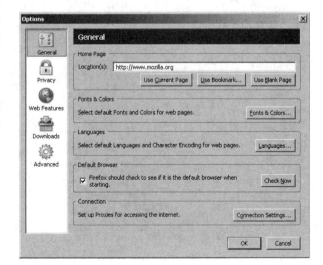

**Figure 2-16**

*The Options screen with the General options displayed.*

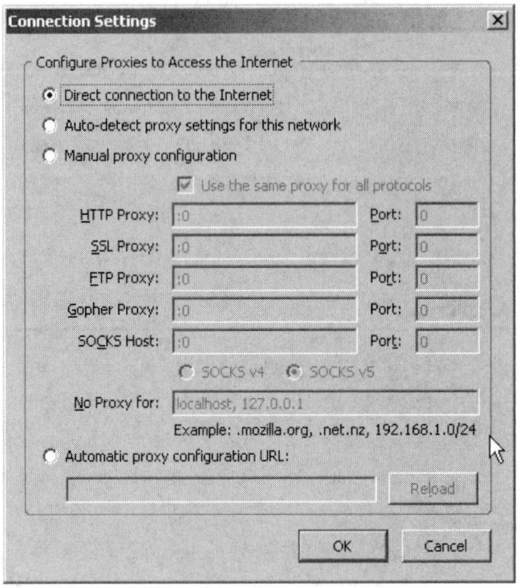


**Figure 2-17**

*The Connection Settings screen.*

Click **Connection Settings** to display the Connection Settings dialog box (shown in Figure 2-17).

Click the **Manual proxy configuration** radio button, which activates the fields in the middle of the Connection Settings screen. Uncheck the **Use the same proxy for all protocols** checkbox.

In HTTP Proxy, enter a message like "Proxy set for limiting web access." (This message is for your own reference.) Enter 80 in the corresponding Port field. Next, in SSL Proxy, enter the same message you entered in the HTTP Proxy field, and set the corresponding Port field to 443.

In **No Proxy for**, enter the names of the websites you want to allow access to. You can enter specific websites, such as www.mozilla.org and www.google.com, which will allow you to access anything within these domains. You can enter broader ranges of websites as well. For example, entering .gov lets you surf to any website ending in .gov. You can be even more specific as well: entering www.mozilla.org/support lets you go to any of the pages in the mozilla.org/support subdomain. Figure 2-18 shows an example of what the Connection Settings screen looks like with the whitelist information added.

When you are satisfied with your entries, click OK. At this point, you can only go to the specified websites. If you try to access any other website, you'll see the message shown in Figure 2-19.

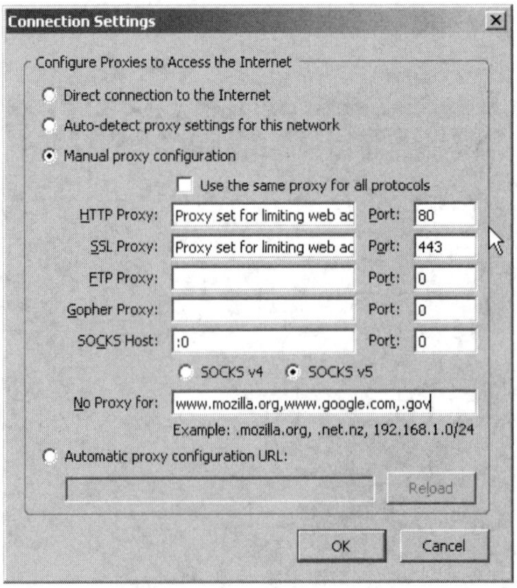


**Figure 2-18**

*The Connection Settings screen with proxy information entered.*

**Figure 2-19**
*Alert for a website blocked by the whitelist.*

You can always go back to the Connection Settings screen and check the **Direct connection to the Internet** radio button to remove the access limitations.

There's another way you can use whitelists. Suppose you want to set up a dedicated terminal at a conference or a public information kiosk. You can use a whitelist together with a list of bookmarks on the Bookmarks toolbar (a technique you'll see in Chapter 5) to point the users to a specific and very limited group of websites on the Internet.

## Setting Other Security Options

In addition to what you've seen so far, you can set a few additional security options. Start by going to Tools | Options | Advanced. The Advanced options are displayed, as shown in Figure 2-20.

**Figure 2-20**
*The Options screen with the Software Update option displayed.*

The Advanced options cover a lot of ground, not all of it security-related. As with the other options screens, you can expand an option by clicking the button next to the option. For now, you only need to worry about software updates and security.

## Software Update

The software update option lets you tell Firefox to check for updates to the Firefox software itself for any extension or theme you may have installed. (Extensions and themes are discussed in Chapter 7, "Customizing Firefox with Third-Party Extensions and Themes.") When these two boxes are checked (the default), Firefox checks periodically for updates to the software. When there's an update, a small icon appears in the top right of the Firefox screen near the Google search bar. If the icon is red, a critical update of Firefox is available for download. A green icon indicates that there are up to four updates to extensions and themes; a blue icon indicates that there are more updates than that. Click the icon and follow the instructions to update the assorted software. If you don't want to wait, you can click **Check Now** to force Firefox to check for updates. If there's an update, Firefox displays a small screen telling you what's been updated and asks if you want to install the update.

No matter what your settings or the updates, Firefox always requires you to approve the installation of *any* software on your computer.

## Security

The Security option (shown in Figure 2-21) specifies how information is transmitted between your computer and a website. *Secure Socket Layer*, or *SSL* for short, is a standardized protocol for sending and receiving information over the Internet in an encrypted form. There are several levels of SSL security. The most common is SSL 2.0, but there is a more secure version, SSL 3.0. Transport Layer Security, or TLS, is an open security protocol that is similar to SSL 3.0. Both SSL and TLS are used to encrypt your data using an encryption method agreed upon by your browser and the website you're communicating with. This ensures that the data can be read only by your browser and the website, and no one else.

You can select SSL 2.0, SSL 3.0, and TLS 1.0 (the two SSL options are already selected by default) for the Security option. SSL and TLS are most commonly used by shopping websites for transmitting and receiving confidential information, such as credit card numbers. Every secure website these days supports SSL 2.0, which provides server authentication. SSL 3.0 and TLS 1.0 are better—they provide server and client authentication—but they're not

universal. If you select all three options, Firefox will use the best security communications option available, depending on the capabilities of the website
you're talking to at the moment.

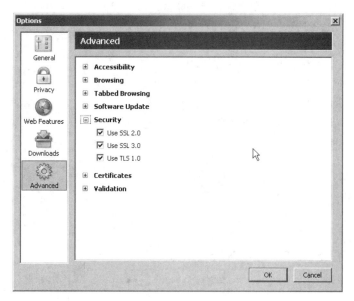

**Figure 2-21**
*The Options
screen with
the Security
option dis-
played.*

**TOOL
KIT.**

**Getting Really Secure**

For the hyperconscious, Firefox offers a number of settings for working with
digital certificates and validation. Almost everyone who uses Firefox will be
completely happy—and secure—with the default settings, but if you want to
be impeccable, check out the technical information on using digital certificates in Firefox in Appendix F, "Security, Certificates, and Validation."

# Setting Web Features Options

The final set of security options appears on the Web Features Options screen,
shown in Figure 2-22. To display the Web Features options, go to Tools | Options |
Web Features.

The options described in the following sections can give you more control
over your web security.

**Figure 2-22**

*The Options screen showing the Web Features options.*

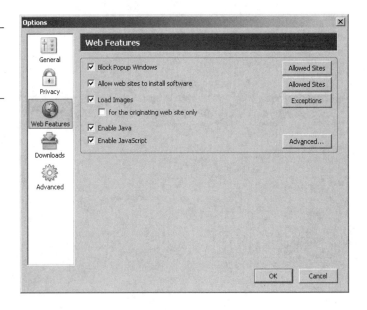

## Block Popup Windows

This option, which blocks popups, is described in Chapter 3.

## Allow Websites to Install Software

When you install Firefox, websites can install extensions and themes on your computer. Adding extensions and themes is a pretty good thing, because you can augment Firefox's capabilities and change the way it looks. (Extensions and themes are discussed in Chapter 7.) However, the installation process isn't completely uncontrolled. Firefox blocks any website from installing software until you've added the website to a whitelist of allowed sites. A small bar appears at the top of the screen telling you that Firefox has blocked the website from installing software on your computer. You can click **Edit Options** to display the Allowed Sites screen, shown in Figure 2-23, to add the website.

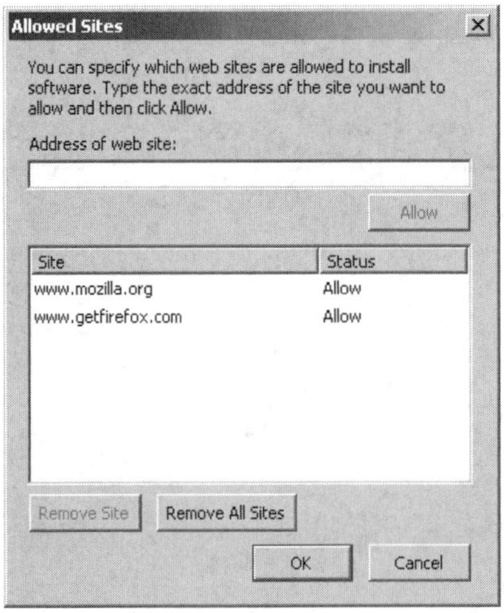

**Figure 2-23**

*The Allowed Sites screen.*

When a website has been added to the list, click the link again to install the software. Firefox displays a small confirmation screen to ask if you want to download this specific piece of software (an example appears in Figure 2-24).

Figure 2-24

*The Software Installation screen.*

The Allowed Sites screen lets you edit the list of websites that are allowed to install extensions and themes on your computer. To manually add a website to the list, click **Allowed Sites** on the Web Features Options screen, enter the website address in the Allowed Sites screen's address field, and click **Allow**. (Any websites that you've previously allowed already appear on the list.) You can remove previously allowed websites from the list by highlighting the site(s) in question and clicking **Remove Site**, or click **Remove All** to block every website from installing software on your computer. When you are satisfied with your entries, click OK.

Themes are handled a little differently: when you try to install a theme and you have this option checked, Firefox does not require you to add the website name to the whitelist. You're just asked to confirm the download in a simple message like the one shown in Figure 2-25.

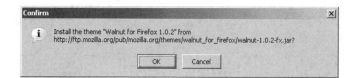

Figure 2-25

*Confirming a theme download.*

By default, downloads are allowed, but unchecking **Allow websites to install software** prevents any downloads from occurring unless you first re-enable this option.

## Load Images

The Load Images option lets you selectively display or block banner ads and other images and is described in Chapter 3.

## Enable Java

Java is a programming language developed for web programming by James Gosling of Sun Micrososystems. Java is very portable: the same Java program can run on a wide variety of computers, making it unnecessary to create multiple versions for differing platforms. Java programs that are downloaded and run in web browsers are typically known as *applets*. Lots of websites use Java applets to add custom features, such as dropdown menus, web buttons, image scrolling, and other features, such as animation and slide shows. Many online, web-based games are written in Java. There are lots of complex and more esoteric Java applets as well; for example, many online accounting systems and other web-based systems make extensive use of Java for reporting and printing information.

By default, Firefox allows Java applets to run, but you can prevent this by unchecking Enable Java.

> **Note**
>
> If you want to run Java applets of any kind, you must also install the Java plug-in in Firefox. For information on installing plug-ins, see Chapter 8.

## Enable JavaScript

JavaScript is a simple, effective scripting language created by Brendan Eich while he was at Netscape. It isn't the same as Java. JavaScript and Java have some things in common (that would only be of interest to a programmer—trust me), but the biggest difference is that JavaScript is used for small things like checking and formatting input on web forms. JavaScript code is integrated in the web page's HTML code, so a lot of functions can be done directly on your computer within the browser without having to go back to the server for computing power. (In contrast, Java applets are compiled programs that are separate from web pages, although they can be called from a web page and downloaded to your computer.)

There probably isn't any good reason to stop JavaScript from running on your browser: it's clean, it's pretty secure as things go, and a lot of websites depend on JavaScript. On the off chance you know why you want to disable JavaScript on your computer, uncheck Enable JavaScript. However, you may want to disable only certain features of JavaScript, which you can do by clicking **Advanced** to display the Advanced JavaScript Options screen (shown in Figure 2-26).

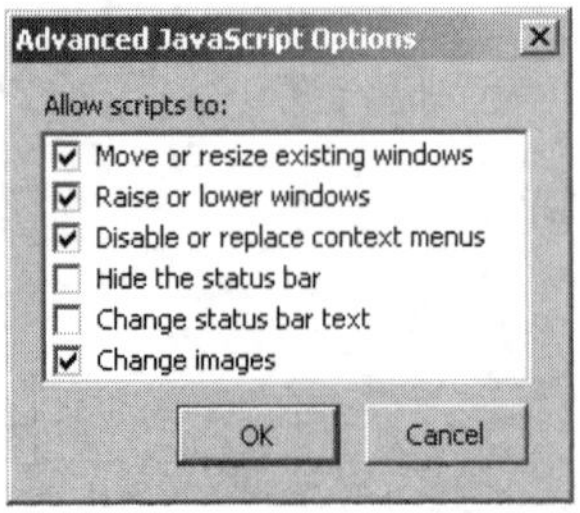

Through this screen, you can enable and disable any of the following:

**Figure 2-26**

*The Advanced JavaScript Options screen.*

- Move or resize existing windows: Enables or disables moving and resizing windows with scripts.

- Raise or lower windows: Enables or disables raising and lowering windows with scripts.

- Disable or replace context menus: Enables or disables web pages from changing or disabling the Firefox context menu.

- Hide the status bar: Enables or disables forcing the display of the status bar in popup windows.

- Change status bar text: Enables or disables status bar text scrolling and hiding web addresses when you hold the mouse over them.

- Change images: Enables or disables changing images. These are often called *rollover* or *mouseover* images; they change when you move the mouse over them. Use this carefully, because disabling this feature can make it difficult to navigate some menus.

Even with all these security and privacy options, Firefox isn't absolutely, totally secure. No web application is 100% risk-free. Nevertheless, Firefox is pretty darned good: it excludes the riskiest technologies found in other browsers, and, while it's not impossible for someone to come up with a way to attack Firefox's security, the amount of effort to do so is much greater because of Firefox's better architecture.

---

I know what computers are supposed to be: they're supposed to be like the computer on *Star Trek*. I should be able to talk to it in plain English and have it sift through my idioms and syntax and implied questions and still come up with exactly what I really want to know. That computer operates like an appliance: efficiently, accurately, with only very rare hiccups in its otherwise seamless performance. Unfortunately, that's not the computer I have on my desk. (I don't think they're going to sell the *Star Trek* make and model for quite a while, darn it!) As a result, I have to know a lot more about how it works, how it connects to the Internet, and what I need to do to protect it from bad people doing bad things. All of this is work that doesn't add anything to the task at hand. It's all overhead. Ugh.

With that in mind, I'm glad that using Firefox means that I don't have to worry about half as many security problems as I used to. As you've seen, it's relatively simple to set up a number of basic security and privacy options that you usually don't have to worry about again. The next chapter gives you the other part of this picture by telling you how to deal with two of the biggest annoyances on the web these days: popups and banners. These aren't security risks of the same caliber as spyware, but they're just as pestiferous. You'll be glad to know that Firefox offers several direct ways of dealing with these problems, too.

## Dealing with Popups

There are many annoyances on the web today, but for my money, the biggest annoyance for web surfers has to be unwanted popups. (If you do a Google search for the phrase "annoying popup," you get over half a million hits, so that should tell you something.) You're looking at a website for an article on tropical fish or your favorite columnist's latest editorial, and suddenly you're interrupted by some popup trying to sell you a subscription to some magazine, tell you about low mortgage rates, or any of a zillion other irrelevant and irritating things.

There are actually three different kinds of popups: popups themselves, which pop up a separate window on the screen; *popovers*, which are like popups except that they aren't a separate window and are harder to control; and *popunders*, which hide behind the current window so that you don't see them until you minimize the window. All three kinds are pretty annoying.

## FAQ

### Are all popups bad?

Not *every* popup is a bad thing. Some websites use popups to display additional information or relevant links. Some web-based messenger services use popups to display message windows. You can think of these as "requested popups" because you usually click a link that is explicitly designed to open a popup for a help tip or comment field or the like.

Unfortunately, requested popups are few and far between by comparison. The popups that are evil and often dangerous are in the class of "unrequested popups," which is what most of this section covers. Unrequested popups are displayed automatically by many websites with the general intent of selling you a product or service, whether you're interested in it or not. Happily, Firefox does a great job of protecting against unrequested popups without disabling the requested popups.

## FRIDGE

All this talk about popovers is making me hungry, so let us pause briefly so I can share with you Eunice's popover recipe:

**Eunice's Popovers**
2 eggs
1 cup milk
1 cup flour, sifted
1 tsp. salt
2 Tbs. melted butter

Sift flour with salt. In separate bowl, beat the two eggs. Add sifted mixture and stir. Add milk. Blend to make a fairly smooth batter. Add melted butter.

Pour into 12 small or 6 large greased cups or a muffin tin (a 6-cup popover tin is perfect for this recipe). Pour no more than 2/3 full. Place in cold oven (not preheated at all) set at 425 degrees. Bake 30-35 minutes. Check at 30 minutes, because you might need to cover the popovers with foil if they're browning too quickly. When done, pierce them to let them dry out a little—watch out for the vent of steam when you do—and serve with any kind of jam and a big pot of hot tea. If you haven't tried it before, splurge and buy a container of Devonshire clotted cream, which should be room temperature.

If you've never made popovers before, remember that the less the batter is stirred or mixed, the better the popovers will be. And I'm not kidding about starting with a cold oven.

Yum!!

Popups are usually just a waste of time, but they can actually be dangerous, too: popups can be used to transmit spyware. Many popups, when clicked,
attempt to download spyware. Popups are also frequently *caused* by spyware,
which loads them whenever you start a browser.

One of the great features in Firefox is its built-in popup blocker. To turn on
popup blocking, go to Tools | Options | Web Features. The Options screen with
the Web Features options appears, as shown in Figure 3-1.

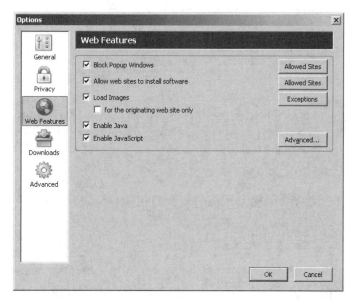

**Figure 3-1**

*The Options
screen show-
ing the Web
Features
options.*

Check Block Popup Windows to block popups from appearing. (Actually,
Firefox figures that you don't want to see popups and checks this by default.)
That's all there is to it! When you're surfing and a website tries to display a
popup, a bar appears under the toolbars; in addition, a small icon showing a
screen with an X on it appears in the right corner of the status bar to indicate
that a popup was blocked. Examples of both of these are shown in Figure 3-2.

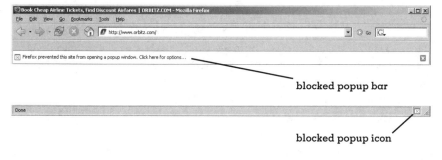

**blocked popup bar**

**blocked popup icon**

**Figure 3-2**

*The blocked
popup bar.*

Firefox, being the helpful little product that it is, gives you some options for what to do when you get a blocked popup. When you click the popup bar, Firefox displays a context menu of options. If you click to allow popups for the website, the popup bar disappears (although the popup icon still appears in the lower-right corner). From now on, Firefox allows any popups that appear for this website to be displayed. (You can get the same menu by clicking the popup icon in the status bar.)

The only problem with allowing popups is that from now on every popup from every website below this, which includes (here's the important part) every website that's displaying popups on subordinate web pages, can now display popups on your screen without being blocked. If you allowed www.findareallycoolhouseforyourself.com to display popups, you might also get popups from www.gimmeareallycheapmortgage.com. This could allow way too much.

You can narrow things down by selecting **Edit Popup Blocker Options** from the context menu (or click **Allowed Sites for the Block Popups** option on the Web Features screen shown in Figure 3-1). The Allowed Sites screen appears, as shown in Figure 3-3.

**Figure 3-3**

*The Allowed Sites screen.*

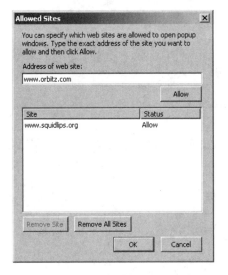

The Allowed Sites screen lets you edit the list of websites that are allowed to display popups even when popup blocking is turned on. You can add a website to the list by entering the website address in the address field and clicking **Allow**. (Any websites that you previously allowed through this screen or by clicking the **allow popups** option on the context menu already appear on the list.) If you've got a website setting that lets too much happen, you can restrict it, allowing just specific pages to display popups. You can remove previously allowed websites from the list by highlighting the site(s) in question and clicking **Remove Site**, or you can click **Remove All** to block every website from displaying popups. When you are satisfied with your entries, click OK.

As I said, many popups are relatively innocuous. Some websites use popups to ask if you got everything you wanted from your visit and to suggest alternative sources of information (admittedly, these are usually paid advertisers, but you really could want to explore these, too). There are popups that provide quick indexing of a website's features. Some websites won't even work right if you don't allow popups, such as a website that displays the site index or menu options in a popup that's designed to float over the screen. But the majority of popups are designed to be difficult to close (ever try to find the "close" option on some of the popups advertising movies?), easy to click by accident, or just plain obnoxious. I leave popup blocking on all the time and don't usually allow any website to circumvent it.

Although the Firefox popup blocker is pretty good, popups continue to evolve and get more sophisticated at skirting attempts to suppress them. You may still have a few popups here and there from uncouth sites.

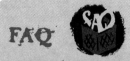

**FAQ**

**What if I just don't care that much about popups?**

If you just don't care that much about popups and don't want to be bothered by their existence when they're blocked, select "Don't show this message when popups are blocked." The popup bar disappears, but popups are still blocked. If you want the popup bar to reappear, you can always click the popup icon in the lower-right corner of the screen and uncheck this option on the context menu.

# Blocking Images

If popups are the number one annoyance, banner ads can't be far behind. Banner ads are the long thin graphic images that are frequently displayed at the top or bottom of web pages, offering any of a zillion different services you probably don't want or need. They're billboards on the information superhighway, and they're about as culturally devoid as real billboards, too.

You can block images from appearing on web pages fairly easily. From the Web Features Options screen (shown earlier in Figure 3-1), uncheck **Load Images**, and click OK. From now on, all images are suppressed. As an example, take a look at the mozilla.org main page, displayed in Figure 3-4. Graphics appear in the title bar and throughout the page.

When images are blocked, Firefox displays the page without the images. If alternative text is supplied in the page's source code, Firefox displays that instead of the picture. For example, in Figure 3-5, you see that text is entered for the various icons missing under the "Other Mozilla Software" section, but the big Firefox logo on the right of the screen is gone without a trace. Missing graphics may show a border with the standard "X" icon in the upper-left corner, showing that there's a missing graphic, but for the most part, you see plenty of nothing.

**Figure 3-4**

*The mozilla.org main page without images blocked.*

**Figure 3-5**

*The mozilla.org main page with images blocked.*

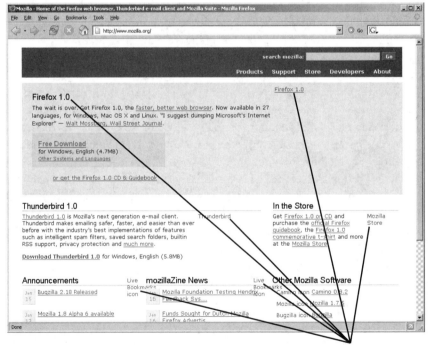

**alternative text**

While this prevents banner ads, it prevents everything else in the way of graphics, too. Websites aren't just text, by a long shot, so you may want to split the difference and try blocking images that do not come from the website itself. Check **for the originating website only** and you'll start seeing graphics that originate from within the domain. Most banner ads and advertising graphics are linked from other domains—even if they're under the company's control—so this will probably block most of the advertising graphics.

**TOOL KIT**

### A Few Words About Domains and Subdomains

A website's domain is identified by its web address. For example, the domain in the address http://www.abcdef.com/about_us.html is abcdef.com. When you enter a web address in Firefox, the address is looked up in a huge table that lists all the known domains and the corresponding IP (Internet Protocol) addresses. The IP addresses uniquely identify every computer connected to the Internet, so your request is routed through the various connections until you get to the computer in question. While you can enter an IP address in the address field and get to where you wanted to go, it's a lot easier to remember a domain name than a string of numbers—and frequently a lot more fun, too. (Domains are sometimes referred to as "servers," which isn't precisely accurate, but it's usually close enough for hand grenades and horseshoes.)

You can have subdomains as well. For example, www.abcdef.com might have subdomains of www.phillip.abcdef.com, www.greg.abcdef.com, and www.elisabeth.abcdef.com. Subdomains are easy to link to a different directory in the computer's file system, making it easy to differentiate between various areas of interest on the website. Just to complicate things, though, you could have a subdomain at the same location as its parent domain. For example, when you enter www.dictionary.com, you actually get www.dictionary.reference.com. It's still the site you want, but it serves a purpose for the website owner. Many websites prefer to avoid subdomains and use subdirectories instead, so instead of www.elisabeth.abcdef.com, you might have www.abcdef.com/elisabeth.

This information probably won't be very useful unless you're doing a lot of web design, but it does give you some background for when you're figuring out what popups and images to block.

Unfortunately, while this technique of blocking images is good for a well-organized website with all its graphics within the domain, it's not so good if you're dealing with a website that pulls graphics from all over the web. If you're blocking too many graphics because of a relatively small number of banner ads, try this: first, check **Load Images** and uncheck **for the originating website only**. Next, right-click the graphic for a banner or other ad you want to block, and from the context menu, select **Block images from**. Firefox adds the domain to the Exception list, so any time a web page tries to load a graphic from that domain, Firefox says, "Not so fast, Buster!" You can add and remove locations just like you did earlier when allowing sites for popups by clicking **Exceptions** and working with the sites on the Exception list (shown in Figure 3-6). With this technique, you can build up a list of the most common offenders in your world and eventually filter almost all the banner ads and the like automatically.

**Figure 3-6**

*The Exceptions screen.*

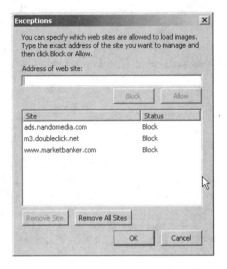

One other image blocking feature is very handy. Suppose you display a web page with an obnoxious image. Right-click the image and select **Block images from <domain>** on the context menu. Firefox adds that domain to the list on the Exceptions screen so that any images coming from the domain in the future will be blocked. No muss, no fuss, and you don't even have to display the Exceptions screen to do this.

### TOOL KIT
### If Image Blocking by Itself Isn't Good Enough...

Firefox's image blocking feature is pretty good, but it's kinda brute-force: you block nothing, everything, almost everything, and/or flag domains individually for blocking. If you need a little more control, you may want to look at an *extension*—an add-on for Firefox—called *Adblock*. *Adblock*, available at http://adblock.mozdev.org, gives you extensive filtering options so that you can see only the content you want to see. You can filter individual ads, all ads from a domain, and even Shockwave Flash ads.

*Adblock* is discussed in Chapter 7, "Customizing Firefox with Third-Party Extensions and Themes."

So now you should be able to control two of the biggest annoyances of the web, popups and banner ads, using built-in Firefox options. You can block popups and banner ads and filter for selected domains when blocking them. You even learned about *Adblock*, a Firefox extension that can dramatically enhance Firefox's ability to filter banner ads and other graphics.

Coming up next on the program is information on how to search the web with Firefox. You can use web search engines like every other browser, but Firefox lets you build any search engine into the toolbar so that you just type in the thing you're looking for rather than having to go to the search engine's site first and then type in your search term. There's also information on the Firefox "find" option. You'll also learn about using and customizing Smart Keywords, a Firefox feature that gives you shortcuts to your favorite websites.

# Searching the Web

**DO OR DIE:**

>> Find stuff on the web

>> Find more stuff on the web

>> Come up with ways to find still more stuff on the web

>> A fun web searching game

No matter how recently you started surfing the web, you've likely been overwhelmed with the amount of information available. (If you're like me, you've also thought that the web is living proof that too many people have too much free time on their hands.) Given that there are at least 40 million websites and over 8 **billion** web pages to choose from, finding the right piece of information requires some sophisticated search tools.

Firefox has incorporated some of the best search technology available—the Google search engine—into the navigation toolbar. Searching is built in. The Firefox address field looks like any other address field: it's a field you enter a web address into. Ho-hum. But if you enter a search word or phrase, Firefox looks up the phrase using Google's "I'm Feeling Lucky" option and takes you to the page Google thinks will most likely meet your search criteria. For example, entering "Mason Williams" takes you to MasonWilliams-online.com, the official Mason Williams web page.

This feature is really helpful (I'm lazy and I hate having to always type in the "www." and ".com" for basic addresses), but you don't always get what you expect. While the "I'm Feeling Lucky" option frequently takes you to the domain of the same name—"banjo" goes to www.banjo.com—this isn't always the case. While you might expect that entering "Weavers" would take you to www.weavers.com or maybe a website about weaving or even the Tannahill Weavers, currently it takes you to a NASA web page for the NASA Advanced

Supercomputing division. The word "Weavers" is nowhere to be found on the page, which seems to make no sense at all, until you look up "Weavers" in Google and discover that this page is a redirected web page from the address www.nas.nasa.gov/NAS/WebWeavers/. Okay, *now* it makes sense… sorta.

There is a downside to "I'm feeling lucky" searches. For example, if you entered "whitehouse" as a search term, you'd probably get what you want: http://www.whitehouse.gov, the President's website. However, until recently, entering "whitehouse.com" would take you to a wholly unexpected and quite child- and work-unfriendly website. Sometimes entering the plain search phrase gives you what you want but adding ".com" to the end of the phrase doesn't.

## Using the Search Toolbar

Probably everyone who's used the web has used Google at one time or another, or even daily, like many of us do. I'd be crippled online without it; it's *that* good. Rather than going to the Google website for a quick search, though, I can simply enter my search criteria in the Google search toolbar and bang the Enter key, and I get a standard Google search results window like the one shown in Figure 4-1. As you can see, the first page in the list is the Mason Williams website, but I can now explore the listings for the other 28,900 search results at my leisure.

When you enter a search phrase in the search toolbar, Firefox remembers it by default. The next time you start typing something in the search toolbar, Firefox tries to match it with previous entries that appear on a dropdown list. You can always type the first few characters of a long search phrase, double-click the phrase or press the down arrow to highlight the phrase, and press Enter. It's a lot easier typing "Lin" and selecting the phrase than having to type "Lincoln's doctor's son's dog" a second time. You can clean out the search list by right-clicking in the search toolbar itself and selecting **Clear Search History**.

For really fast searching, you can highlight a phrase, any phrase, in a website, and then right-click it. A small context menu appears from which you can select **Search web for…** and display a Google search results page. You don't have to type anything.

**Figure 4-1**

*A typical Google search results page.*

If you prefer using keyboard shortcuts to mousing around, you can press Ctrl+L, F6, or Alt+D to jump to the address field. To get to the search toolbar quickly, use Ctrl+K (if you're using a Mac, use Ctrl+E; for Linux, use Ctrl+J). Your hands never leave your wrists or the keyboard, either.

The search toolbar isn't limited to just Google searches. If you click the Google icon in the search toolbar, you see a selection of search engines that are built in, as shown in Figure 4-2.

**Figure 4-2**

*The list of built-in search engines.*

Simply select the search engine you want to use the search toolbar for. The icon for the new search engine now appears in the search toolbar field instead of the Google icon. Table 4-1 lists the search engines and what they do.

| SEARCH ENGINE | WHAT'S THERE |
|---|---|
| Google | The Google search engine, www.google.com |
| Yahoo | The Yahoo search engine, www.yahoo.com |
| Amazon | Amazon, the online bookseller, www.amazon.com |
| Creative Commons | A nonprofit organization that offers "flexible copyright" on publicly licensed photographs, writing, and code, creativecommons.org |
| Dictionary.com | A collection of online dictionaries (although not, alas, a slang dictionary), www.dictionary.com |
| eBay | eBay, the auction site, www.ebay.com |

Table 4-1    Built-in search engines in Firefox.

Click the search engine you want to use. (To change the search engine using the keyboard instead of the mouse, press Ctrl+Up or Ctrl+Down to scroll through the selections.) The icon in the search toolbar changes appropriately, and Firefox now uses the specified search engine to look up the word or phrase you enter.

**FAQ**

**How many search engines do you want?**

If you don't think the built-in Firefox search engines give a wide enough range, you can add search engines to the list by clicking Add Engines at the bottom of the context menu. The web page you go to lets you download even more search engines, including

- IMDB, the Internet Movie Database, something I use daily
- CDDB, the CD Database, which lets you find information on albums, artists, and songs
- Merriam-Webster, a dictionary different from the ones available through dictionary.com
- LEO, an English-to-German translation tool
- WikiPedia, an online free encyclopedia so amazingly different that you'll have to see it for yourself to appreciate it

*Still* not enough choice? You can also go to the Mycroft Project (http://mycroft.mozdev.org) and look at its latest downloadable search engines. There are well over a thousand search engines in about two dozen categories, including Arts, News, Reference, Business & Economy, Games, Religion, and Travel.

# Searching Pages

The preceding section told you how to search for the right web page, but what do you do if you found the right page but need to skim for the phrase in question? Time to press Ctrl+F to find something. (You can also select Edit | Find, but it's not worth the effort—just about everyone presses Ctrl+F.)

Unlike many other browsers, Firefox doesn't display a window in the middle of the text to get in the way of what you're searching for. Instead, you see a small, well-behaved Find bar at the bottom of the screen, like the one shown in Figure 4-3.

**FRIDGE**

Instead of Ctrl+F, you can just press "/" to display the Find bar. This is faster, but there's a catch: the Find bar disappears after about 5 seconds of inactivity. I usually prefer the Find bar to stay there until I'm done with it—at which time I press Esc—but you may prefer the automatic cleanup of your browser screen.

Find field

Figure 4-3

*The Find bar.*

When the Find bar appears, the cursor is automatically positioned in the Find field. Enter the word or phrase you want to find. As you type, Firefox automatically starts finding the first word or phrase on the web page that matches what you've typed. As it does so, it highlights the word in bright green, as shown in Figure 4-4.

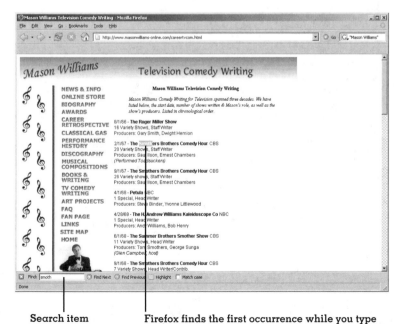

Search item       Firefox finds the first occurrence while you type

Figure 4-4

*Find results highlighted in green.*

As you type more of the word or phrase, Firefox highlights the corresponding letters. If you had typed "the" at first, Firefox would highlight the first occurrence of those three letters, whether it was "*the*" or "*anathema.*" If the next letter is "r," Firefox then finds the first occurrence of "there," "other," or "rather."

After you find the thing you're looking for, you can click Find Next or Find Previous on the Find bar to find and highlight the next or previous occurrence of the search word or phrase. (Keyboard afficionados will press Ctrl+G or Ctrl+Shift+G to do the same thing.) When you run out of instances on the page, Firefox starts searching again at the top of the page.

If you're just plain impatient, you can click **Highlight** on the Find bar. Firefox then highlights every occurrence of the search word or phrase in yellow so you can quickly pick through them to find the very thing you're looking for. An example of this appears in Figure 4-5.

**Figure 4-5**

*Highlighting every match for the search item.*

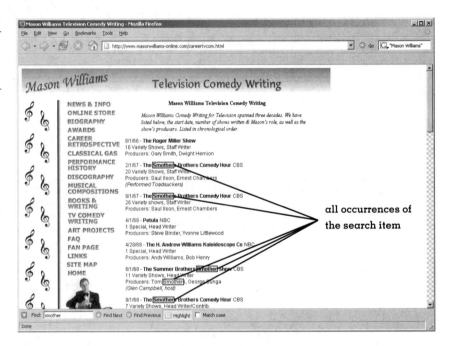

If you end up typing something in the Find field that isn't on the page, the Find field changes color, and "Phrase not found" is displayed on the Find bar, as shown in Figure 4-6.

**Figure 4-6**

*The search item was not found.*

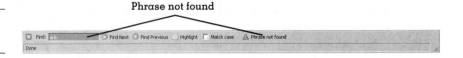

One other thing you can do with the basic search is to make it case-sensitive. The default is for Firefox to find any example of the word or phrase without regard to capitalization, so entering "The" as the search item will find "the," "THE," and even "tHe" on the web page. Checking **Match case** on the Find bar guarantees that you find only instances of the search item that are capitalized in exactly the same way.

You can close the Find bar by pressing Esc or clicking the X icon on the left side of the Find bar, or you can just leave it up until you need it again if you prefer. You can display another page and then click Find Next to find the "next" (first) occurrence of the search item on the new page.

## Using Find as You Type

If you're doing a lot of searching, you can tell Firefox to search for anything you type while surfing. Go to Tools | Options | Advanced. The Options screen with the Advanced options appears. If it's not already visible, expand the selection for Accessibility at the top of the list, as shown in Figure 4-7.

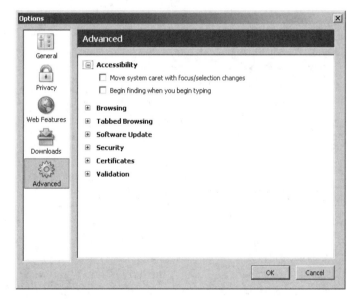

**Figure 4-7**
*The Options screen with the Advanced options displayed.*

Check Begin finding when you begin typing, and then click OK. Now, whenever you start typing, Firefox opens the Find bar and enters whatever you type in the Find field. You can use the find options and the keyboard shortcuts as usual. If you don't do anything for about five seconds, the Find bar closes on its own.

**TOOL KIT**

**Cool Google Tricks**

Google has a selection of *advanced operators*—words and phrases that do special things when you add them to the Google search bar. The operator intitle: finds the subsequent word or phrase in the URL's title. Try entering "intitle:Index of" in the Google search bar. You'll see links such as LibDex, the world index of library catalogues, the Iowa State Entomology Index of Internet Resources, and the Index of Native American Resources on the Internet, along with 12,400,000 others. You can also try the inurl: operator, which looks for the search phrase in the website's URL. Entering "inurl:firefox" lists websites that have "firefox" in the address. Not only does this find www.firefox.com, but it also finds www.mozilla.org/firefox and www.firefox-browser.de. Advanced operators can be combined. Entering both "intitle:firefox" and "inurl:gov" displays all government websites (.gov) that have page titles containing "Firefox."

There are a number of other Google advanced operators that you may find useful. Look for more information in the Google help files at www.google.com/help.

## Finding Links

Most of the time you'll be looking for a word in a web page—you Googled this web page, and the thing you were searching for has to be here somewhere!—but you can also search for links on a web page. Without opening the Find bar, type an apostrophe. Firefox opens the Find bar, which looks like it always does. Start typing in the Find field. Rather than highlighting the first occurrence of the search item, Firefox highlights the first occurrence of the search item in a link. After you've found a link, you can press Enter to follow the link. You can use all the standard next/previous options with this feature, but be aware that the Find bar vanishes automatically after five seconds of inactivity.

## Using Smart Keywords

As you've seen already, Firefox offers more search options and features than most other browsers, but there's still more to go. You can use Smart Keywords to search directly from the address field rather than selecting the search engine you prefer in the search toolbar and then entering your search criteria.

To use Firefox's Smart Keywords, type one of the predefined keywords, such as "google," into the address field, followed by the thing you're searching for. (An example of looking up "five-string banjo" in Google appears in Figure 4-8.) Press Enter, and Firefox looks for your search item as if you'd gone to Google.com and entered the search phrase directly.

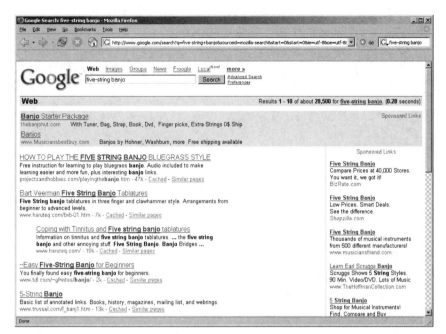

**Figure 4-8**

*Searching on Google using a Smart Keyword.*

Firefox comes with five keywords for popular websites, as shown in Table 4-2. Give each of these Smart Keywords a try!

| | |
|---|---|
| **Table 4-2** | **Standard Smart Keywords in Firefox.** |

| SMART KEYWORD | WHAT IT DOES |
|---|---|
| Google | Searches on Google.com for the word or phrase you enter. |
| Goto | Does a Google "I'm Feeling Lucky" search (this is the same as just entering something in the address field). |
| Dict | Looks up the word or phrase in the online dictionaries at Dictionary.com. |
| Wiki | Looks up the word or phrase in Wikipedia, the free online encyclopedia. |
| Quote | Looks up the stock symbol on a variety of stock services: Yahoo Finance, Fool.com, MSN MoneyCentral, and ClearStation. |

## Doing It Yourself

The built-in Smart Keywords are convenient, but you may want to be able to search for many other things. You can actually set up Smart Keywords for any website that has a search field so that you can quickly search for any of the following:

- Auto parts
- Old record albums
- Fine tea
- Matchmaking
- Butterfly wing art
- Montblanc pens
- Cell phones
- Plumbing supplies
- Tulip bulbs
- Quilt fabric

It's very simple to set up your own Smart Keywords. Go to a website you want to create a Smart Keyword for, and right-click in the search field. From the context menu that appears, select **Add a Keyword for this Search**. The Add Bookmark screen appears. Enter the name you want to assign to the bookmark in the Name field. In the Keyword field, enter the keyword you want to use for this. For example, if you had set up a keyword for eBay, the name might be "eBay.com," but the keyword would almost certainly be "ebay." (An example of this appears in Figure 4-9.)

Click OK to save the bookmark in the Bookmarks folder for now. (You'll see how to put bookmarks into other folders in Chapter 5, "Bookmarks and History.") Now when you type "ebay banjo five-string" in the address field, Firefox goes to www.ebay.com and does a search using the search criteria you entered.

**Figure 4-9**

*The Add Bookmark screen with an entry for eBay.*

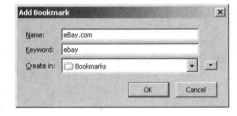

# FRIDGE

## Search Games People Play

After you get the hang of searching on the web and feel like you're a pro, you should try a game called NetBullseye, described on Harold Chaput's web page at http://www.cs.utexas.edu/users/chaput/netbullseye/welcome.html. (I've also seen this game called Googlewhacking, described on http://www.googlewhack.com.) The basic idea of both is that you and any number of friends do a search on two unrelated words or phrases on a search engine. The first person to enter a search request that produces exactly one found document wins the round.

Here are some other rules:

- Search terms must be mandatory, so they should be preceded by a plus sign (+).
- Phrases must be enclosed in quotes to make sure that the exact phrase is found.
- Words and phrases must be spelled correctly.
- You can use any search engine you like, as long as everyone uses the same engine. Harold's web page recommends AltaVista, but this is probably because it's an older page; I (and the folks at Googlewhack.com, obviously) prefer Google. Any search engine will do, really.

Here are some examples of search pairs that do pretty well, though not all are perfect:

- "Disneyland" and "Rockwell scale"
- "left-handed banjo" and "ice cream"
- "bardolatry" and "particle physics"
- "Spanish-American war" and "Michigan J. Frog"
- "Fibonacci series" and "eleemosynary"
- "Mad Magazine" and "two-toed sloth"
- "mediocre superstar" and "big money" (heyyyyyyy, does this sound like a prime-time game show or what?)

As a variation, you can have everyone come up with their pair of search terms in a round and the winner of the round is the person with the lowest number of hits. If you're using Google, for example, you'd grab the number of hits off the top-right corner of the Google search screen.

I really like this game. The more trivial, random, and disjointed you can be with your search phrases, the better... usually. Coming up with a search pair that doesn't have any hits at all is a disqualifier for that round, so you can't be totally bizarre in your guesses.

For a better chance of winning pairs, use phrases that represent opposite ends of some real or imaginary continuum, such as "red heat" and "blue Christmas" or "high road" and "low motives." This technique is so easy and formulaic that there's not a lot of sport in it sometimes. You can also go for two *completely* unrelated ideas (my preference), such as "Moody Blues" and "Hall effect" or "diffraction jewelry" and "Space Needle." The latter technique is more in the spirit of the original game and is a good deal harder to pull off successfully.

As I write this, Harold Chaput doesn't appear to be updating the NetBullseye website any more, but you can check out a number of former winners on his "Hall of Fame" page. (Karen Mulholland, who told me about this silly game in the first place, has a few winners under the name Mnemosyne.) The Googlewhacking site has lots of entries in its "Whack Stack," too. Keep in mind that things on search engines change frequently. When first created, the Disneyland/Rockwell scale pair was a winner with only one hit. Three weeks later, it had two hits. If you play this regularly, you may want to try pairs that are almost perfect every so often just to see if they improve.

As you can see, whenever you sit down to use Firefox, you'll probably start by searching for something somewhere online. Firefox has so many different built-in ways to search that you'll find yourself thinking of ways to customize it just for what you do.

After you've found things, you need to know how to find them again. The next chapter is my favorite: how to create and organize bookmarks that let you find a website the next time you need it. You'll learn how to create bookmarks that update themselves automatically and put bookmarks on the toolbar for fast reference. There's also a description of the Firefox sidebar, a quick reference for bookmarks and your browsing history.

# BLOG

## Websites to Waste Your Time With

The web has forever solved the problem of "There's nothing to do!" There is always something fun to do on the web that nevertheless wastes time and productivity. The following list gives you a few ideas for things to do when you don't feel like doing anything more useful.

> **Note**
> The websites listed here have been screened for anything particularly rude or offensive and are likely to be reasonably office-safe, but you should always keep in mind that things on the web change and tastes are variable. If you find something that offends you—and there's a lot to be offended by on the web—go to another website and don't return to the one that offended you. And, if any of these links don't work by the time you try them, try searching Google for the name or a description to see if they've moved or if you can find something similar elsewhere.

## Cartoons and Movies

**Albino Blacksheep**
http://www.albinoblacksheep.com    Amazing and silly animations of all kinds.

### AtomFilms

http://atomfilms.com   Independent films of all sizes and shapes. Be sure to check out Bill Plympton's cartoons (start with "Your Face" and "25 Ways to Quit Smoking") and Nick "Wallace and Gromit" Park's claymations. Caution: not everything on this site is office-safe.

### User Friendly the Comic Strip

http://userfriendly.org   This comic strip focuses on life at an Internet service provider and tech support facility. Deliciously funny if you work in high-tech or know anyone who does.

### Pot-Shots

http://www.west.net/~ashleigh/index.html   Those wonderful postcards from Ashleigh Brilliant that we all know.

### IFILM—Movies, Trailers, Music, and Viral Videos

http://www.ifilm.com   Where AtomFilms feels a bit fringier, IFILM is a little more mainstream... well, at times, anyway. You can find movies, music videos, TV clips, even SuperBowl ads. Be sure to check out the Viral Videos collection.

### Stick Figure Death Theatre

http://www.sfdt.com   Evolving from just a few simple computer animations into a website with thousands of cartoons, all of which seem to involve one or more stick figures being horribly killed in more ways than Kenny on "South Park."

### Badmovies.org

http://www.badmovies.org   "A website to the detriment of good film." If your tastes run to the B-movie or lower, find out how to reach new heights in low taste with the recommendations here.

### Oh, the Humanity!

http://www.ohthehumanity.com   More bad movies (aka "The Ghost of the Son of New Heights in Low Taste Returns Again Once More!").

### Golden Age Cartoons

http://www.goldenagecartoons.com   A collection of cartoons and comic strips from Hollywood's Golden Age.

### Singing Horses

http://svt.se/hogafflahage/hogafflaHage_site/Kor/hestekor.swf   A charming little Shockwave animation. Click each of the horses in turn to get it singing its part of the quartet. It takes a little practice to get the timing right, but it's worth it.

### Calvin and Hobbes

http://www.ucomics.com/calvinandhobbes   "Calvin and Hobbes" strips, run 14 years to the day after they originally appeared in syndication.

# Music

### The Arrogant Worms

http://www.arrogant-worms.com   One of my favorite groups! They're Canadian and have written several alternatives to the Canadian national anthem, "O, Canada!," including "Canada's Really Big," "Rocks and Trees," and "We Are the Beaver." The Arrogant Worms have released about a dozen CDs, but, as far as I know, they've yet to perform a serious song.

### MerleFest: the Americana Music Celebration

http://www.merlefest.org   An annual Americana music festival held in North Carolina in honor of Doc and Merle Watson, with over a hundred scheduled bands and artists. If you're into fiddle, banjo, or folk guitar, plan on being there.

### PolkaJammer.com

http://www.polkajammer.com   An Internet radio station that gives you non-stop polka music.

### Whole Wheat Radio

http://www.wholewheatradio.com   An Internet radio station based in Talkeetna, Alaska, with a rich and varied collection of alternative and folk music. They have highly eclectic tastes are open to listener suggestions.

### Kelly Wright

http://www.kellywright.com   Kelly Wright, a fabulous vocalist. Not only does she sing beautifully and really belt out the numbers on stage, she's got a dazzling career doing voiceovers for commercials, computer games, and children's toys.

### Lorne Elliott

http://www.lorne-elliott.com/music.htm   Lorne Elliott is a very funny singer and entertainer. You can periodically hear one of his songs, "Morris the Moose," on Dr. Demento's show. (Check out http://www.drdemento.com or listen to shows online at http://www.thedoctordementoshow.com.)

### New Zealand Symphony Orchestra Amusements

http://users.actrix.co.nz/dgold/fun/index.html   Jokes, stories, and fun stuff for musicians. Some of the links on this page are inactive, but keep looking; there are some gems here.

# Silliness and Entertainments

### Welcome to Archie McPhee Online

http://www.mcphee.com    Archie McPhee is probably the world's biggest and best novelty store. I buy all my rubber chickens here.

### Dribbleglass.com

http://www.dribbleglass.com    "Sips from the dribbleglass of life." Pictures, jokes, trivia, silly e-cards.

### Zeeks

http://www.zeeks.com    Lots of fun online games specifically for kids.

### Office Humor links from ishouldbeworking.com

http://www.ishouldbeworking.com/office.htm    The epitome of ways to waste your time, by pulling pranks on your coworkers to waste their time as well.

### Bad Cookie—Real Web Chinese Fortune Cookie

http://www.badcookie.com    People being too nice to you? Feeling sure of yourself? Each time you hit this website, you'll get another little ping to your self-confidence in the form of a bad fortune cookie fortune.

### Internet Oracle

http://cgi.cs.indiana.edu/~oracle/index.cgi    If you need advice, ask the Internet Oracle, an ancient Net tradition.

### Kooks Museum Lobby

http://home.pacifier.com/~dkossy/kooksmus.html    Donna Kossy's Freeze-Dried Kooks Museum serves to highlight some of the lesser-known and stranger theories and opinions available on the web. Or maybe it just serves as a good laugh; who knows?

### MyCatHatesYou dot com

http://www.mycathatesyou.com    He really does. There are pictures to prove it.

### I-Tarot

http://manor.york.ac.uk/cgi-bin/cards.sh    The Internet Tarot is the hand-distilled wisdom of the moderns. "The Queen of Bobbins. The judgement: A proud supervisor, crossing a stream, falls back. It furthers one to wash up."

# Science and Technology

**Short Words to Explain Relativity**
http://www.muppetlabs.com/~breadbox/txt/al.html    Relativity is explained in words of no more than four letters.

**Animated Engines**
http://www.keveney.com/Engines.html    This is both fun and educational. You can see how all kinds of engines really work.

**The T.W.I.N.K.I.E.S. Project**
http://www.twinkiesproject.com    Scientific things you can do with America's snack food with a shelf life of years, such as gravitational response tests, radiation tests, and Turing tests.

**Welcome to Heavens-Above!**
http://www.heavens-above.com    For stargazers, this website gives you times and locations to spot all kinds of satellites, the International Space Station, comets, planets, and constellations.

**Mechanical Confections**
http://www.ginakamentsky.com/workpg1.html    Gina Kamentsky's handmade mechanical banks.

**Ig® Nobel prizes**
http://www.improb.com/ig/ig-top.html    The official website of the Ig Nobel Prizes, sponsored by the Annals of Improbable Research (AIR).

**HubbleSite**
http://hubblesite.org/newscenter    Enjoy the site and see why the Hubble Space Telescope must be saved.

**HowStuffWorks—Learn How Everything Works!**
http://www.howstuffworks.com    Just what it says: how everything works, from snowflakes to TiVo to handcuffs to building muscle mass.

**Patents—Patent Full-Text and Full-Page Image Databases**
http://www.uspto.gov/patft/index.html    You can look up every U.S. patent ever issued.

**The Buckminster Fuller Institute**
http://www.bfi.org    Look at this and be inspired by Buckminster Fuller and his ideas.

# What Time Is It?

### Time

http://entries.the5k.org/365/t.htm   An unusual digital clock. This makes a nice display for a pseudo-screensaver.

### Today Date and Time

http://www.ecben.net/calendar.shtml   Today's date and time, including moon phase and some other interesting information.

### Industrious 2001

http://www.lares.dti.ne.jp/~yugo/storage/monocrafts_ver3/03/index.html   A really unusual form of "digital" clock. I always wonder about the eventual stack of eraser crumbs that'd build up, but that's just me.

### The Death Clock

http://www.deathclock.com   How long will you live? Log on here and find out.

# Words

### Famous Quotes and Quotations at BrainyQuote

http://www.brainyquote.com   Quotes from all sorts of people on all sorts of topics.

### World Wide Words

http://www.worldwidewords.org/genindex.htm   For those of us fascinated with the anfractuous and the sesquipedalian in English.

### High Tech Quotes

http://www.sysprog.net/quotwrit.html   A large collection of quotes, all dealing with some aspect of computers and high tech.

### The (sort of) official Daniel Pinkwater Home Page!

http://pinkwater.com/pzone   Daniel Pinkwater is one of the world's greatest authors of children's books. He's very strange. I am one of his millions of devoted fans.

### Says You!

http://www.wgbh.org/radio/saysyou   The website for the NPR radio quiz show for the frivolously overeducated.

### Bookfinder

http://www.bookfinder.com   The best online used bookstore in my opinion, Bookfinder combines listings for the inventories of over 60,000 booksellers and makes them searchable with a simple and effective interface. Everyone else you may have used online is already part of this list, so use just this one site for used books and be assimilated.

### The Endeneu.com Filter Collection

http://www.endeneu.com/funstuff/miguel   Enter text and translate it into various "dialects," including goth, superhero, and pirate. "Now be the time fer all hearrty corsairs ta come ta the aid o' their party! Arrrh!"

### The Dialectizer

http://www.rinkworks.com/dialect   Like the Edeneu.com filter collection, but this has a completely different selection of filters, including redneck, Elmer Fudd, and Swedish Chef. You can translate a whole web page at a time.

### The Zompist Phrasebook

http://www.zompist.com/phrases.html   How to be snide in nine different languages.

### Wordscapes® Interesting Assorted Sites

http://www.wordscapes.net/assorted-1-sites.htm   A large collection of interesting sites in case you run out of things to look at from this list.

### The Bulwer-Lytton Fiction Contest

http://www.bulwer-lytton.com   You know: "It was a dark and stormy night…" Check out the annual contest results here.

# News, Information, and Vaguely Educational Things

### NewsIsFree: Your Personal News Portal

http://www.newsisfree.com   Search the news or build your own customized news feed from 18,000 online news sources.

### Roadside America

http://www.roadsideamerica.com   Going somewhere? This is "your online guide to offbeat tourist attractions." Always check this whenever you're planning a road trip to find out what to see on the way.

### Coudal Partners

http://www.coudal.com/moom.php   The Museum of Online Museums. This site provides links to a wide variety of online museums and shows.

### Snopes

http://www.snopes.com   If you get email that sounds like it's possibly an urban legend (particularly if it says "Pass this on!"), check it out first on Snopes and make sure you're not just cluttering up other people's in-boxes with mythology.

### Primitive Ways

http://www.primitiveways.com   Look here to find out more about bow scraping, fire drills, and other ancient and fascinating skills.

### Chuck Shepherd's News of the Weird

http://www.uexpress.com/newsoftheweird   For when life is looking just a little too sane.

### Bathroom Readers' Institute

http://www.bathroomreader.com/home.html   The BRI publishes several dozen large books of short articles and trivia specifically designed to be read in the bathroom.

### The Institute of Official Cheer

http://www.lileks.com/institute/index.html   Pop culture re-examined, including the classic Gallery of Regrettable Food. Also check out the parent site, http://www.lileks.com, for more strange excursions into parts of our collective pasts.

### The Baby Name Wizard's NameVoyager

http://babynamewizard.com/namevoyager/lnv0105.html   How popular is your name now? How popular was it 10, 50, or 100 years ago? What are people naming their babies now? Fun stuff to see how times change.

### Panoramic Photographs (American Memory from the Library of Congress)

http://lcweb2.loc.gov/ammem/collections/panoramic_photo   Approximately 4,000 panoramic photos between twenty-eight inches and six feet long with an average width of ten inches. These photos were taken between 1851 and 1991 and feature American cityscapes, landscapes, and group portraits. They're wonderful slices of life and history that will almost certainly put you in a reflective mood.

### Flickr

http://www.flickr.com   An online digital photo site for blogging and sharing digital photos under a Creative Commons license.

# Other Websites

**Chivalry Sports**

http://www.renstore.com   The finest store in the world for meeting all your Renaissance and medieval needs.

**Mo Hotta, Mo Betta**

http://www.mohotta.com   If you like hot sauces, check this out. Temperatures range from Lukewarm to Grim Reaper. They're not kidding about the high end; some of this stuff should be classified "For external use only!"

**The Budget Traveller's Guide to Sleeping in Airports**

http://www.sleepinginairports.net   Probably more for the young and flexible, but a valuable thing to know for that time when you get stranded in an airport overnight by bad weather, bad connections, or bad service. (Why does an image of O'Hare come indelibly to mind as I type this?)

**The Teacup**

http://seattleteacup.com   A great tea shop. I buy all my tea there online.

**Freeoldies—The Abandonware Search Engine**

http://www.freeoldies.com   Ever feel an urge to try some of the really old computer games from 10, 15, 20, 25 years ago? You can download all kinds of abandonware—games that were removed from business distribution and abandoned by their authors—at this site. The oldest game is Adventure from 1977, a classic text-based game written when men were men and women were women and cars were cars and the railroads ran on time.

**TvTix.com Free TV Tickets—Print Television Tickets Online!**

http://www.tvtix.com   A clearinghouse of information for getting tickets to tapings of all kinds of TV shows. Be a member of Jay Leno's audience! Watch people get the right question on "Jeopardy!" It's all here.

# Finding Other Unusual Websites

You can find still more websites to waste your time by doing a quick search on Google for lists of links: try searching on "strange websites" or "unusual websites" or even "bizarre websites." All three turn up different lists of websites that are guaranteed to leave you thinking, "Boy howdy, there are some people who really need to find a girlfriend and get away from the darned computer occasionally!"

# Bookmarks and History

iven that there are over 8 billion web pages out there, it's important to be able to flag the pages you like so that you can get back to them again. Firefox uses bookmarks (IE and Safari call these "favorites") to save web addresses. It's much easier to find the needle in the haystack a second time when you have a reminder of where it is. This chapter shows you how to find needles in haystacks over and over again.

## Creating Bookmarks

As part of the Firefox installation procedure, Firefox gives you the option of copying bookmarks from your previous browser, so it's likely that you'll already have a few bookmarks waiting for you. But assuming for a moment that you chose to start with Firefox or that you didn't import previous bookmarks, the Bookmarks menu looks like the one shown in Figure 5-1.

The default Bookmarks menu shows three things: the Bookmark This Page command, the Manage Bookmarks command, and an empty folder for the

**Figure 5-1**
*The Bookmarks menu.*

Bookmarks toolbar. The best way to see how these options work is to add a few bookmarks and experiment with them.

When you have found a web page you want to keep, you can create a bookmark simply by going to Bookmarks | Bookmark This Page or by pressing Ctrl+D. The Add Bookmark screen appears, as shown in Figure 5-2.

**Figure 5-2**

*The Add Bookmark screen.*

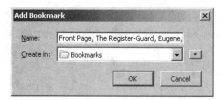

Firefox uses the web page title as a proposed name for the bookmark. You can change this to something shorter and/or more memorable if you wish. For now, just click OK and ignore the other option on the screen. Firefox saves the bookmark in the bookmarks list, which is updated immediately to show the new bookmark, as shown in Figure 5-3.

**Figure 5-3**

*The Bookmarks menu with a bookmark added.*

Most web addresses (aka "URLs" or "Uniform Resource Locators") aren't very easy to remember. We all can manage the easy ones—flowers.com, alaskaairlines.com, and honda.com—but start getting into websites with addresses like http://www.west.net/~ashleigh/currentpotshots.html and you can see why bookmarks are such a good idea. Even if you could remember that exactly, you'd never want to have to type it more than once.

Tim Berners-Lee, the inventor of the World Wide Web, said that had he known how popular the web was going to be, he might have thought harder about the way in which URLs were designed. URLs are wonderful things for reading by computers, but they're somewhat less convenient for people.

Now, all you have to do to display the web page is to click the bookmark to display the web page again. As a matter of fact, you can right-click the bookmark and select Open in New Window to start a new instance of Firefox and open the bookmark in it. (Clicking **Open in New Tab** opens the bookmark in a new tab. Tabs are covered in all their glory in Chapter 6, " Harnessing the Power of Tabbed Browsing.")

# Modifying Bookmarks

You can change bookmarks by right-clicking the bookmark entry and selecting Properties from the context menu to display the Properties screen (shown in Figure 5-4).

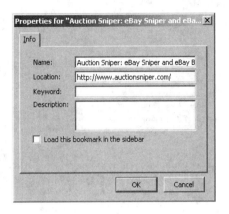

**Figure 5-4**
The Properties screen.

The Properties screen lets you edit the name (which is too long in this case; "Auction Sniper" is fine for the bookmark list), the location (for example, if the web address changes to a new domain), and the keyword. Although keywords (aka "Smart Keywords") are discussed in detail in Chapter 4, "Searching the Web," here's a taste: you can enter a keyword that you type in the address field to bring up the website quickly. You might assign the website in Figure 5-4 a keyword of "AS"—short, simple, and easy to remember. Keywords are very helpful for websites you go to frequently. Entering a description is purely optional, but if you've got several bookmarks that are similar and you need additional information, you can enter a description. The description doesn't appear in the bookmark list, but it's there if you look at the properties. When you are satisfied with your entries, click OK.

You can add a bookmark from scratch by right-clicking the bookmark list and selecting **New Bookmark** from the context menu. You then enter all the information—the name, the web address, and so on—manually in the Properties screen rather than having Firefox pick up the name and location from the web page displayed on the screen. It's useful if you're setting up a few bookmarks offline that you want to look at later, but it's probably not practical for adding bunches of bookmarks to the list.

Someday you'll click a bookmark and get a 404 error. The website's gone away. If you don't have a new address you can enter through the Properties screen, it's time to delete the bookmark. Highlight the bookmark and press **Delete**. (You can also right-click the bookmark and select **Delete** from the context menu if you prefer.)

## Moving Bookmarks

You can add as many bookmarks as you like. Firefox keeps adding them to the bottom of the list. Unfortunately, you'll have problems: pretty soon, you'll have a big list of bookmarks. You can do some simple organization by dragging and dropping a bookmark to a new location on the list, as shown in Figure 5-5.

A line appears where the bookmark will appear when you drop it

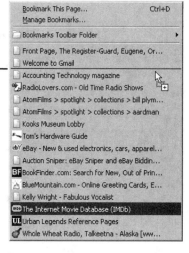

**Figure 5-5**

*Dragging and dropping this bookmark...*

*...to a new location on the Bookmark menu.*

**FRIDGE**

Some websites have really cool icons—known as *favicons*—that help identify the address. If the website doesn't have a favicon, you just see the browser's standard icon. In Firefox, this is an icon of a page with a corner turned down (you know, a bookmark for people who dog-ear books). The favicons show up after you've used the bookmark the first time. Personally, I think favicons are pretty and really useful when looking for a specific bookmark, and I would like more websites to use them.

You can also cut or copy and paste a bookmark from one place on the list to another in about the same way. Right-click the bookmark and select **Cut** or **Copy** from the context menu, and then right-click in the bookmark list and select **Paste** from the context menu to paste the bookmark in the new location. When you copy a bookmark, it shows as the same thing: if you wanted to, you could have five bookmarks on your bookmark list that all say "Kelly Wright—Fabulous Vocalist" and that all point to www.kellywright.com. The only real value to this would be if you wanted to put the same bookmark into several different bookmark folders (described in the next section) or if it would be easier to modify copies of the one bookmark for several slightly different locations.

## Adding Separators

While dragging and dropping is helpful, it really helps to be able to organize your bookmarks into groups. If you've got just a few bookmarks, you can add separators to the bookmark list that break the list into groups. Figure 5-6 shows a bookmark list with separators added between some of the groups.

You can't move or delete separators directly from the bookmark list. You'll see how to move and delete separators with the Bookmarks Manager later in this chapter.

## Adding Bookmark Folders

Between separators and dragging and dropping bookmarks to sort them, you're probably okay... but only as long as you've got only a dozen or two book-

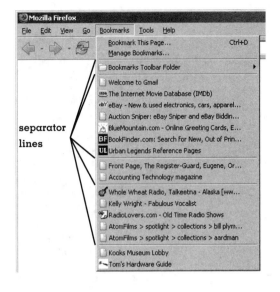

**Figure 5-6**
*Bookmark list with separators added.*

marks. But I'm certain that you'll want to add a lot of bookmarks to your list and that the list of bookmarks will end up rolling off the bottom of your screen, out across your desk, and down to the floor before your list ends. You need to create *bookmark folders*.

Bookmark folders are a lot like folders on your computer or desk: you use them to hold a bunch of similar items so that you can more easily find them all easier and so that you don't have them all skittering around on your desktop. To create a bookmark folder, right-click in the bookmark list where you want the new folder to appear, and select **New Folder** from the context menu. The Properties for "New Folder" screen appears. Enter the name for the new folder (which will appear on the bookmark list) and the description (which won't). Figure 5-7 shows an example of how this might look.

When you are satisfied with your entries, click OK. Firefox creates the folder in the bookmark list. As you can see from the example in Figure 5-8, there aren't any bookmarks in the folder yet.

**Figure 5-7**
*The Properties for "New Folder" screen.*

**Figure 5-8**

*The Book-
marks menu
with a new
folder added.*

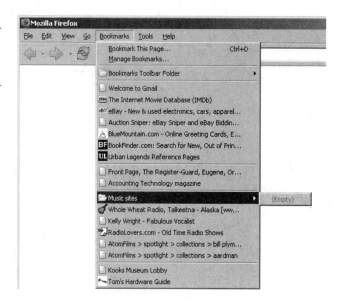

You can drag bookmarks over the folder (which opens conveniently),
whereupon you can drop them into the folder. When you click the folder, the
bookmarks in the folder now appear in the submenu, where you can select
them as usual (as shown in Figure 5-9).

**Figure 5-9**

*Folder with
bookmarks
added.*

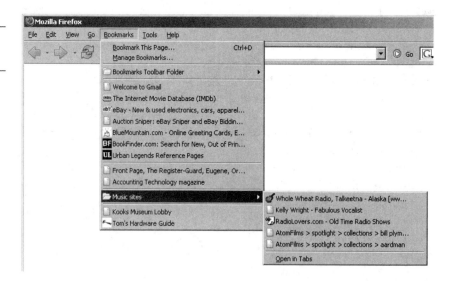

If a folder has lots and lots of bookmarks, you may want to create one or more subfolders in the same way and then add bookmarks to the subfolder, and so on. There's no practical limit to the number of folders you can create. You can't drag and drop bookmark folders, although you can cut or copy and paste them to a new location. Copying and pasting can be particularly useful when you've got subfolders of bookmarks that need to show up in different main folders.

One other thing you can do from the context menu is sort the bookmarks by name. This affects only the folder you're in at the moment. While this may be helpful for folders, it's probably a bad idea to do this to your entire bookmark list, because it's rare that your bookmarks and folders will benefit from being in straight alphabetical order.

**TOOL KIT**

### Cleaning the Garage

Bookmarks are computer clutter incarnate. After you get used to them, it's almost automatic to do a fast couple of keystrokes and bookmark whatever nifty web page you're currently looking at because

- It's interesting
- It's relevant
- It's funny (one of my favorite excuses)
- It's of professional interest
- You think you should be interested in it (even if you aren't really)
- You don't have time to look at it now but you'll look at it Real Soon, When You Have More Time
- You want to show it to someone else later
  ...and any of a dozen other reasons.

The problem is that you'll inevitably end up with a truly colossal bookmark list. And even if you do a good job of sorting bookmarks into the appropriate folders as you save them, many bookmarks are like many people: they don't age gracefully. web pages are deleted (particularly true for bookmarks to articles in online newspapers and magazines), websites expire and are no longer active, or the website might move to a new address.

Every so often (for some value of "often"), you need to check your bookmarks and folders to make sure that you're not keeping a bunch of dead links and links to websites with information that is no longer interesting, relevant, or funny. This takes a little while because you have to check most of the links to make sure that they're still active and you still want to keep them. On the other hand, this is a wonderful exercise for those days at work when you feel like you ought to be doing something productive but you don't really want to undertake anything large. Be sure to open *every* folder, because it's amazing what can sometimes get buried two or three levels deep.

Digging through the bookmarks list to get to each subsequent link is a bit annoying if you've got zillions of links to pursue. However, with this feature, you can go into the Bookmarks Manager and reset the Bookmarks Toolbar Folder for each round of surfing. That way, all the relevant bookmarks for, say, relocating appear on the Bookmarks Toolbar while you're working on relocating issues. You can then change to the jobs folder and so on, finally coming back to the Bookmarks Toolbar Folder when you're done. (In the middle of doing one thing, if you need to look up a link in another venue, you can always dig it out of the bookmark list like always.)

## Changing the Bookmark Display

The bookmark display on the right side of the Bookmarks Manager shows some information about the bookmarks by default: the name of the bookmark, the bookmark's location or address, and the description. You can go to View | Show columns and display other columns of information as well: keyword, bookmark added, last modified, and last visited.

The context menu in the bookmark list lets you sort bookmarks and folders in ascending alphabetical order, which is occasionally useful, but this is nothing compared with the sorting options you have in the Bookmarks Manager. You can view items unsorted (however they are at the moment) or sorted by name, location, keyword, description, date added, date last modified, or date last visited, all of which can be in ascending or descending order.

*Be careful!* When you sort bookmarks, the Bookmarks Manager sorts *all* the bookmarks in the current view, so if there are 75 bookmarks and folders in the main bookmark list and you sort them by location, you may destroy lots of manual organizing. This could be one of those times when undoing your last action may be really helpful.

## Importing and Exporting Bookmarks

When you installed Firefox, you probably imported bookmarks from your current browser as part of the installation process. You also saw in Chapter 1, "Getting Started," how to import additional sets of bookmarks from other browsers. Importing can be done in the Bookmarks Manager (go to File | Import and you can import bookmarks from Internet Explorer or from a bookmark file), but what's more exciting is that you can *export* bookmarks to a file, too!

To export your bookmarks, go to File | Export, identify the name of the file you want to save to (the default is **bookmark.html**), and click OK. Firefox saves the bookmarks as HTML. You can open the file itself (go to File | Open File on the Firefox main menu) and then click any of the links. You may want to go so far as to save your bookmarks to an HTML file with a standard name in some standard location, add a bookmark to the file of bookmarks on your Bookmarks toolbar, and then open this file. Every one of the bookmarks is displayed in a plain but effective nested format that you may find more convenient than the standard bookmark list.

### FRIDGE

The normal way of searching for bookmarks in the Bookmarks Manager is to enter the search term in the Bookmarks Manager's Search field. Unfortunately, this only lets you look through the names of the bookmarks. If you've exported the bookmarks into a file, you can open it in a text editor and look for any kind of information you like. It's a bit messy, but it works.

Actually, now that I think of it, the Firefox bookmarks file itself is stored in an HTML file, so you could open that directly in an editor... but I recommend that you not do this. It's all too easy to get distracted, make a few minor edits, and save the file without thinking, whereupon you realize that you've just damaged your bookmark file. It's better to make a copy and play with that.

Apart from the value of backing up your bookmarks periodically—a good thing in case of a system crash—exporting your bookmarks gives you a convenient way of sharing your bookmark list with other people. For example, you could post a bookmark file—or a portion of one—on a website and let other people download the file and then use the File | Import command to add this to their own bookmarks. The bookmark names, folders, and structure all remain the same; the information is just added to the bottom of the existing bookmark list.

### FAQ

**What do Opera, Galeon, and Konqueror have in common?**
Some browsers, such as Opera, Galeon, and Konqueror, store their bookmarks in formats that don't lend themselves to easy conversion. For example, Galeon and Konqueror use the XBEL format to store their bookmarks. Firefox can't directly import these files, because Firefox bookmarks are stored in HTML, whereas XBEL is XML. However, both Galeon and Konqueror offer the possibility to export your bookmarks to the Mozilla/Netscape format (which is the one used in Firefox).

Fortunately, there are workarounds: third-party bookmark conversion tools can bridge the gap for you. If you're using Windows, you can convert bookmarks with Magnus Brading's Bookmark Converter (http://www.magnusbrading.com/bmc) or Phillip Perkmann's BookmarkPriest (http://homepage.uibk.ac.at/homepage/csab/csab3666).

> Linux users can use a program called bk_edit (http://freshmeat.net/projects/bk_edit and a zillion other places) to edit and convert bookmarks from Opera 6, Netscape, Mozilla, Firefox, and Galeon. After having exported your bookmarks, you can import them directly into Firefox by going to File | Import. Other bookmark conversion programs can be found at websites such as http://www.shareware.com.
>
> You can copy encrypted Mozilla passwords directly to Firefox by copying the files xxxxxxxx.s and key3.db from your Mozilla profile folder to your Firefox profile folder and renaming xxxxxxxx.s to signons.txt. If you need help locating the Firefox profile folder, check out the support document at http://www.mozilla.org/support/firefox/edit#profile.

Exporting your bookmarks is not a bad idea for another reason. When you open the `bookmarks.html` file, all the folders are expanded and every bookmark at every level appears, something like the example in Figure 5-21.

**Figure 5-21**

*Exported bookmarks file opened in Firefox.*

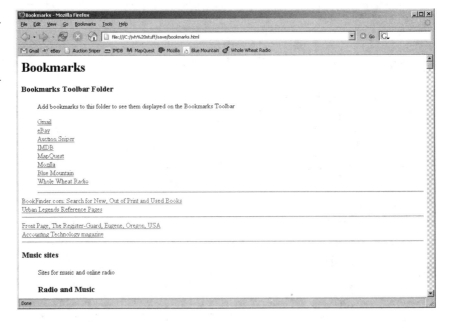

The descriptions for the folders are included in this example immediately after the folder name. Some of the links shown in Figure 5-21 still have the original default name, such as the entry for BookFinder—you'd never type anything that long for a name yourself. You can click any of the links in this page and go to the referenced website.

If you're like me, you'll discover whole pockets of bookmarks buried two or three levels down that you'd completely forgotten about. Some of them may be worth keeping; more (like the name for BookFinder and the Eugene Register-Guard) are worth editing, but you'll probably find a lot of stuff that's just so many wasted bits of storage. There's a good chance you'll find several folders in different places with the same focus and maybe even a few of the same bookmarks. Periodically pruning and decluttering your bookmark list makes it easier to find the bookmarks you're really interested in.

**TOOL KIT**

### Bookmarklets: the Cocktail Peanuts of Web Applications

For the real HTML hacker, exporting gives you a chance to edit your bookmark list like a manly man in a manly manner. You can open the HTML file in the editor of your choice and make all kinds of changes and then delete the existing bookmarks from Firefox and import the revised file. But because bookmarks are not much more than HTML code, it stands to reason that you can expand their basic capabilities using JavaScript and so on. As a result, you can add a number of little bitty mini-applications called *bookmarklets* to your bookmark list.

Bookmarklets usually do one small thing: give you the date and time, show you the links on a web page, email the current page's URL to someone, or change font colors or size to something more readable. They look just like bookmarks on your bookmark list, except they actually contain two or three lines of JavaScript code that does whatever it is. Because they're JavaScript, they're platform-independent—and browser-independent, for that matter; you can use most bookmarklets in a variety of browsers.

You can do all the usual things with bookmarklets that you can with bookmarks: rename them, put them in folders, give them keywords, add them to the Bookmarks toolbar, and so on. And, like bookmarks, bookmarklets don't do whatever it is they do until you click them.

You can find bookmarklets at many websites, including

- www.bookmarklets.com
- www.squarefree.com/bookmarklets
- www.guyfisher.com/builder/bookmarklets

Here's an example of how to use a bookmarklet. Gmail doesn't let Firefox save passwords using the Password Manager, because it has the autocomplete webform option set to off. The *remember password* bookmarklet (available at www.squarefree.com/bookmarklets or at http://ostermiller.org/bookmarklets/utilities.html) forces this on again, with the result that the Firefox Password Manager asks if you want it to remember your login information.

# Getting Something Going on the Sidebar

Instead of viewing your bookmarks in a dropdown list that you have to trigger each time, you can leave them on display with a *sidebar*, an area on the left side of the Firefox window. To view your bookmarks in the sidebar, go to View | Sidebar | Bookmarks, or just press Ctrl+B. Figure 5-22 shows the bookmarks displayed in the sidebar.

**Figure 5-22**

*Bookmarks displayed in the sidebar.*

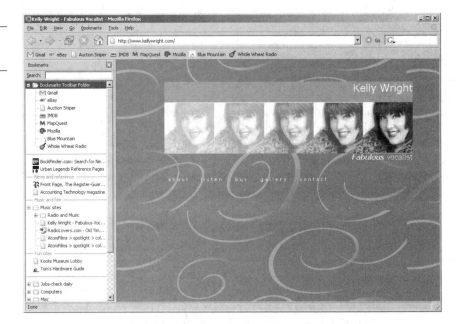

The bookmark list displayed in the sidebar has the folders and separators that appear on the bookmark list. One of the handy things about viewing the bookmarks in the sidebar is that any names you've assigned to the separators appear in the list (they are just lines in the regular bookmark list). The order in which the bookmarks appear in the sidebar is whatever the most recent viewing order was in the Bookmarks Manager, so you can have the bookmarks sorted by name in the sidebar and in your standard order in the dropdown bookmark list. You can open and close folders and click bookmarks as usual with this. The web page appears in the window on the right side.

One of the options when creating a bookmark is to check **Load this bookmark in the sidebar** on the Properties screen, shown near the beginning of this chapter in Figure 5-4. The next time you click this bookmark, the website appears in the sidebar. You can then click a link in the website displayed in the sidebar and have that link displayed in the main Firefox window. (A sample of this appears in Figure 5-23.) You're most likely to use this option if you've book-marked a website that shows things like lists of links or short summaries of information.

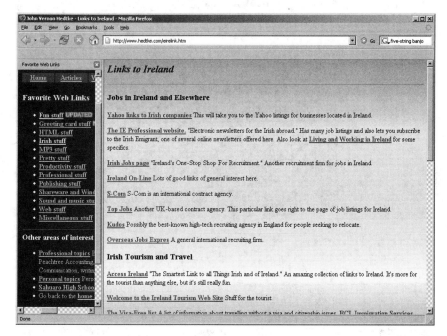

**Figure 5-23**

*Loading a website in the sidebar.*

The sidebar has a Search field, which lets you search for the bookmark name (the same as the Search field in the Bookmarks Manager). You can close the sidebar by clicking the X at the top of the sidebar.

## Viewing Your Browsing History: Where Have You Been Today?

You can also use the sidebar to display your browsing *history*. Your history is the list of the websites you've visited. Firefox automatically tracks your history according to the privacy options you set (as discussed in Chapter 2, "Protecting Your Security and Privacy"). Displaying your history is very helpful when you need to track down that one website you stumbled onto a few days ago but didn't think to bookmark.

To view your history, go to View | Sidebar | History, Go | History, or just press Ctrl+H. The browsing history appears in the sidebar, as shown in Figure 5-24.

Figure 5-24

*Browsing history displayed in the sidebar.*

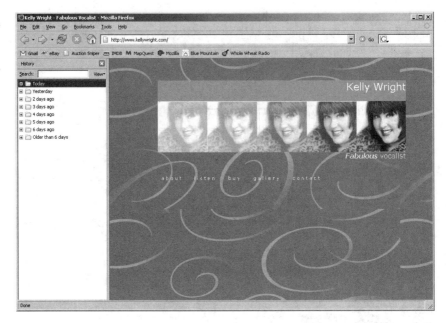

The default is for history to be displayed sorted by date. You can expand the folders to show the history bookmarks for each of the websites you've visited, as demonstrated in Figure 5-25.

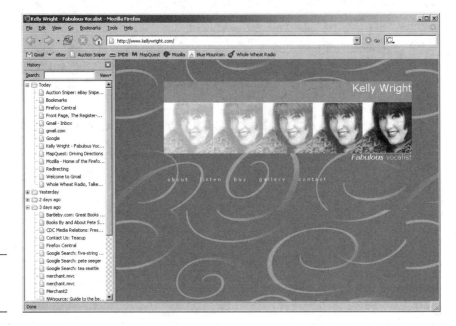

**Figure 5-25**

*Expanding a folder in the browsing history.*

When you're displaying the history in the sidebar, you have the option of sorting the display using the View button. You can also sort the history by date and site, by site, by most visited site, or by last visited site. Each of these sort options affects how the history is displayed.

As when you're displaying bookmarks, you can search for specific history items by entering an item in the Search field, and you can close the sidebar by clicking the X at the top of the sidebar. You can right-click history items and delete them, which is a big help.

The big disadvantage of using the sidebar is that it uses up a lot of screen real estate. You can drag the sidebar divider over to the left to minimize the amount of space the sidebar uses, but this shrinks the room for the sidebar display and makes it harder to read the information. You'll probably end up using the sidebar only when you really need it and leaving it off the rest of the time.

---

Creating and organizing bookmarks is a lot of fun. There's something satisfying about being able to create lots of bookmarks and have them filed Just Right so that you can find whatever you need with a minimum of effort. Firefox's many bookmark features and options are one of the best reasons to use it over any other browser.

The next chapter tells you about my absolute favorite Firefox feature: tabbed browsing. Sure, Firefox may have great security, dazzling search features, password management, and all the rest, but for my money, the instant I saw how tabbed browsing worked, I knew I'd never go back to IE. You'll learn how to open tabs, open an entire suite of related websites at once, and even how to create multiple home pages. Trust me—tabbed browsing is worth the price of admission all by itself.

# Harnessing the Power of Tabbed Browsing

## DO OR DIE:

>> Tabs and goatees

>> Tabbed browsing options

>> Multiple home pages

>> Tabs and windows

Whenever I'm surfing, particularly when I'm doing research on some topic, whether for business or pleasure, I like having multiple threads of inquiry. I've tried doing things in one window—a single instance of the browser—but it's often too much work: I have to remember where I was, and if I back up and go a different direction even for a moment, I've lost the pages I was working with in the other thread. It's better to have several copies of the browser open at once so that I can navigate back and forth along several different lines. But I can't have everything open at once on the screen, and if it's all minimized, there's not a lot of indication about what's open. I have to switch between all the browsers to find the one I want at that moment. What a pest! Fortunately, Firefox lets you create and use *tabs*, which are basically additional browser screens that have all the power and features of a separate instance of the browser.

Like goatees and spiral staircases, it's easier to show you how tabs work for browsing than to describe them. To open a new tab, go to File | New Tab (or make it easy on yourself and press Ctrl+T). As you can see in Figure 6-1, a tab bar appears with tabs for the original window and the new window. The new tab doesn't have anything in it when it's first created, so the tab title is "(Untitled)" and the address field is blank. As soon as you enter something in the address field or click a bookmark, Firefox loads the new web page and adjusts the title of the tab to reflect the new web page.

**Figure 6-1**

*A new tab in Firefox.*

tab bar          new tab

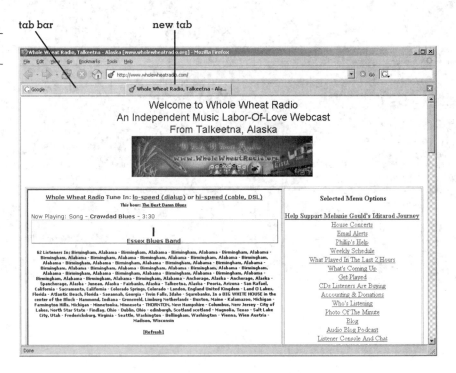

You can repeat this process as many times as you like, creating new tabs as you need them. In fact, you may choose to do this as matter of course: every time you think of something else to look at, just open a new tab and start afresh. Figure 6-2 shows an example how Firefox looks with several tabs open at once.

The biggest advantage of opening multiple tabs is that each tab has its own history that lets you browse back and forth without affecting what appears on the other tabs. You can switch between tabs by clicking the tab in the tab bar, pressing Ctrl+Tab (appropriately enough) to cycle to the next tab, or pressing Ctrl+Shift+Tab to cycle to the previous tab. If you have a lot of tabs open at once, you can press Ctrl+the number of the tab, such as Ctrl+3 to go to the third tab on the screen.

Another delightful aspect of tabbed browsing is that slow Internet connections or sites that take forever to load aren't nearly so much of a problem anymore. Try this: open a tab, click the bookmark you want to load, open another tab, click the bookmark, open another tab... and so it goes until you've got a bunch of bookmarks happily loading their respective websites. You can look at one web page while the other five are chugging along.

**Figure 6-2**

*Multiple tabs
open in
Firefox.*

# Opening Links in New Tabs

You can speed up the whole new tab process by opening links in a new tab on-the-fly. Suppose you're trying to find the perfect place to buy tea in Seattle (harder to find in a city where they buy more than twice as much coffee per capita as any other U.S. city). You might start by searching on Google for " tea Seattle." When you get the page of links, open a link by doing any of the following:

- Right-clicking the link and selecting **Open Link in New Tab** from the context menu
- Middle-clicking the link (if you've got a three-button mouse or a mouse with a scroll wheel)
- Holding down Ctrl (or Cmd on a Mac) and clicking the link

Regardless of which way you do it, the link opens in a new tab.

You can do this any number of times. Figure 6-3 shows a search that's four tabs deep: from Google to a list of reviews to one review that looks interesting to the website for Seattle tea shop.

Figure 6-3

*Opening links in new tabs.*

From Google...     to review site...     to review...     to tea shop site!

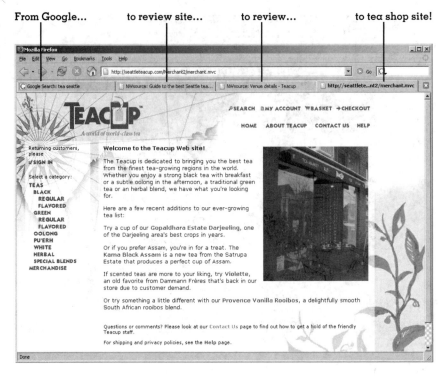

## Closing Tabs

You can close tabs by clicking the standard X icon on the tab bar, which closes the active tab. You can also press Ctrl+F4 or Ctrl+W or even go to File | Close Tab. You can also middle-click a tab to close it quickly (except on Linux, which loads the text into your clipboard as if it were a web address). You can also close all but the current tab by right-clicking the tab and selecting Close Other Tabs, sort of like cropping the tabs.

## Setting Tabbed Browsing Options

You can set a number of browsing options in Firefox by going to Tools | Options | Advanced. The Options screen with the Advanced options appears, as shown in Figure 6-4.

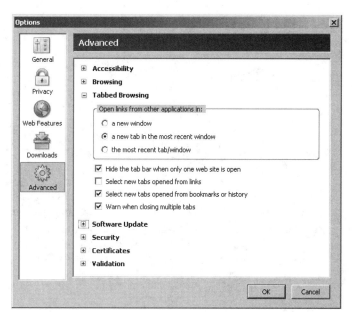

**Figure 6-4**
*The Options
screen with
the Tabbed
Browsing
selections
displayed.*

The first tabbed browsing option, **Open links from other applications in**, lets you set Firefox to open web pages called by other applications (such as your email program) in a new window, a new tab in the most recent window (the default), or the most recent tab or window. With the first selection, Firefox opens a new instance of the browser each time you open a link in another application. The default selection opens a new tab in the Firefox window each time. The last selection opens the website in the tab or window most recently created. (While this may be handy, it's not very good if you're opening a bunch of websites one after another.)

Unchecking **Hide the tab bar when only one website is open** displays the tab bar at all times. (Normally, it's not displayed when only one website is open.)

If **Select new tabs opened from links** is checked, opening a link in a new tab also makes the new tab the active one. If it's not checked—the default—the link opens in a new tab, but the tab containing the link remains active.

If **Select new tabs opened from bookmarks or history** is checked, it does the same thing as **Select new tabs opened from links**, but it's for links that are opened from bookmarks or from history. (If it's unchecked, whatever tab was active remains active.)

If **Warn when closing multiple tabs** is checked, you'll get a warning like the one shown in Figure 6-5 if you try to close Firefox when multiple tabs are open.

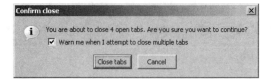

**FRIDGE**

If you find yourself so taken with tabs that you constantly have half a dozen open, you may want to get the *Tabbrowser Preferences* extension (http://www.pryan.org/mozilla/site/TheOneKEA/tabprefs/). It adds an entire suite of tab options to the Tools | Options screen and gives you control over things you wouldn't have even thought of. *Tabbrowser Preferences* is described in Chapter 7, "Customizing Firefox with Third-Party Extensions and Themes."

## Reloading Tabs

Reloading a web page in a window is easy: press F5 or Ctrl+R or go to View | Reload. You can use the same technique to refresh the information in a tab, too: just select the tab and do the reload procedure of your choice. But what if you want to reload the information in all the tabs at once? (You might; who knows?) Right-click a tab—any tab—and select **Reload Tab** to reload the website in this tab, or go for the gold with **Reload All Tabs**. Firefox refreshes the information in all the open tabs at once.

## Putting It All on My Tabs

You saw in the previous chapter how to add a folder to the bookmarks toolbar. You can open all the bookmarks in separate tabs just by right-clicking the folder and selecting **Open in Tabs** from the context menu. All the bookmarks in the bookmark folder open in separate tabs.

You can even open multiple bookmarks in multiple tabs as your home pages by going to Tools | Options | General and clicking **Use Bookmark** in the Home Page section. The Set Home Page screen (shown in Figure 6-6) appears.

Select the folder you want to open, and click OK. The next time you start Firefox or click the Home Page icon, all the bookmarks in the folder will be opened in separate tabs on the screen. You could use this trick for things like

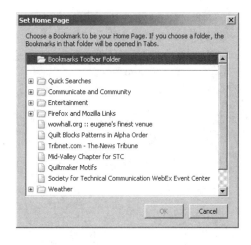

Figure 6-6
*The Set Home Page screen.*

- Job hunting—looking at half a dozen job search websites every morning

- Financial news—how the market is doing

- Headlines—what's happening in the world

- Online realtor listings—searching for that perfect house

Keeping your bookmarks organized in categories is not only a good idea in general, it can make tabbed browsing a lot easier... which in turn can make your surfing that much more effective. If you have bookmarks organized into discrete groups, it's easy to open an entire folder in tabs without a lot of extraneous or outdated websites.

## Bookmarking a Bunch of Tabs All at Once

Suppose you've opened a bunch of tabs to search for information on something or other and, what the heck, you struck pay dirt. Now you want to create a folder of bookmarks for all the tabs so you can open them as a group. Here's how:

When you've got all the websites displayed that you want to make bookmarks for (and no others!), go to Bookmarks | Bookmark This Page or press Ctrl+D. It really doesn't matter which tab you do this from; you're going to put all of them into a folder anyway. The Add Bookmark screen appears.

Enter the name of the folder you want to create for the bookmarks. This is a little different from what you saw in the previous chapter, where the name is applied to a new bookmark. What makes the difference is that you also check

**Bookmark all tabs in a folder** on the screen. Figure 6-7 shows an example of what this looks like.

When you click OK, Firefox slurps up the addresses for all the open tabs and puts them in a new folder with the name you entered. If you created this in the Bookmarks folder, the new folder is right on the bookmark list; otherwise, the new folder is a subfolder in the specified folder. You can then open individual bookmarks or the entire folder all at once.

**FRIDGE**

Want a tiny extension that makes tabs a little easier to read when you've opened a lot of them at once? You can try *Unread Tabs* (http://blog.codefront.net/mozilla/unreadtabs), which has one function: it italicizes the title of the unread tabs. When you click the tab to view it, the title changes back to normal text. This makes it easy to open a whole bunch of tabs and keep track of what you've read.

## Opening Live Bookmarks in Tabs

Opening a live bookmark in a tab is as easy as opening any other bookmark. Click the live bookmark to display the news items, right-click the news item you want to open, and then select **Open in New Tab** from the context menu. The selected story appears in a new tab. You can even open every news item in the live bookmark in tabs all at once by right-clicking the live bookmark, selecting **Open in Tabs** from the context menu, and poof! you're instantly well-informed on the topic of your choice.

## Using Windows and Tabs Together

All through this chapter, I've been saying "Tabs good! Use tabs, not windows!" But I have to say that there are some really great uses for multiple windows, too. For example, you might want to have two instances of Firefox, each of which has a group of tabs on a single subject. This makes working on two disparate subjects easier. Another reason might be the sheer volume of your search: it's entirely possible that you could have 10 or 12 tabs that you want to have open, and being able to sift through them can be difficult. And if I've got one instance of Firefox open with my Gmail account, there's a certain satisfaction in just closing another instance of Firefox and the half dozen tabs I opened for another topic in one fell swoop.

———————————————

Whenever I try to tell someone what's so special about Firefox, I always tell them about tabbed browsing first. Tabbed browsing allows the user to multitask vigorously: whenever I think of something else I want to look into, I just open a new tab and start a new line of inquiry. It's fast, powerful, and amazingly useful.

After I gush about tabbed browsing, the next thing I talk about is the ability to augment Firefox by adding extensions and themes. The following chapter introduces you to the enormous variety of extensions with which you can expand Firefox's capabilities. You'll learn about the many types of Firefox extensions, as well as my favorites from each category. You'll also see how to use themes to change icons, toolbars, and Firefox's overall look and feel to suit your needs or even your mood.

# Customizing Firefox with Third-Party Extensions and Themes

**DO OR DIE:**

>> Want fries with that extension?

>> To bug me, or not to bug me... that is the question.

>> What color is your browser? Go get some themes and find out!

>> When a Magpie isn't a bird

Think of Firefox as a cool car (perhaps a black Mazdaspeed Miata?) that can get you wherever you want to go on the web in the fastest way possible. When you want to customize your car, you might add a supercharger to make it go faster, or some outrageous rims to set it apart from the other cars on the road. The same is true of extensions and themes—when you are feeling as if there might be something you need to enhance your browsing experience, third-party extensions are at your disposal to make the browser fit your specific needs. When you want your browser to look a little different, third-party themes are available that can make your car shine brighter than the best custom paint job around.

Here I'll discuss what you need to know about extensions and themes and how to install them in Firefox. I will also recommend some fun extensions and themes that you can take out for a test drive. So, back your car out of the garage, and get ready for some fun!

## What Are Extensions?

Extensions are essentially mini-programs that are written to add some kind of extra functionality or features to the browser. Extensions add a wide range of features—some add icons to the toolbar while others add items to the context menus. Some actually run as powerful applications within Firefox. Some examples of extensions that run as applications include *ChatZilla*, *Mozilla Calendar*, and the *Mozilla Amazon Browser*.

Third-party extensions are written in the XPI (Cross Platform Installable File) format, which means they install as an add-on to the Firefox browser. In all cases, you must download the extension and install it in the browser before it can be used. Installed extensions are managed via Firefox's *Extension Manager* interface, discussed later in this chapter.

Like all software you might download and install, Firefox extensions could contain potential security vulnerabilities or other bugs (or even intentionally malicious features). Although no extensions have been reported to contain security vulnerabilities (and some even offer additional security and privacy features), you should always do some research and evaluate the extension you want to install, the author, and the site it originates from. Extension sites frequently offer information, ratings, and postings from users about their experience using the extension. Use these as a guide, and ask questions in newsgroups and forums if you have any questions before installing.

## Why Are Extensions Created?

The numerous third-party extensions available for Firefox are created for a variety of reasons. In many cases, extensions are created by members of the open source community who might have a passion for a particular element that they think will help all Firefox users. Other extensions, such as the *Mozilla Amazon Browser*, are created as a "proof of concept" to showcase the power of XUL and what you can do to develop web applications with Mozilla. Other extensions are created to satisfy the needs of a particular target audience. A good example of such an extension is *Biobar*, a search toolbar for searching bioinformatics databases that also provides links to bioinformatics tools. In other instances, the popularity of sites such as Google has spawned a number of extensions that help optimize the Google search experience.

**FRIDGE**

Google is popular, and extension developers have definitely taken notice, because many extensions have been developed for Firefox that are aimed at Google power users. For example, the *Google Pagerank Status* extension displays the Google page rank in the Firefox status bar. The *GooglePreview* extension provides a little more visual information because it inserts preview images of websites, Amazon products, and stock charts when you return a set of Google search results. The following are some other extensions you can check out to add some horsepower to your Google experience:

- *Googlebar* (discussed later in this chapter)
- *Google Preview*
- *Google Pagerank Status*
- *SearchStatus*
- *FireluckyBox*
- *LookAhead*
- *McSearchPreview*
- *Define Word*

**FAQ**

**What is XUL?**

XUL (pronounced "zool") is an abbreviation for Extensible User-Interface Language. In the world of software development, XUL is used to help define what the UI (User Interface) will look like. The XUL language defines things like where scrollbars and text boxes will appear, but it doesn't drill down to the level of what that scrollbar or text box will look like. The best-selling feature of XUL is the fact that developers can build applications that are cross-platform, and these applications can also be run without being connected to the Internet. Both the *Mozilla Amazon Browser* and the *Mozilla Calendar*, which are discussed later in this chapter, are excellent examples of the power of XUL at work. To learn more about XUL and to access some tutorials, head to http://www.xulplanet.com.

## Extension Conflicts

While third-party extensions can be very beneficial (and many can often be great time-savers), occasionally you may encounter issues with extensions conflicting with each other. In the same way that your car occasionally needs a tune-up, you may have to examine your extensions if you have many installed and you begin to experience browser problems. If you notice any problems, the first place you should look is your list of installed extensions. Just like when your mechanic has to troubleshoot a problem, you may have to disable or uninstall each extension to uncover the extension that is problematic. Remember that Firefox does not have control over third-party extensions, and the Firefox developers cannot resolve issues with third-party extensions. If you are having difficulty with a particular extension, contact the extension author or visit one of the many *forums* available (referenced in Chapter 1, "Getting Started") that can help you with the issue you are experiencing.

# Locating Extensions on the Web

Your recommended first stop for extensions is the official Mozilla repository, *addons.update.mozilla.org (UMO)*, which can be accessed directly from the **Get more Extensions** link on the right side of the Firefox Extension Manager. *UMO* contains a categorized list of extensions that are updated frequently and can be sorted by platform and version number. *UMO* also breaks down extensions into several categories, including top-rated, most popular, and newest.

In addition to *UMO*, there are a number of other places on the web that you can find extensions for Firefox.

# Installing Extensions

Thanks to a robust Extension Manager that is built into Firefox (as shown in Figure 7-1), it is a breeze to install extensions.

**Figure 7-1**

*The Firefox Extension Manager.*

Here are the steps for installing an extension:

1. Locate the relevant extension, either at *UMO* or at another site.
2. At *UMO*, select the **Install** link.

3. A software installation dialog box launches and requests your permission to install the extension. Because Firefox prides itself on security, this measure is built into Firefox to protect you from possibly installing malicious software by confirming that you actually want to install the file. Other sites that list extensions may require that you click a link, but you should still see the dialog box shown in Figure 7-2, and the remainder of the install instructions listed here should be the same.

**Figure 7-2**

*The Software Installation dialog box that launches when you install an extension in Firefox.*

4. After a brief delay, the Install button becomes active, and you should be able to click it. This delay is intentional and was installed as a security measure to protect users from accidentally installing an extension.

5. The `.xpi` file now installs in the Extension Manager. A progress meter shows the progress until the extension installation is complete.

6. After installation, you **must** restart the browser to enable the extension.

> **Tip: Another Way to Install Extensions**
> If you prefer to save the .xpi file to your hard drive, you can drag and drop the saved file into an open browser window, which also triggers the Software Installation dialog box.

## Managing Extensions

After extensions have been installed, they can be managed in a number of ways. Right-clicking any installed extension launches a context menu that allows you to set preferences for the extension as well as visit the home page and learn more about the extension author and version number. There are also three context menu items that allow you to move the extension to the top of the list in Extension Manager or up or down. This lets you sort your extensions alphabetically if you wish.

Some extensions actually add a label to the File menu and can be accessed from the File | Tools menu selection. For example, both *Mozilla Calendar* and *ChatZilla* can be accessed from File | Tools after they have been installed.

# Disabling and Uninstalling Extensions

Firefox permits you to temporarily disable any extension in the event that you don't want to uninstall it completely. Here are the steps to disable an extension:

1. Go to Extension Manager, right-click the extension, and then select **Disable**.
2. Restart Firefox.
3. The extension should now be grayed out in Extension Manager.
4. To re-enable the extension, right-click the extension, select **Enable**, and restart Firefox.
5. To uninstall the extension, you can either right-click the extension or select the extension and click the **Uninstall** button at the bottom of the Extension Manager.

# Updating Your Extensions

Extension developers frequently offer updates to their extensions. Firefox offers a number of ways to update your extensions. If you are like me and need constant reminders, your best bet is to configure Firefox to check for updated extensions automatically. This preference is on by default, so if you decide you don't want Firefox to check for updates automatically, you must go into the Advanced Preferences and uncheck the box under **Software Update** that is labeled **My Extensions and Themes**.

If updates are available, Firefox alerts you by displaying a color-coded icon in the upper-right corner of the browser window. Here is the breakdown of what the color codes mean:

- Red: Critical updates are available (this appears only if there are updates for the Firefox application itself)

- Blue: Five or more updates are available
- Green: Less than five updates are available

If you decide you want to check for extension updates manually, you can click the **Update** button in Extension Manager. The update wizard launches and guides you through the process.

> **Firefox Profile**
>
> Because extensions are stored as part of your Firefox profile, if you delete your profile, you will lose all your extensions and will have to reinstall them.

# Featured Extensions

Now that you know the ins and outs of extensions, I took the liberty of scouring the Internet for some of the more interesting third-party extensions that are available for Firefox. Because Firefox runs on Mac, Windows, and Linux, so do most (but not all) extensions. The extensions discussed here are all cross-platform, with the exception of *Bookmark Backup*.

The extensions are divided into the following categories:

- Tabbed browsing
- Security and privacy
- Bookmarks
- Toolbar
- Sidebar
- Downloading
- Navigation
- Email
- Extensions that are applications
- Extensions that improve the browsing experience
- Search
- Miscellaneous

> **Extension Development and Version Numbers**
>
> Remember that extensions are continually under development and may contain different features by the time this book goes to press. Make sure when you download an extension that it is compatible with the version of Firefox you are running. The dropdown box in UMO allows you to select the version of Firefox for which you want to search extensions.

You'll find the official web page link next to the name of each extension, but the best way to get all these extensions is through *addons.update.mozilla.org (UMO)*, which can be accessed by launching the Extension Manager within Firefox.

## Tabbed Browsing Extensions

Tabbed browsing is truly one of the more unique features of Firefox. In looking for extensions in this category, I sought out ones that would extend the already powerful tabbed browsing features that are found within Firefox.

## Tabbrowser Preferences
### (http://www.pryan.org/mozilla/site/TheOneKEA/tabprefs/)

As a companion to Firefox, the *Tabbrowser Preferences* extension is a great tool for users who really want to harness the power of tabbed browsing. Not only can you configure some of the hidden tabbed browsing preferences in Firefox, but you can also control the handling of internal and external links as well as tab focus issues by using this extension.

The *Tabbrowser Preferences* extension settings are managed through the Tools | Options | Tabbed Browsing menu. Some of the cool things you can do with this extension include: opening URLs in the URL bar, moving the tab bar to the bottom portion of the browser window, and tweaking the focus/unfocus of some of the tab-creating functions. If you grow weary of a lot of repetitive mouse clicks, *Tabbrowser Preferences* lets you select a tab by simply hovering the mouse over the tab, eliminating at least one click. Of note, *Tabbrowser Preferences* also permits you to open URLs from the Extension/Theme Manager and the Help window into new tabs.

## Linky
### (http://gemal.dk/mozilla/linky.html?ver=2.2.0)

Links, links, and more links—and so many ways to manage them. Sometimes web surfing is nothing more than a big link-o-rama. When you need a great extension to manage this morass of links, you can install *Linky*, a nifty extension that allows you to exercise great power over how you handle links. Need to open all the links on the page you are viewing in a set of tabs? No problem— *Linky* can do that and a lot more, and it is as simple as right-clicking the link or web address and accessing the *Linky* menu. *Linky* also gives you a summary of how many links and images are present on the page that you are viewing.

*Linky* has a preferences menu that allows you to manipulate a number of features, including the link and image menus and the Select Links dialog box. This extension can be especially beneficial when you view any type of web galleries.

## miniT
### (http://extensionroom.mozdev.org/more-info/minit)

Sometimes things that come in small packages aren't so bad after all. The *miniT* extension seems like it doesn't add much at first glance, but it actually adds quite a bit of extra functionality to Firefox's tabbed browsing feature. The most useful part of this extension is being able to drag and drop tabs. The next best part of this extension is being able to double-click any tab and have a new tab open instantly. Finally, a context menu is available that allows certain attributes of `docShell.allow*` to be changed, such as the ability to not allow images and plug-ins to load. If you use a mousewheel, you can also switch tabs by turning the mousewheel on the tab bar. *miniT* is a great addition to your extensions repertoire—give it a try!

## Security Extensions

Currently in the browsing realm there is a definite heightened awareness of security and privacy concerns. While Firefox does its part to try to help out in this area, there are also extensions available that can help you browse safely and securely.

I recently attended a presentation given by an Internet security consultant. I remember his reiterating the point that there is no "magic bullet" to protect yourself from being a victim of Internet fraud. The best thing you can do to try to protect yourself is to be as *aware* as you can when you are surfing, and that is why I believe *Spoofstick* is an extension that could be useful in this area.

### Spoofstick (http://www.corestreet.com/spoofstick)

Protecting your privacy and security is important, and one of the most important things you need to know while you are browsing is exactly where you are. Scammers and hackers create fake websites known as *spoofed sites* and try to drive traffic there to try to see if they can obtain some of your personal information. This common practice is known as *phishing*.

The *Spoofstick* extension (see Figure 7-3) attempts to combat this problem by adding a display under your toolbar that shows only the relevant domain name you are visiting. *Spoofstick* should let you know if you are not on eBay but visiting a spoofed site. It isn't the magic bullet, but it will help you be more aware of exactly where various links take you while you are surfing the web.

*Spoofstick* has a minimal set of options you can configure, including changing the color and size of the display. One caution—*Spoofstick* can take up some real estate, even with the "medium" size setting, so if you have other items or toolbars installed, you should opt for the "small" setting.

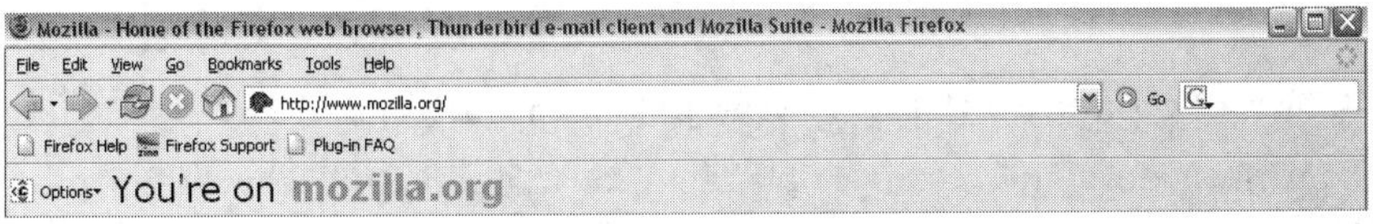

**Figure 7-3**

*The Spoofstick extension.*

### x (http://extensionroom.mozdev.org/more-info/x)

I like extensions that make it easy to accomplish tasks you would otherwise have to go to the File menu or Preferences to complete. *x* extension is a great solution that allows you to erase your tracks quickly and easily with the simple click of a button on the toolbar.

Installing *x* adds a "*Paranoia*" button to the toolbar that lets you quickly delete history, form information, stored passwords, download history, cache, and cookie information (see Figure 7-4). Clicking the button launches a simple context menu that allows you to check the parameters you want to clear. This extension really is a time-saver if you like to clear things out regularly and don't want to bother navigating to Preferences each time to purge information.

**Figure 7-4**

*The Paranoia button.*

## Bookmarks Extensions

Chapter 5, "Bookmarks and History," showed you some of the many ways bookmarks can make it easy for you to find a needle in a haystack when you are searching the web. The following extensions allow you to enhance your bookmark experience, giving you even more management options. Finally, after you have spent time finding all those needles in a haystack, the Bookmark *Backup extension* allows you to back up your bookmarks, thus preserving all that hard work.

### Automarks (http://www.ticklespace.com/)

Firefox offers a number of powerful ways to manage and organize your bookmarks. *Automarks* can be useful when you want to find a bookmark without having to go directly into the Bookmarks menu. Firefox already uses your browsing history to autocomplete URLs when you type them in. What the *Automarks* extension does is allow you the luxury of having your bookmarks included in the autocomplete search.

*Automarks* is a snap to use. After installing the extension, go to the Bookmarks menu and choose the option that says **Copy bookmarks to Autocomplete**. You receive a confirmation prompt and then a success dialog box, and then you are good to go. Simply type a few letters in the URL bar, and you should see one of your saved bookmarks autocomplete.

### Bookmark Backup (http://www.pikey.me.uk/mozilla)

*Bookmark Backup* is another simple extension that can be a lifesaver. If you are like me, your bookmarks are your life, and after some time you can accumulate quite a few of them. If for some reason your bookmarks file becomes corrupted, *Bookmark Backup* is ready to spring into action to help. This extension takes a snapshot of your bookmarks file and saves it to a backup location on a regular basis. You can then find the most recent backup copy and not be shaking your head in utter disgust after you have lost your bookmarks and you find you can't remember the name of a site someone sent you two years ago in an email.

*Bookmark Backup* stores the backups in a folder inside the Firefox profile folder, but you can change this location in the Options dialog box. Thanks to some additional code that was added to this extension, you can also back up other files at the same time you back up your bookmarks by checking various boxes or by alternatively listing the files in the text box using the | character to separate the files. Some of the additional files that can be backed up include history, passwords, preferences, cookies, and download history. This is an excellent, proactive extension that could be of help some day in the future.

> **Note**
>
> At the time of this writing, *Bookmark Backup* is supported only for Windows and Linux.

## Toolbar Extensions

Toolbars are like traffic-free highways—they allow you to get where you want to go in a hurry, without having to go through the extra step of using the File dropdown menus. A number of extensions can help you customize your toolbar experience. While some just add a set of icons that may be useful, others actually allow you to control the placement of toolbars.

### Toolbar Enhancements (http://extensionroom.mozdeve.org/clav/#tbx)

Toolbars can definitely make your browsing life easier. A few extensions out there offer some powerful configuration options for the user interested in an icon-centric world rather than a dropdown-centric one. I think I probably fall into that category, since after writing all day I sometimes just like gazing at pictures.

The *Toolbar Enhancements* extension (see Figure 7-5) lets you add a wonderful array of useful toolbar enhancements to Firefox, including extra toolbar items and the ability to manage toolbar placement. Some of the toolbar items available include JavaScript, Images, Plugins, and Redirections, and all work on a per-tab basis.

**Figure 7-5**

*The Firefox toolbar with several Toolbar Enhancements icons installed.*

The *Toolbar Enhancements* extension permits quite a bit of latitude in toolbar placement, allowing toolbars to be placed in a variety of window locations, including the left, right, and bottom of the window and directly below the tab bar. One of the neat features of *Toolbar Enhancements* is that you can do quite a bit of customization from the context menu (setting icon size and mode) while you are setting up a new toolbar. You can also move toolbars around by right-clicking while you are customizing. This extension's author does warn that you may experience difficulty if you place Bookmarks toolbar items in a toolbar on the left or right or in a toolbar that is placed below the tab bar.

## ResizeSearchBox
### (http://dragtotab.mozdev.org/resizesearchbox/)

Have you ever run out of real estate in the search box? No need to fret any longer, because when you install this extension you can resize the toolbar by using a resizing widget that can be added to the toolbar. After installing this extension, you will have to right-click **Customize** and add the resizer to the right side of the search box as shown in Figure 7-6. After this has been done, you can resize to your heart's content.

**Figure 7-6**

*The ResizeSearch Box extension in action.*

resizer

## Web Developer
### (http://www.chrispederick.com/work/firefox/webdeveloper/)

If Firefox has a "showoff" extension, the *Web Developer* extension just might be it (see Figure 7-7). Even though the target audience for this extension is web developers, so many features nested in *Web Developer* are useful for everyday browsing I felt it was worthy of being mentioned in this chapter. In fact, so much is packed into this extension that you might be able to devote an entire book just to discussing its features. *Web Developer* focuses on the following areas:

- Disable features
- CSS features
- Forms features
- Images features
- Information features
- Miscellaneous features
- Outline features
- Resize features

- Tools features
- View Source features
- Options features

**Figure 7-7**

*The Web Developer extension installed in Firefox.*

*Web Developer* allows quick access to things like View Source, View Cookie information, and zooming in and out, among other things. Even if you are not a web developer, I encourage you to install this extension and give it a test drive—you might find it useful in your everyday browsing.

## Sidebar Extensions

The Firefox sidebar allows you to manage your browser real estate in a number of interesting ways. A few extensions can help you further refine what you do with the sidebar space. *SiteBar* is one extension that allows you to operate on your bookmarks while you are in the sidebar, and *WebPanel Enhancer* adds a rich feature set to the sidebar. Give these extensions a try to see how they can help you manage your sidebar experience.

### SiteBar (http://www.sitebar.org)

*SiteBar* is an interesting extension that adds a sidebar to Firefox that allows you to share bookmarks with your friends and family. When installed, *SiteBar* is added as a menu selection under the Tools menu option. You have to sign up if you want to share your bookmarks with others. It offers user group support and lets you autojoin new members, as well as providing the ability to configure access rights to bookmarks at the user group level.

SiteBar has a well-designed icon bar that allows you to navigate through the sidebar. It also includes a search bar that allows you to search the various bookmarks and folders and a handy widget that collapses or expands the bookmark folders.

This extension can be extremely helpful to users new to the Internet who don't know how to power surf (I could have used this extension long ago when my grandmother first started her journey on the Internet). In other instances, you might be planning a vacation with a bunch of friends, and this might be a good way to share travel information while you are in the planning stages of your vacation. *SiteBar* has quite a bit to offer and may be a useful extension to add to your Firefox sidebar.

## WebPanel Enhancer (http://editcss.mozdev.org/indexwpe.html)

The sidebar can be your best friend, especially when there are extensions such as *WebPanel Enhancer* around. This extension adds a number of useful features to the sidebar, including the ability to open links, view your extensions and downloads in the sidebar, and view source. *WebPanel Enhancer* adds these options to the View | Sidebar dropdown list. One interesting extension I was able to add to the sidebar was a calculator—you might find it useful if you need to do some number crunching while you are browsing.

**FRIDGE**

If *WebPanel Enhancer* is not enough for you, the author of this extension recommends *Content Holder* (http://piro.sakura.ne.jp/xul/_contentholder.html.en) as another extension that you can take for a test spin. *Content Holder* may be particularly useful if you need to compare two sets of pages—an original and a translated page.

## Downloading Extensions

There is certainly an abundance of content on the web for you to download, and although the Firefox Download Manager can handle the load with relative ease, there are extensions that can further help out in this space. The lead engineer of the Firefox browser created *Magpie*, which is one extension you can try out if you want a little extra functionality when you are downloading content. If you want a different way to view your downloads, the *Download Status Bar* gives you the chance to manage your downloads in a status bar. It's all about different strokes for different folks.

## Magpie (http://www.bengoodger.com/software/tabloader/)

*Magpie* is an extension developed by Ben Goodger, the lead engineer of the Firefox browser project (see Figure 7-8). This extension lets you save images, videos, and documents that you come across on the Internet. The best part of this extension is that it is designed to download these files quickly and efficiently, in large part due to its support of the *Bukster protocol*. *Bukster* is a freeware web application that allows users to scan web pages and quickly download only the specific content they are interested in.

*All-in-one Gestures* is a well-designed and well-maintained extension that should provide you with all the horsepower you need to browse the web at warp speed.

## Search Keys (http://www.squarefree.com/extensions/search-keys/)

Many times navigation is about getting to what you want quickly and efficiently. I find that I have a tendency to click the wrong link when I have performed a Google or Yahoo search. *Search Keys* is a handy extension that adds a number next to the individual items in a search, allowing you the ability to type the number and go right to that search result. At the time of this writing, *Search Keys* supports Google, Yahoo, and del.icio.us searches. Even though it doesn't support all search engines, it still can be useful when you're trying to wade through pages and pages of search results, especially when you can hold down the Alt key to open your set of results in new tabs or the Shift key to open the results in new windows.

## Email Extensions

There are a multitude of email choices out there, but enough web surfers are using webmail services these days that extension developers have definitely taken notice. The following two extensions should make it infinitely easier for webmail users to manage and respond quickly to email while they are in the confines of the Firefox browsing environment.

## Gmail Notifier (http://nexgenmedia.net/extensions)

The *Gmail Notifier* is an extension that allows you to log into your Gmail account (Figure 7-9 shows the login screen) and then receive notification when you have messages. This notification is shown in the status bar and includes the number of new email messages you have received, subject, sender, as well as the amount of space you are using. You can also tweak a few other preferences, including how often you want it to check your email in addition to whether to open it in a new tab, an existing tab, or a new window. If your status bar is getting cluttered and you don't want to see the Gmail icon there, you

**Figure 7-9**

*The Gmail Notifier Login.*

can also add an icon to the toolbar so you can manage your mail from that location. *Gmail Notifier is* a clever extension that will definitely improve your email management.

### WebmailCompose (http://www.jedbrown.net)

*WebmailCompose* is a handy extension that allows you to configure `mailto:` links so that they load in your webmail's compose page. You can set your preferences for the major players in the webmail space, such as Yahoo, Gmail, Netscape, and Hotmail. By virtue of a simple right-click, you can launch your webmail app and be on your way to speedy email composition. I can see this extension being very useful for anyone who clicks on "Contact Us" links on a regular basis.

## Extensions That Are Applications

One of the great things about Firefox is that you can install extensions that actually run as applications within the browser. Two of the best examples of applications that integrate with Firefox are *ChatZilla* and *Mozilla Calendar*. The best thing about these two applications is that you can manage your chatting and scheduling without ever having to leave the browsing environment— no need to be switching back and forth between external applications.

### ChatZilla (http://www.hacksrus.com/ginda/chatzilla/)

*ChatZilla* is a well-designed cross-platform *IRC* client that fuses Internet Relay Chat (IRC) with existing web standards, such as JavaScript, HTML, and CSS (see Figure 7-10). *ChatZilla* adds a menu option under Tools that allows you to launch the client and get right to chatting. If you prefer to add an icon to the toolbar, you can do that too. There are a number of preferences that can be configured—enough to satisfy even the most savvy IRC user. The author of this extension has a fairly comprehensive FAQ that should answer any questions you have related to the program: http://www.hacksrus.com/~ginda/chatzilla/faq/chatzilla-faq.html. /msg you: Use it!

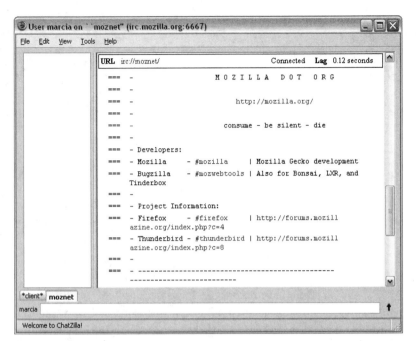

Figure 7-10

*The ChatZilla
login window.*

## What is IRC, and how can it be useful in relation to Firefox?

*IRC* stands for *Internet Relay Chat*. After you connect to an IRC network (which is composed of a variety of IRC servers), you can join a channel where you can chat about a variety of topics related to Firefox. On IRC, channel names begin with the # sign. There are a number of developer and help channels that you might find useful on IRC. Under the Mozilla IRC network (moznet, or irc.mozilla.org), *#mozillazine* is particularly beneficial if you have questions regarding Firefox. *#firefox* is primarily a developer channel,

## Mozilla Calendar
## (http://www.mozilla.org/projects/calendar/)

The *Mozilla Calendar Project* is a XUL-based calendar that is built for the entire suite of Mozilla products, including Firefox, Thunderbird, and the Mozilla suite (see Figure 7-11). The calendar is based on the iCal standard, which is an open source calendar effort. There is also a standalone version of the calendar that is known as Sunbird, which uses the same codebase as the Mozilla calendar.

**Figure 7-11**

*The Mozilla Calendar.*

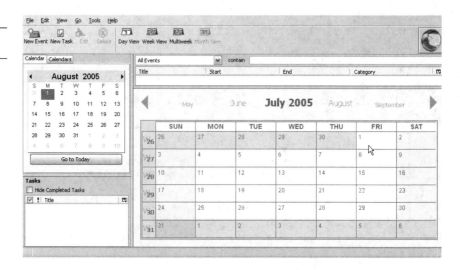

*Mozilla Calendar* provides some useful documentation in its FAQ. Because the product is still under development, some users may find that it is lacking in certain areas (as of this writing, there is no support for Palm Pilot synch and no direct support for Outlook), but it is still a great way to be able to manage your calendar without ever having to leave your browser. You can also install the *Mozilla Calendar* in Thunderbird.

## Extensions That Improve Browsing

Browsing can be fun, but there are still annoyances that can get in the way, and you need things to help you neutralize these annoyances. The extensions in this category do just that: they help you deal with the distractions and easily get on to what you want to do—they let you see content on the web without interruptions. *Adblock* helps you control images, and *BugMeNot* helps you when you don't have the patience to deal with website registrations. Once you try these extensions, I think you will see how they can make your web surfing much simpler.

### Adblock (http://adblock.mozdev.org/)

Of all the extensions discussed in this section, *Adblock* might be the one that is a *must-have* for Firefox, because it contains more powerful capabilities than Firefox's built-in image blocker. Web surfers can often be overwhelmed by sites that contain more ads than their eyes can handle. The *Adblock* extension serves as an elegant content filtering plug-in for Firefox, allowing you to construct filters that remove images, banner ads, and so on so that you can get to the content you want with a minimum amount of distraction. When you install *Adblock* and start using it, you will definitely see the difference.

**FRIDGE**

Remember, the Internet is all about revenue, and many sites live or die by their ad click-throughs. So if you have a favorite site that you visit regularly, you might consider turning off *Adblock* for that site in order to support it.

After you've installed *Adblock*, just right-click any ad and select *Adblock* from the menu. You then can block that particular ad or all ads coming from that domain. *Adblock* also lets you put an overlay on Flash ads.

*Adblock* installs under the Tools menu option. You can set your various filter preferences through the Preferences menu item.

**FAQ**

**Is the AdBlock tab missing?**

If for some reason you come across a plug-in but don't see the *Adblock* tab, this means that the plug-in has been cropped. Simply select Overlay Flash from the Tools menu, or type its shortcut and you'll be able to click directly on the overlay to manage the plug-in.

## BugMeNot
(http://roachfiend.com/archives/2005/02/07/bugmenot/)

Not long ago, I came across an email thread where someone recommended going to a website to read an article about Firefox. Apparently the website required the user to register before the article could be accessed. In the email reply the person said that they didn't "do" website registrations.

Rather than have him miss reading the article, someone else replied to this email and included a link to *BugMeNot*, an extension that allows the user to bypass this type of web registration by virtue of a simple right click in a username/passworld field. *BugMeNot* fills in the website fields with the first username/password combination it finds in its database. If *BugMeNot* can't locate a valid username/password combination, it leaves the fields open and gives you the opportunity to register for the site. I tried *BugMeNot* on a number of newspaper sites and was able to get a username/password just about every time.

This is a definite must-have extension if you do a lot of online reading and you don't want the hassle of having to register for a site you might not otherwise go to on a regular basis.

## Search Extensions

Every day, Internet users all over the world enter keywords into search engines to try to wade through the plethora of information that is available on the Internet. A number of search extensions are available for Firefox, but two of the more interesting ones are the *Mozilla Amazon Browser* and *Googlebar*.

### Mozilla Amazon Browser (http://www.faser.net/mab/)

The *Mozilla Amazon Browser* (MAB) is a XUL application that is installed as an extension. When installed into Firefox, it adds a MAB selection to the Tools menu. When you select MAB, it launches a web app interface that allows you to search amazon.com (UK, DE, and JP versions as well) without all the image clutter that might otherwise distract you from your shopping experience. Think of the *MAB* as amazon.com with the *AdBlock* extension installed, because in a way it distills information to the simplest level—a no-frills text search. In addition to being able to do price comparisons across different Amazon stores, MAB allows you to also search Google in case you need a little more information regarding the item you have selected.

MAB has a lot of great features, but the best thing is that while you are shopping you can add items to your cart and then check out using the normal Amazon method. While MAB might not be for everyone, I found it to be a slick way to navigate the amazon.com waters as well as a great example of a powerful application that can run within Firefox.

### Googlebar (http://googlebar.mozdev.org)

If Google is the Cadillac of search engines, the *Googlebar* might be the Rolls Royce of extensions (see Figure 7-12). Originally available only for IE users, the *Googlebar* team (not affiliated with Google, Inc.) decided to bring that functionality to Mozilla users so that you can manage all of Google's specialty searches from one handy toolbar.

**Figure 7-12**

*The Googlebar installed in Firefox.*

The *Googlebar* is well designed, with crisp icons and a bevy of features that even the most savvy searcher will enjoy. It includes a number of interesting options that can be set in the *Googlebar* preferences, which can be accessed from the Google icon located on the left side of the toolbar. Some of these options include the ability to configure keyboard shortcuts, site options, and save history. International users will love the ability to be able to select their countries in the options. Even better, if you want the *Googlebar* to be language-specific, you can visit the Googlebarl10n Project to see which foreign language packs are available.

If you are looking for the Holy Grail of search toolbars, the *Googlebar* just might be it.

## Miscellaneous Extensions

So many other categories could have been included in this book, but I had to limit the number, so this category became a catchall for other fun Firefox extensions that you can explore. *ForecastFox*, *MapIt!*, and *FoxyTunes* are all practical extensions that can help you in your everyday Internet surfing, so that is why I chose to include them in this book. All of them are definitely more fun than the game Barrel of Monkeys that I used to play incessantly when I was a child.

### ForecastFox (http://www.forecastfox.mozdev.org)

This was one of the tougher categories for which to recommend extensions, simply because there are so many interesting extensions out there for Firefox. So just consider the kinds of things you might do on a daily basis. Checking the weather is one of them, so *ForecastFox* fits the bill nicely (see Figure 7-13).

All you have to do is enter your zip code into *Forecast-Fox*, and, thanks to weather.com, you can embed weather forecast information for your area into the browser. When installed, it adds a series of three icons to the location you specify in the options. (I used the status bar because that seemed

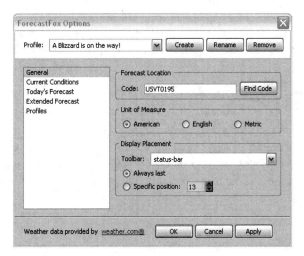

**Figure 7-13**

*The ForecastFox options screen.*

to be the place that was least intrusive in my browser configuration.) The icons show you the weather now, today's forecast, as well as the following day's forecast. Now there's no excuse for going out without your raincoat.

### MapIt! (http://mapit.mozdev.org)

I have a terrible sense of direction and no GPS installed in my Miata, so I rely on online mapping to get me to my destination. *MapIt!* is a handy extension that pulls maps from MapQuest, Yahoo! Geocode, Terraserver, and GlobeXplorer. When you right-click an address, *MapIt!* generates a street map of an address you have selected. At this time, *MapIt!* supports only U.S. addresses, but there are plans to support international addresses in a future release. *MapIt!* is a great extension that allows you to navigate the highways and byways of the world as easily as you can navigate the web with Firefox.

### FoxyTunes (http://www.iosart.com/foxytunes.firefox)

I would be remiss if I didn't include at least one extension that allows you to listen to music while you are web surfing. *FoxyTunes* allows you the ability to control your music experience within the Firefox browser. It supports a variety of different media players on all three platforms including *iTunes*, *Windows Media Player*, *Winamp* and *Real Player*. *FoxyTunes* allows you to position its set of controls in a number of places in the browser, including the toolbars and the status bar. Figure 7-14 shows *FoxyTunes* installed in the Firefox status bar. Other features include the ability to configure keyboard shortcuts, the ability to pop up/hide the player with a mouse click, a sleep timer, and an alarm clock. Now I just have to decide what song to wake up to when I am napping at my desk—my guess is that it will be something from Nirvana.

**Figure 7-14**

*The FoxyTunes control panel.*

## Themes

One of the coolest features of Firefox is that you can customize the browser's look and feel by installing third-party themes. Think of themes as the best custom paint job you could ever get for your browser. Figures 7-15 and 7-16 demonstrate how themes can be used to make Firefox unique.

**Figure 7-15**

*The Charamel theme—a creamy, sugary experience.*

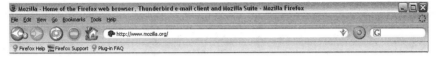

**Figure 7-16**

*Noia Extreme theme.*

**FRIDGE**

Check out http://www.grapple.net.tf/ if you are looking for some cool Mac OS X themes. The author has also provided skins for several extensions, including *Sage*, *Scrapbook*, and *Web Developer*.

## Locating Themes on the Web

Your recommended first stop for themes is the official Mozilla repository, *addons.update.mozilla.org* (*UMO*), which can be accessed directly from the **Get more Themes** link on the right side of the Firefox Extension Manager. *UMO* contains a categorized list of themes that are updated frequently and can be sorted by platform.

In addition to *UMO*, there a number of other places on the web that you can find themes for Firefox.

## Installing Themes

Firefox provides a theme manager that makes installing themes very easy. Here are the steps:

1. Locate the relevant theme, either at *UMO* or at another site.

2. At *UMO*, select the **Install** link.

3. Clicking the **Install** link should launch a confirmation dialog box, as shown in Figure 7-17, that requests your permission to install the `.jar` file that contains the theme.

**Figure 7-17**

*The theme
installation
confirmation
dialog.*

Other sites that list themes may require that you click a link, but you should still see the confirmation dialog box come up, and the remainder of the install instructions listed here should be the same.

4. After a brief delay, the **Install** button becomes active and you should be able to click it.

5. You should then see the .jar file install in the Theme Manager. A progress meter shows the progress until the theme install is complete.

6. Click the theme that you want to use, and then click on the button that says **Use theme**.

After installation, you must restart the browser to enable the theme.

## Switching Themes

To switch to a new theme, follow these steps:

1. Highlight the new theme you want to use.

2. Click the **Use Theme** button at the bottom of the Theme Manager. You may also right-click the theme and select **Use Theme** from the context menu.

3. After selecting **Use Theme**, you should now see a message underneath the theme name that indicates you must restart Firefox to use the new theme.

4. Restart Firefox, and voila! Your new theme should now appear.

## Uninstalling Themes

To uninstall a theme you have been using, follow these steps:

1. Highlight the new theme you want to uninstall.

2. Click the **Uninstall Theme** button at the bottom of the Theme Manager. You may also right-click the theme and select **Uninstall** from the context menu.

3. After clicking **Uninstall Theme**, you should now see a message under the theme name that indicates you must restart Firefox to use the new theme.

4. Restart Firefox, and voila! Your new theme should no longer be present.

> **Tip**
>
> If you never installed a theme and you elect to uninstall the theme, it disappears completely without your having to restart Firefox.

  **Something For the Mac Crowd: FireFoxy** (http://homepage.mac.com/amake/software/fireFoxy.html)

Firefoxy is a cool addition to your Mac repertoire—after you download this application to your desktop, you can drag and drop it on the Firefox application to give Firefox a more native Mac feel. So if you fancy having an improved experience with buttons, menus, and other controls, this might be something you want to install.

## Updating Themes

Updating themes in Firefox is managed the same way as it is in extensions. See the description in the "Updating Your Extensions" section for an explanation of how to configure automatic updates as well as how Firefox alerts you to the fact that theme updates are available.

If you decide that you prefer to check for theme updates manually, you can always click on the **Update** button in Theme Manager. You can also highlight the relevant theme and right-click to get the Update option. The Update Wizard launches and guides you seamlessly through the update process.

---

Wasn't that a wild ride? This chapter has shown you some of the many ways you can customize Firefox with extensions and themes to add a wide range of functionality and personality to your browsing experience. But more customization can be done. In Chapter 8, "Other Interesting Features," you will uncover additional ways you can customize the UI (user interface) in Firefox, including making your toolbars as complex or as minimalistic as you want. Ladies and gentlemen, start your engines—we're heading into the final Firefox chapter, looking for the checkered flag!

# Managing Your Blog with Extensions

'm out in my garage, trying to repair my 2000 Mazda Miata. There is a tool I need to fix my Miata, but I have a few choices of which tools I can pick from. I can try an SAE wrench (which might work), or I can try a tool that is optimized for my particular car (a Japanese car that uses the metric system-size tools).

When managing my blog, I am faced with a similar scenario. A number of third-party extensions can help me manage my blog, but which one do I reach for on a regular basis?

The answer to that question partially depends on which blogging format your blog uses. If you happen to use Google's Blogger format, *BlogThis* should be your extension of choice. *Deepest Sender* is also a good choice, but only if you use *livejournal.com*. The *Bloglines Toolkit* is another choice if you happen to use the Bloglines News Reader.

But my favorite extension by far is *JustBlogIt*, simply because it allows me to select from a number of popular blog formats right from the context menu (http://blog.warmbrain.com/justblogit/). My blog happens to use the *Movable Type* format, so with that set as the parameter, *JustBlogIt* makes it a snap for me to highlight any URL and then immediately paste it into my blog (http://weblogs.mozillazine.org/marcia/). If your blog format isn't listed, you can use *JustBlogIt's* custom setting to add any blog type you desire.

If you're trying to post from a news reader, just right-click with text selected (or not) and *JustBlogIt* determines which news reader you are coming from and handles the data appropriately.

Simply put, *JustBlogIt* is the best tool right now to manage blogs, in large part due to its support of multiple blog formats. So start using it today, and you will be happily blogging away to your heart's content, or until you run out of witty things to say. Suffice it to say that I don't often have that problem.

# 8

# Other Interesting Features

**DO OR DIE:**

>> Downloading

>> Printing

>> Customizing your toolbars

>> Does this font make me look fat?

>> Great art and you

The web is for more than just your viewing pleasure. You can get files of all kinds from it: MP3 files, movies, documents, programs, pictures, and much more. Firefox makes it easier to download files with the built-in Download Manager and a variety of downloading options.

## Setting Download Options

You already saw how to set some Download Manager options in Chapter 2, "Protecting Your Security and Privacy," that were focused on keeping your download history discreet. There are several additional options for downloading that you should know about. Go to Tools | Options | Downloads to examine the download options (shown in Figure 8-1).

The following sections show you how to set the download options on this screen.

**Figure 8-1**

*The Options screen with the download options displayed.*

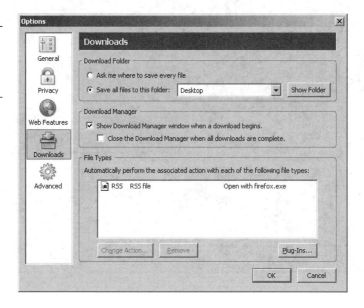

## Download Folder

The default option is to automatically save all files to the Desktop. You can select **My Computer** from the dropdown list or **Other** if you wish to browse for a folder. What I disagree with about this default is that I don't always want to save files in the same directory or even on the same drive, so I recommend you select **Ask me where to save every file**. Subsequently, each time you download a file, you'll tell Firefox where to save it.

## Download Manager

This option determines when you see the Download Manager screen. The default is to show the Download Manager when a download begins and not to close it when the download ends. (Your choices on this will probably also be affected by the privacy options you've selected for the Download Manager.) Leaving the Download Manager up after downloading a file is probably a good idea while you're finding out what you prefer.

## File Types

The File Types option lets you set file associations for types of files from within Firefox. When Firefox sees a file of a type that's registered in the list, it tries to open it with whatever application is associated with it. Firefox does a pretty good job with file associations—the work's actually done by the operating system; Firefox just tags along—but you may want to change the way in which Firefox handles one kind of file.

To change the action for a specific type of file, highlight the file type in the list and click **Change Action**. The Change Action screen (shown in Figure 8-2) appears.

The default setting changes from file type to file type. Selecting to open the file using the default application tells Firefox to use whatever your computer thinks is the standard application for this file. (For example, for an AVI file, the computer's default movie player would be used.) If you prefer to have Firefox override the system's default, select **Open**

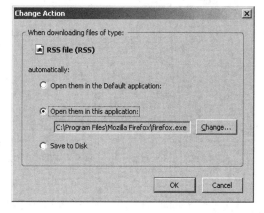

**Figure 8-2**
*The Change Action screen.*

**them in this application** and specify the application you want to use instead. (For example, if your system opens AVI files with the computer's default movie player, you can still open AVI files from within Firefox with a different movie player.) Finally, you can tell Firefox not to open the file—even if your computer's perfectly willing to have a go at it—but just to save it to disk. Click OK to save your entry for this file type.

You'll usually leave your plug-ins alone on the "Firefox knows best" principle, but you might want to disable a plug-in to try a different application or just to avoid opening the file in the plug-in. To see which plug-ins are installed and to view and change plug-in settings, click **Plug-Ins**. The Plug-Ins screen appears, as shown in Figure 8-3.

You can scroll through the list of plug-ins that are installed and the file type(s) associated with each one. To disable the plug-in without uninstalling it, click the check mark in the Enabled column. The check mark changes to a bullet. You can enable previously disabled plug-ins by clicking the bullet to change it back to a check mark. Click OK to save your changes.

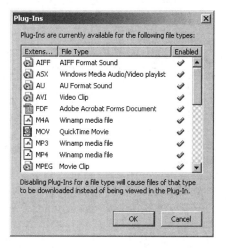

**Figure 8-3**
*The Plug-Ins screen.*

## What are plug-ins?

Firefox is a smart application that can open, display, and process a wide variety of files. However, as slick as Firefox is, it doesn't know how to handle absolutely everything. Plug-ins are add-on applications that focus on helping Firefox open and process files that it can't handle alone. They tend to be fairly mainstream and are usually available for many browsers, not just Firefox. (In contrast, extensions are generally smaller and are more focused on enhancing some specific aspect of Firefox rather than many different browsers.) Examples of typical plug-ins are Sun Java, Macromedia Flash, Macromedia Shockwave, RealNetworks RealPlayer, and Adobe Acrobat Reader. Each of these applications adds the ability to process types of files that Firefox can't handle alone.

Plug-ins aren't usually standalone applications, although there are standalone versions of many plug-ins. (A complete list of downloadable plug-ins can be found on the Netscape website at https://pfs.mozilla.org/plugins.) You also don't need to have a particular plug-in installed on Firefox to download and save a file that needs that plug-in to run, but you won't be able to run it in Firefox until you install the plug-in. To see a list of plug-ins that are currently installed in Firefox, all you have to do is type about:plugins in the URL bar.

When files cannot be opened within Firefox, you can choose to launch helper applications that open outside of Firefox. For example, to play MP3 files, programs like Winamp can be opened outside of Firefox.

If for some reason you don't want Firefox to be able to handle a particular file type, you can remove it from the list by highlighting the file type and clicking **Remove**. Confirm that you really want to do this and Firefox will forget that it ever knew that file type and will deny it thereafter.

# Downloading Files

Downloading a file of any kind is generally a matter of clicking a link on a web page and letting Firefox blaze away. Actually, there's a step or two in between, but it's still awfully simple.

Start by clicking the link of the file you want to download. Firefox asks you how you want to save it on the Opening screen, as shown in Figure 8-4.

You can choose to open the file on-the-fly or save the file to disk. Firefox suggests opening the file with the default application for your setup, but you can select a different application from the dropdown list. If you choose to save the file to disk, Firefox either saves the file to the default directory or lets you specify the drive and directory you want to save the file to.

Figure 8-4

*The Opening screen.*

> **Note**
>
> If you're downloading any kind of executable file—a program, a batch file, a script file, a screen saver, a help file, or the like—Firefox only lets you save the file to disk. This is to prevent you from accidentally downloading a program or script infected with a virus or that's a trojan horse. You'll see how to run the file right after downloading it if you want to, but this is a pretty good safety feature for that one time when we're all not quite awake at the switch and say "Yes" when we shouldn't have.

Unless you've changed the default, Firefox automatically displays the Download Manager when the download starts, as shown in Figure 8-5.

The Download Manager shows you the download progress: how much of the file has been downloaded at what speed and the estimated time remaining for the download. Most of the time, I just look at the histogram (the bar) to see how the download is doing.

You can pause the download in progress by clicking **Pause**. The histogram freezes and the dis-

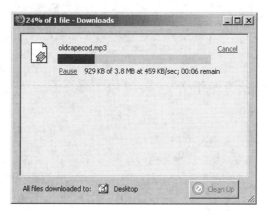

Figure 8-5

*The Download Manager screen.*

play shows how much of the file has been downloaded so far (as shown in Figure 8-6). You can resume the download by clicking **Resume**, whereupon the Download Manager picks up where it left off. Clicking **Cancel** at any point during the download process stops the whole thing.

**Figure 8-6**

*Pausing a download.*

When the download is complete, the Download Manager looks like Figure 8-7.

You can click **Open** to open the file (or, in this case, to play the MP3 file you've just downloaded). This is the same as going to the downloaded file on your hard drive and running it. Clicking **Open** for any potentially dangerous executable file causes a message like the one shown in Figure 8-8 to be displayed.

Go ahead and click OK if you're reeeeeally sure it's okay to do so.

**Figure 8-7**

*A completed download in the Download Manager.*

**Figure 8-8**

*Warning before running an executable file.*

**Warning**

You can click "Don't ask me this again" so that Firefox won't ask you again when you open a file of whatever type, but don't do this casually: you'll be shortcutting a valuable last-gasp protection against possibly running a harmful program or file.

As you download more files, the Download Manager shows the most recent at the top of the list. Figure 8-9 shows the Download Manager after three consecutive downloads of demo music files from a website.

Because the Download Manager keeps track of the files you've downloaded until they're cleared from the download history, you can always display the Download Manager (go to Tools | Downloads or press Ctrl+J) and right-click the name of a file in the list to display a small floating menu. You can open the file or remove it from the float-

**Figure 8-9**

*The Download Manager showing several down-loaded files.*

ing menu, but you can also open the containing folder the file is in to see where the file is located on your computer. For more information, you can select **Properties** to display the Download Properties screen (shown in Figure 8-10) that shows where the file came from, where it's been stored, and when the file was downloaded.

You can't change any of the information on the Download Properties screen, but it's very help-ful for showing you where a file came from so you can go back to that website.

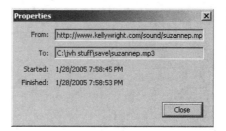

**Figure 8-10**

*The Download Properties screen.*

Keeping all the files in your Download Manager may present a privacy problem. Setting the Down-load Manager history retention to three days will help expunge the list auto-matically, but it can also be a good idea to clean up your tracks so no one knows you've been downloading Barry Manilow tunes. (Ohhhh, Maaanndy!) To remove the record that you've downloaded a specific file with the Download Manager, click **Remove**. This removes the listing in the Download Manager but does not delete the file from your hard drive. If you prefer, you can erase your entire download history all at once by clicking **Clean Up**, which scrubs the entire list at once (but doesn't delete any of the files).

One other thing to know about the Download Manager: lots of extensions are available that augment the Download Manager's capabilities in a variety of ways. Look for *Magpie* (http://www.bengoodger.com/software/tabloader) and *Download Status Bar* (http://downloadstatusbar.mozdev.org), both of which are described in Chapter 7, "Customizing Firefox with Third-Party Extensions and Themes."

# Printing

Sooner or later, you'll want to print a web page or two. I typically print maps to places I haven't been, confirmations of online transactions, and the occasional biscotti recipe. Most of the time, I'm comfortable just spitting things out on a piece of paper so I can keep track of whatever it is away from the computer. But every so often, you want something to print looking really nice. You'll be pleased to know that there are, in fact, some things you can do to enhance your printouts of web pages.

When you print a web page, don't just go to File | Print and click OK. This prints the web page, but it has the default print settings. Instead, go to File | Print Preview to see what the page will look like. Figure 8-11 shows a typical website displayed in the Print Preview screen.

**Figure 8-11**

*A website in the Print Preview screen.*

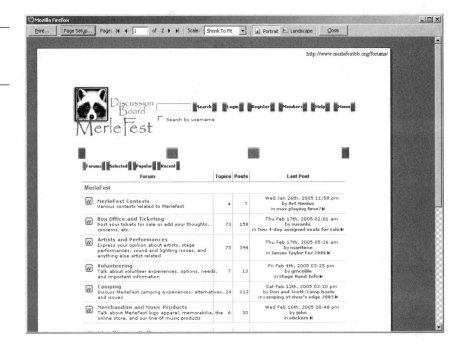

The Print Preview screen has a nice, clean feel to the control bar at the top. You can use the left and right arrows in the Page section to scroll through the pages as they'll be printed. Scaling lets you shrink or expand the web page's content. Figure 8-12 shows the same web page shrunk to 50%. Although the text is harder to read, you can print this entire web page on a single sheet of paper, which is more convenient. The default option, Shrink To Fit, is a pretty good idea: because many web pages aren't restricted in width, you can frequently lose that last little bit of information on the right margin that didn't print.

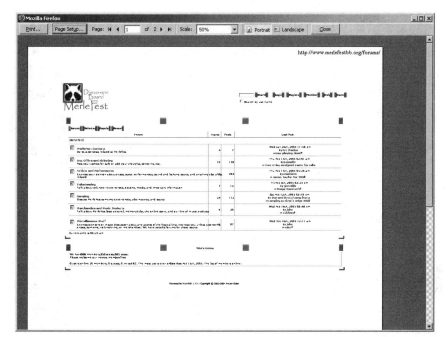

**Figure 8-12**

*Shrinking the website to 50%.*

You can also switch between portrait and landscape printing modes, which, combined with scaling, can give you the perfect fit for printouts that have to be just right.

Firefox, by default, does not show the screen background. If the screen has a watermark or a really dark background with text in weird colors, Firefox drops the background and displays only the text (even if it's colored weirdly—sorry) on a white background. This saves lots of toner and makes printouts much more readable, but the page may not be as pretty. If you just *have* to have the backgrounds printed as well, click **Page Setup** and check **Print Background (colors & images)**. Figure 8-13 shows the same page as shown in Figure 8-11 with the background added.

Some things that most people don't worry about are the page margins and headers and footers. The **Page Setup** option (which you can also get to directly from the Firefox menus by going to File | Print Preview) gives you control over all this, as shown in Figure 8-14.

The 0.5″ defaults shown are standard for most printers. The headers and footers are each set up with left, center, and right elements. The dropdown lists let you quickly select the web page title, URL, date/time of the printout, page number, or page number out of however many pages. You can also leave the field blank (like the center fields in the example) or select **Custom** from the dropdown list and enter your own text.

**Figure 8-13**

*Website with the background added.*

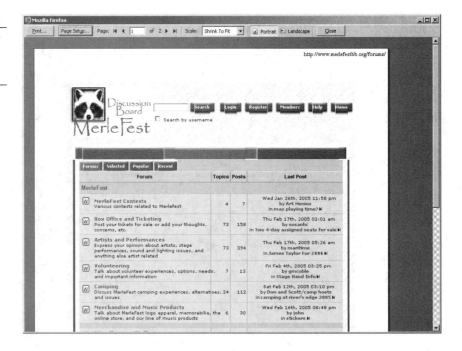

**Figure 8-14**

*Setting page margins and headers/footers.*

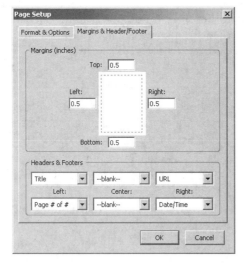

When you're happy with all the adjustments you've made in the Print Preview screen, click **Print** in the upper-left corner and go through the standard print menu for your printer and operating system. Or, if you're like me and you want to print a website, nine times out of ten you'll just go to File | Print from Firefox and click OK to start printing and be done with the whole thing.

# Toolbars

Firefox comes with two standard toolbars: the Navigation toolbar and the Bookmarks toolbar. You can toggle the display of either or both of these by going to View | Toolbars and then checking or unchecking the toolbars you want to display. You already saw in Chapter 5, "Bookmarks and History," how to modify the Bookmarks toolbar. You can also modify the Navigation toolbar and even create new toolbars with your own selection of toolbar icons on them.

To customize the Navigation toolbar, go to View | Toolbars | Customize, or just right-click the navigation toolbar and select Customize from the context menu. The Customize Toolbar screen (shown in Figure 8-15) appears.

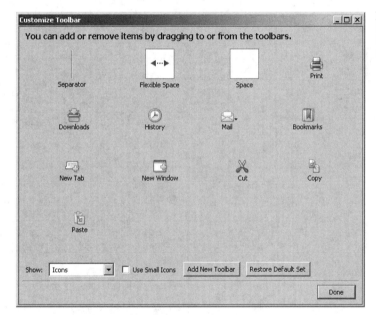

**Figure 8-15**

*The Customize Toolbar screen.*

The items on the Customize Toolbar screen can be added to the Navigation toolbar by dragging and dropping. Table 8-1 shows you the toolbar icons available on the Customize Toolbar screen and their functions.

**Table 8-1    Toolbar icons in the Customize Toolbar screen.**

| Icon | Name | Description |
|------|------|-------------|
| Separator | Separator | Inserts a vertical separator. |
| Flexible Space | Flexible space | Inserts a "flexible space" that tabs anything past it on the toolbar to the right end of the toolbar. |
| Space | Space | Inserts a space. (When you insert the space it appears as a white vertical rectangle for editing purposes, but the space then just appears as space in the toolbar.) |
| Print | Print | Does the same as the File \| Print command. |
| Downloads | Downloads | Does the same as the Tools \| Downloads command. |
| History | History | Does the same as the View \| Sidebar \| History command. |
| Mail | Mail | Does the same as the Tools \| Read Mail command. |
| Bookmarks | Bookmarks | Does the same as the View \| Sidebar \| Bookmarks command. |
| New Tab | New tab | Does the same as the File \| New Tab command. |
| New Window | New window | Does the same as the File \| New Window command. |

| ICON | NAME | DESCRIPTION |
|------|------|-------------|
| ✂ Cut | Cut | Does the same as the Edit \| Cut command. |
| 📋 Copy | Copy | Does the same as the Edit \| Copy command. |
| 📋 Paste | Paste | Does the same as the Edit \| Paste command. |

You can add any or all of these to the Navigation toolbar. When you drag icons from the Customize Toolbar screen to the Navigation toolbar, they vanish from the screen: you can have only one occurrence of the icon in the Navigation toolbar. This rule doesn't apply to the separator, flexible space, and space icons, however; you can add as many of those as you like. Figure 8-16 shows the Navigation toolbar with a selection of these icons added.

**Figure 8-16**

*Navigation toolbar customized with additional toolbar icons.*

When you put more icons in the toolbar, the location and search fields shrink… which is okay, really, because the amount of room you need for a web address isn't nearly as much as you're allotted by default. You can put the icons anywhere you like—in the example in Figure 8-16, the Print icon is off to the right of the toolbar, immediately to the left of the search field.

You can remove icons from the Navigation toolbar, too: drag the icons you want to remove back to the Customize Toolbar screen and drop them. This trick works with the menu bar and the Bookmarks toolbar, too: the icons for the activity indicator and the Bookmarks Toolbar Folder can be repositioned.

As you're working with the toolbars, the flexible space followed by the activity indicator is visible in the menu bar, and the icon representing the Bookmarks Toolbar Folder is visible in the Bookmarks toolbar. These can be dragged to the Customize Toolbar screen and positioned along with other icons that had been on the Navigation toolbar. Table 8-2 lists the default icons and what they do.

**Table 8-2  The default toolbar icons.**

| Icon | Name | Description |
|------|------|-------------|
| Back | Back | Goes to the previous web page. |
| Forward | Forward | Goes to the next web page. |
| Reload | Reload | Reloads the current web page. |
| Stop | Stop | Stops loading the current page. |
| Home | Home | Displays the home page set in the Firefox general options. |
| Location | Location | The field in which you enter web or file addresses. |
| Go | Go | Tells Firefox to go to the location in the Location field. |
| Search | Search | Searches for an item in the specified website. |
| Activity Indicator | Activity Indicator (aka "Throbber") | Goes to the Firefox home page. |
| Bookmarks | Bookmarks | Identifies the position of the Bookmarks Toolbar Folder. Wherever this is placed, the bookmarks in the Bookmarks Toolbar Folder are displayed. |

Although you can't drag the menu items on the menu bar to the Customize Toolbar screen, you can change what appears on the rest of the menu bar and on the Bookmarks toolbar, for that matter. For example, you can add most of the icons and fields currently on the default Navigation toolbar to the menu bar, add a thing or two to the Bookmarks toolbar, and eliminate the need for the (now empty) Navigation toolbar, as shown in Figure 8-17.

**Figure 8-17**

*Customizing the toolbars.*

In this example, the back and forward arrows are now in the Bookmarks toolbar, the bookmarks on the Bookmarks toolbar are pushed off to the right of the screen with a flexible space, most of the remainder of the Navigation toolbar appears in the menu bar, and the rest of the default icons are gone. This works: it's functional and attractive and is fairly economical of your screen real estate.

All this changing of features is fun, but what if you think that this just isn't working for you and you'd like things back the way they were? On the Customize Toolbar screen, click **Restore Default Set**, and all the toolbars are returned to their initial settings and contents.

You can add other toolbar icons: some Firefox extensions also create toolbar icons

**FAQ**

**How do I make things smaller and cleaner?**

If you're really concerned about cutting down the space, you can shrink the icons. Check the "Use Small Icons" box on the Customize Toolbar screen, and the icons, attractive as they are, shrink to about half the width and height of the defaults. For something even more modest, select "Text" from the dropdown list to display text instead of icons. Text is actually a little wider than the icons, so you may want to stick with small icons if you're trying to save space. On the other end of the spectrum, you can show both icons and text on the toolbars, which can be just the thing to help you learn your way around initially. Your call.

when you install them. These icons will appear at the bottom of the standard list of options on the Customize Toolbar screen. You can add these to toolbars just like any other icons. If you have a lot of extension icons, it may be desirable to create a new toolbar that is populated with extension icons. On the Customize Toolbar screen, click **Add New Toolbar**. When the Add New Toolbar screen appears, enter a name (as demonstrated in Figure 8-18).

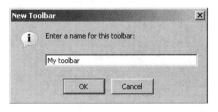

**Figure 8-18**

*The New Toolbar screen.*

The new toolbar can be customized like any of the other toolbars. When you next go to View | Toolbars, the new toolbar's name appears on the list of toolbars to display. (Clicking **Restore Default Set** erases any new toolbars, so be careful when you've created one.)

**TOOL KIT**

### Augmenting Your Toolbar Features

You can augment the toolbar's features and functions by using bookmarklets on the Bookmarks toolbar. Set up a folder in the Bookmarks Toolbar Folder with a name like "Tools" and add helpful bookmarklets to it, such as *Resize Window*, *Send Location*, and some search bookmarklets. Many of the basic navigation functions, such as Back, Next, Stop, and Find, are available as bookmarklets, too. You can then click the Tools folder to access additional commands and functions that aren't directly available on the Customize Toolbar screen without taking up a lot of valuable real estate on the Bookmarks toolbar.

# Tweaking Your Display

Because you've seen all sorts of ways to tweak your Firefox interface in this chapter and with themes in the previous chapter, it's only fair that there should be a brief discussion of a few things you can do with the actual display.

Chapter 1, "Getting Started," showed you how to set options for displaying the website fonts and colors. This is wonderful, but you should also know how to change the size of the text in the display. When you have a web page open, go to View | Font Size and select either **Increase** or **Decrease**. (You can also press Ctrl++ or Ctrl+- to do the same thing.) This cranks the text display up (or down) two sizes. Do this a time or two more and the text will either be very large or very small. Pressing Ctrl+0 (on the keyboard, not the number pad) resets the text to the default size. If your mouse has a mouse wheel, pressing Ctrl while you move the mouse wheel does the same thing. Resizing doesn't work with graphics, but Firefox can resize text even if the size is hard-coded in pixels—another advantage over IE.

Earlier in this chapter, you learned how to get rid of a toolbar to save some screen space. Go to View | Full Screen (or press F11) to hide most of the toolbars and menus to get the absolute most web page on the screen you possibly can. The only toolbar that's left is the Navigation toolbar. Pressing F11 or clicking the restore icon in the upper-right corner brings the screen back to normal. Maximizing the screen works very well in conjunction with a customized Navigation toolbar, so all the buttons you're likely to need are right there.

**FRIDGE**

In addition to the basic Firefox commands, there are bookmarklets that tweak the size and color of the fonts, the windows, and many other display options. Search the bookmarklet websites listed in Chapter 5 for additional ideas on ways to adjust your display.

If you're on a Windows or Linux computer (sorry—Mac users don't have this capability), you can right-click any image you see on a web page and select **Set As Wallpaper**. The Set Wallpaper screen (shown in Figure 8-19) appears.

You can center, stretch, or tile the picture and also tweak the background color. When you are satisfied with the way the picture and background look, click **Set Wallpaper** to change to this.

**Figure 8-19**

*The Set Wallpaper screen.*

 **FAQ**

### Where do people go to look for cool pix?

The web is swarming with wonderful pictures and art that make lovely wallpaper. Try Googling any of the following search categories with the Google Images option (use Google's SafeSearch Filtering option to ensure that anything you download is reasonably office-safe):

- Mucha
- Crystals
- Pre-Raphaelite
- Film noir
- Roman fresco
- Conure
- Illuminated manuscript
- Landscape painting
- Gaudi
- Mola art
- Sunset
- Haida
- Georgian architecture

- Antique map
- Classic rock posters
- Rodin
- Fractals
- Chinese coin
- Still life
- Calligraphy
- Fern
- Crown jewels
- Sister Wendy
- Commemorative stamp
- Wildlife
- Celtic knotwork

- Kandinsky
- The Hudson River school
- Hubble Space Telescope image
- Museum of Bad Art
- Joan Miro
- 67 Mustang
- Semiprecious stones
- Charles Rennie Mackintosh
- Swords
- Tropical fish
- Wooden toys
- Iridescence

If all else fails, you can always display M.C. Escher, Sandra Boynton, or Mary Engelbreit drawings.

This chapter concludes the Firefox half of the book. You've seen all the basics: how to install and configure Firefox; how to use the built-in search features, the Bookmarks Manager, and tabbed browsing; how to augment Firefox with extensions and themes; and how to download and print information. There's still more you can learn, such as how to tweak your user files and ways to use digital certificates (both topics are covered in the appendices), but most people probably won't be interested in that level of technical detail. At this point, you have enough information to use Firefox efficiently and enjoyably.

The next part of this book focuses on Mozilla Thunderbird, the powerful open source email program. Thunderbird gives you a way to send and receive email securely, to stop junk mail, and to follow RSS feeds and access newsgroups. So even if you've been reading this book to learn about Firefox, keep reading: you'll love the features and options available to you in Thunderbird.

# Literary Blogs through the Ages

**B**logging is so many things. For some it is a rambling, often incoherent rendering of the day's events (take a look at http://www.livejournal.com), a type of online diary. For others, it is used as an announcement mechanism—I got a new car, here's the inside scoop on what is happening in my life, and so on. Some blogs are nothing more than travelogues. For a whole other set of users, blogging is something in between—sort of a work in progress that describes them moving from one state to another, a kind of meandering through the meadows of cyberspace. One thing that all people who blog do—they definitely have something on their minds, and they need to speak their piece.

But blogging isn't just about getting something off your chest; it is also a community experience. The fact that people post on their site links to blogs that they read on a regular basis (or their friends' blogs) means that people are reaching out and trying to form some sort of cyberspace community amongst the daunting tsunami of information that is commonly referred to as the Internet. Posting someone else's blog on your blog is a kind of referral—it is basically you acknowledging that you respect this person's work/writings and it is worth the click to read what he or she has to say.

This got me thinking about some of the great literary minds over the centuries and whether they would have participated in writing a daily blog. I thought about whether poets or authors would have been better bloggers, and so far I have decided I have a slight bias toward poets. When I decided to venture into this territory, some writers immediately sprang to mind, and many of them were built around a community or a particular historical movement. Here are some of my thoughts about who I think would have embraced the art of blogging.

Any of the members of the Beat Generation—Allen Ginsberg, Jack Kerouac, William Burroughs, and Gregory Corso—would have been excellent bloggers. If Gregory Corso kept a blog, this poem probably would have made it into one of his blog posts:

### Last Night I Drove a Car

*Last night I drove a car*
*not knowing how to drive*
*not owning a car*
*I drove and knocked down*
*people I loved*
*…went 120 through one town.*

*I stopped at Hedgeville*
*and slept in the back seat*
*…excited about my new life.*

I would have been especially interested in what Burroughs would have written in his blog the day after he shot his wife in the head while trying to imitate William Tell. Knowing Burroughs, he likely would have blogged about it.

Kerouac took a lot of cross-country trips with Neal Cassady, which provided fodder for some of his writing. Rather than trying to fictionalize what happened, he wrote the story exactly as it happened. It turns out that it took quite a while for his editor to see the value of publishing this work (seven years), but eventually *On the Road* made it into print. If he were blogging about this trip the whole time, who knows what would have happened? One thing is for sure—it might have resulted in his novel getting published a whole lot sooner, because another editor would have probably recognized his talent and published it much earlier.

Ginsberg would have done his best blogging in the '60s, when he was protesting against the Vietnam War, causing a ruckus in India, and getting booted out of Prague and Cuba. If he were keeping a blog during this time, it might have been better than some of his poetry.

Another community that would have made excellent bloggers were the Surrealists, especially André Breton. Octavio Paz said of Breton, "'It is impossible to speak of André Breton in a language that is not that of passion." You can be sure that Breton's forceful presence and his penchant for stirring the pot would have produced some thoughtful blogs. And because the Surrealists were so gung ho about manifestos, a blog post would have been the perfect forum for their call to arms.

The style of writing that the Surrealists practiced (Automatic Writing) would have been well suited to the blogging style, as they were continually experimenting with language. Robert Desnos might have included some of his "cooked language," and I would have been curious to see what he would have blogged about on a daily basis. Some of the Cinema poems that I have seen would have made great blog posts. Another reason I know Desnos would have made a good blogger: in 1936, he embarked on a further foray into "Automatic Writing," as he set out to write one poem a day for an entire year. Now that is a true blogger in the making. Finally, the subject of Desnos' poems would have made for good reading, as he continually explored the subject of desire, as well as love and eroticism, which would have meant his blog would have got a lot of hits.[1]

Voltaire, in addition to being a princely writer, would have blogged until there was nothing left to say. As versatile as they come (he wrote poetry, philosophical works, dramas, and scientific novels), Voltaire's particular penchant for ridicule probably would have earned him an earnest blog following. By the way, I often wonder whether Voltaire would have been so successful if he hadn't spent time in the Bastille for various and sundry crimes. Being in prison would have given him plenty of time to blog, assuming that they had Internet access in 1717.

Mark Twain would have been an epic blogger. His world tour to France and Italy would have provided some tremendously interesting travelblog posts. More travel followed in the 1890s as he then embarked on a world lecture tour, which took him to New Zealand, Australia, India, and South Africa. He took on this world lecture tour to try to recover from his personal bankruptcy, which also would have made for interesting blogging. If he had the opportunity to blog about his personal bankruptcy, he might have been able to get donations to sustain him and he might never have had to embark on that world tour.

Kurt Vonnegut would write an interesting blog—he reminds me a little of a modern Mark Twain. Someone once described him as a "word cartoonist," which in my opinion is a perfect characterization for someone who would write in a blog. If Vonnegut had a blog, I would hope he used an RSS feed so I could pull in new content every day, because I would not want to miss a word he said.

Lewis Carroll would probably have posted some interesting blogs. With his verbal wit and his penchant for logic, he might have posted some kind of logical puzzle. If he did, I would probably still be trying to solve it.

---

[1] If you are interested in reading more about the Surrealists, a good first start is the book *What Is Surrealism?: Selected Writings* by André Breton and Franklin Rosemont.

While I am fairly certain that a lot of these writers and poets would have blogged up a storm, there is a whole other subset of writers that I suspect would not have embraced the blogging space. Despite the fact that I am a fan of Shakespeare, I am not convinced that the person(s) known as Shakespeare would have been adept at blogging. Sylvia Plath is one of my favorite poets, but I don't think it is likely she would have kept a blog. Dr. Seuss wrote really cool stories, but I probably wouldn't make his blog a top priority on my list.

Finally, there is one grand assumption here that might not be reasonable to make. I am assuming that all these great writers would have been willing to share their words and witticisms in their blogs. Perhaps that might not have happened. Instead, they might have just written normal, boring prose and saved their better, and more personal, stuff for books. Maybe these writers would have written about buying a new car or spilling coffee on their new carpet. Maybe we wouldn't have gotten any Automatic Writing from the Surrealists in blogs or any marvelous travelogues from Mark Twain. In many ways one could argue that their Zeitgeist was their Zeitgeist and that their expressions and thoughts could never be conveyed in the same way in a blog. Who knows? Perhaps the subject for another book? Whatever the case, if you have never had the opportunity to read any of the works by the authors listed in this piece, I strongly encourage you to sample some of their writing. It seems these days many of us spend plenty of time reading online, but there is a world of printed material out there just waiting to be discovered.

# PART II:
## Mozilla Thunderbird

Y ou have just wrapped up your exploration of the Firefox browser and learned about how you can make every day a fine browsing experience using a safe and customizable browser that will allow you to explore the web in ways you never knew were possible. (If you haven't yet read the Firefox part of this book, I strongly encourage you to do so—you won't be sorry!) Now it's time to introduce you to Firefox's elegant companion, the Thunderbird email client.

Thunderbird is a full-featured email program that allows you to manage your mail in a safe and efficient manner. While setting up an email program may seem like a daunting task, Thunderbird provides a simpler set of controls, and its relative ease of use makes it perfect for beginners as well as advanced users. If you have been using another email client to manage your mail, Thunderbird provides a mechanism for you to import your mail, address books, and other settings, so it is easy to pick up where you left off.

Thunderbird provides a little something for everyone. If you are coming from Outlook or Outlook Express, you will enjoy feature parity because Thunderbird offers many of the same features that are found in both of those clients, such as global inbox, saved searches, filters, and multiple identities. If you are looking for something a little different, Thunderbird has a number of powerful search features that allow you to locate information quickly. In addition, Thunderbird provides a robust spam filter that keeps your inbox spam free.

If you are starting from scratch and and are unfamiliar with Thunderbird, I encourage you to read the entire Thunderbird introduction (Chapter 9, "Getting Started with Mozilla Thunderbird") as well as Chapter 10, "Setting Up Your Mail, RSS, and Newsgroup Accounts Using Mozilla Thunderbird." Remember, email can be somewhat complicated to set up and a little more dif- ficult to manage for a number of reasons, so it is important to read these chap- ters and learn what information you will need to have on hand to set up your email accounts as well as how to migrate from other email clients.

If you have been using Thunderbird and are interested in learning how to get the most out of some of its features, you might want to check out Chapter 12, "Organizing Your Email Topics," and Chapter 13, "Customizing the Look and Feel of Mozilla Thunderbird." Remember, one of the truly unique features of both Firefox and Thunderbird is the ability to customize the programs by using extensions and themes. Depending on how you use your email client, you can likely find an extension that will make your life infinitely easier.

Okay, you are primed and ready for takeoff. Fasten your seat belt—we are about to taxi down the runway and begin our journey into the air, to soar to new heights with an exciting new email program called Thunderbird! Turn the page to get started!

# Getting Started with Mozilla Thunderbird

oes this sound familiar to you? Traffic is snarled, and cars are lined up bumper to bumper as far as the eye can see. A commuter lane is available for cars that have more than two passengers, but few can use it because most commuters are sitting in cars by themselves.

When these hapless commuters finally reach their office, they fire up their computers and immediately begin sifting through their email. Some of these users may have a choice concerning which email client they can use. If they do, which email client will help them get where they need to go?

Think of Thunderbird as the email client that can move you into that commuter lane, get you operating at a more efficient speed, and deliver you to your destination with time to spare!

Fasten your seat belt, and get ready for a whirlwind tour of the Thunderbird email client. I promise after reading this part of the book that you won't be left sitting in a traffic jam. I also promise you that after using Thunderbird you will likely feel a little like Alice in Wonderland did when she reached the Eighth Square. Enjoy the ride!

**DO OR DIE:**

>> How to get to your destination with time to spare

>> The Zen of Thunderbird

>> Don't think: download and install!

>> Need a lifeline? Help is on the way

**FRIDGE**

In case you are not familiar with what happens to Alice when she reaches the Eighth Square, it is the serene place where she realizes she is wearing the golden crown without knowing exactly how it got on her head.

# What Is Mozilla Thunderbird?

Thunderbird is a free open source standalone email and news application that is supported on the Windows (95, 98, Me, 2000, XP), Mac (OS X), and Linux platforms. It is intended to be the perfect companion for Firefox, which is the open source standalone browser discussed in Chapters 1 through 8. Thunderbird includes a number of desirable features and offers numerous ways to manage your email and newsgroups in a fast, safe, and efficient manner. Figure 9-1 shows an example of what the Thunderbird program looks like after it has been installed and mail accounts have been set up.

**Figure 9-1**

*The Thunderbird program.*

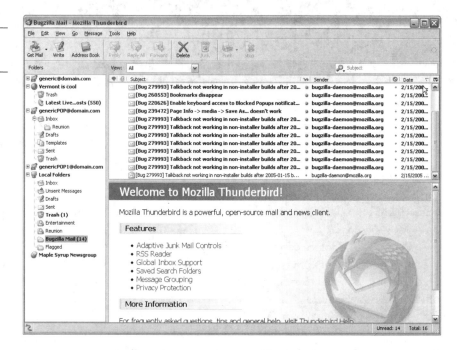

**Why is it free?**

Thunderbird is part of a burgeoning open source effort that promotes the development of innovative software that users can download and use for free. Users are also permitted to view and modify the source code as long as they adhere to the terms of the software license.

To learn more about open source, see Chapter 1, "Getting Started."

To learn more about who works on Thunderbird, go to Help | About Mozilla Thunderbird to see the list of credits.

# Where Did Mozilla Thunderbird Come From?

Thunderbird was borne of Mozilla blood because it is based on the Mozilla codebase. The project started out with the name Minotaur and was later changed to Thunderbird as the project gained momentum. In the same way that the Firefox team set out to make a lean and nimble web browser by redesigning the browser portion of the Mozilla suite, the Thunderbird developers set out to redesign the Mozilla email component with the intent of making an email client that was both faster and easier to use. They decided to focus primarily on the footprint and the performance of the mail application by removing chrome and components that were being shared with the browser. Thunderbird's user interface (UI) was also reworked to make it easier to navigate. Thunderbird is built on the stable core of Gecko, which is the Mozilla layout engine. Thunderbird's UI is built from the same powerful XUL technology as Firefox. (For more information about XUL, see the FAQ in Chapter 7, "Customizing Firefox with Third-Party Extensions and Themes.")

# Why Use Mozilla Thunderbird?

There are a multitude of reasons to use Thunderbird as your email application. Here are a few reasons, all of which will be discussed in depth in subsequent chapters.

## It's Secure

Worried about security? Relax. Thunderbird has powerful security features that will help keep you out of harm's way. First, because it *does not* permit scripts to run by default (JavaScript is switched off by default), it makes it more difficult for worms, trojan horses, and viruses that are running rampant on the Internet to block your productivity or, worse yet, cause irreparable damage to your computer and files. Additionally, Thunderbird's remote image-blocking capabilities add a further layer of protection to your privacy and security. This does not mean that you shouldn't take proper precautions and use a good anti-virus program on your computer system to make sure you are fully protected.

Thunderbird also contains a number of other desirable security features, such as message encryption, support for certificates (both personal certificates as well as certificate authorities), and digital signing. You can also manage security devices such as smart cards by using the Thunderbird preferences.

## It's a Time-Saver

Thunderbird features accurate junk mail management. When trained, Thunderbird's adaptive filter is amazingly accurate and can save you time by identifying messages that are most likely to be spam. Thunderbird employs what is known as "Bayesian filtering," which essentially means that the user "trains" the mail client to identify messages that are spam. Chapter 11, "Protecting Your Privacy and Blocking Spam," explains more about how you can use Thunderbird's junk mail controls to keep your inbox free from spam.

## It Has a Robust Set of Features

Thunderbird offers a wealth of features, including an integrated spell checker that was developed by the *Mozdev Project*. It also features an integrated RSS reader, saved searches, message grouping, message filtering, and powerful overall search capabilities. If you want to manage your mail using POP, Thunderbird offers a handy *Global Inbox* feature that makes managing your mail a breeze. If you need to manage multiple email accounts (or perhaps you are having a personality crisis), Thunderbird serves up a tasty *Manage Multiple Identities* feature that helps you control all your accounts and leaves you time for fun things like trying to figure out where Alice really went when she fell down the rabbit hole.

**What is mozdev.org?**

mozdev.org (http://www.mozdev.org) is an organization that provides a free centralized host repository for projects that use Mozilla source code to create applications, extensions, and themes, as well as other add-ons. A number of active projects are hosted on mozdev, and anyone can start a new project as long as it is related to Mozilla in some fashion.

## You Can Customize and Personalize to Your Heart's Content

Thunderbird gives you the ability to install extensions to make the client serve your individual needs. Chapter 13, "Customizing the Look and Feel of Mozilla Thunderbird," shows you some extensions that can extend Thunderbird's already powerful capabilities. Thunderbird also lets you choose numerous mail window layout options. Finally, if you think Thunderbird needs a makeover, themes are available to add a whimsical touch to your inbox. A number of helpful extensions and themes are easily accessible through a search mechanism that can be launched from the Thunderbird Extension Manager.

## It Encourages Dynamic Development

Thousands of users across the world are giving the development team feedback on Thunderbird every day. End users are filing bugs in the Bugzilla bug system (https://www.bugzilla.mozilla.org) and also are making requests for enhancements to the product. This collaborative process produces dynamic software that is never stale and always forward-thinking. Not every request for an enhancement can be implemented in Thunderbird, but the mere fact that end users have a mechanism for suggesting improvements is a quantum leap forward from the way other software is typically developed. Bugzilla also has a voting mechanism that allows users to vote for the bugs that are most important to them.

FAQ

**What is Mozilla Mail, and how is it different from Thunderbird?**
Mozilla Mail is part of the Mozilla suite, an integrated application suite that includes a web browser and a toolkit. While the Mozilla Mail client contains many of the same features as Thunderbird, Thunderbird includes a number of features not found in Mozilla mail. Also, it is important to distinguish that the Mozilla application suite is *not* a combination of Firefox and Thunderbird, but rather an entirely different application. For a brief history of Mozilla Mail, visit http://www.mozilla.org/mailnews/intro.html.

# System Requirements

The requirements for installing Thunderbird are almost identical to those for Firefox (see Chapter 1).

## Operating Systems

### Windows

Thunderbird supports the following operating systems. If you are using Windows, you should probably consider using XP because it is the recommended system according to the Mozilla reference page.

- Windows 98
- Windows 98SE
- Windows Me
- Windows NT 4.0
- Windows 2000
- Windows XP

### Mac

OS X is the only operating system that is supported. You can use Mac OS X 10.1.x or Mac OS X 10.2.x and beyond.

### Linux

Note that Linux distributors may offer distribution packages that contain different requirements than the ones listed here:

- Linux kernel 2.2.14—The following libraries or package minimums are needed:
  - glibc 2.3.2
  - gtk+ 2.0
  - XFree86 3.3.6
  - fontconfig (also known as xft)
  - libstdc++5
- If you are using Red Hat Linux 8.0 and later, Thunderbird has been tested and should work with no problem.

## Hardware

Listed next are the *minimum* recommended configurations and recommended configurations according to the Mozilla website.

### Windows and Linux

*Minimum* recommended configuration:

- Pentium 233 MHz with 64 MB RAM and at least 52 MB of available hard drive space. For Linux, the Mozilla site recommends an Intel Pentium II or AMD K6-III+ 233 MHz CPU.

Recommended configuration:

- Pentium 500 MHz or greater and 128 MB of RAM or greater. Remember, it never hurts to have more RAM.

### Mac

*Minimum* recommended configuration:

- PowerPC 604e 266 MHz with 64 MB RAM and at least 72 MB of available hard drive space.

Recommended configuration:

- PowerPC G4 that is at least 667 MHz or greater with 256 MB RAM or greater.

Don't forget that if you elect to save your email messages to your hard drive, you have to budget additional storage space to accommodate all your email messages and attachments.

## Downloading and Installing

You should always download the latest version of Thunderbird from the official Mozilla site: http://www.mozilla.org/products/thunderbird/.

> **Need Thunderbird on a CD?**
> If you are unable to download the file, you may purchase a CD that contains Thunderbird from the Mozilla Store (http://www.mozillastore.com/products/software).

### Unofficial Thunderbird Builds/Localized Builds/Downloading Thunderbird From Other Locations

A number of organizations may offer unofficial Thunderbird builds that can be downloaded from the mozilla.org FTP site:

http://ftp.mozilla.org/pub/mozilla.org/thunderbird/releases/1.0/contrib/

You should be aware that these builds may be configured differently from the official builds distributed by mozilla.org. These builds may also be optimized and/or tested for specific platforms, such as Solaris and Java Desktop for Linux.

A number of localized builds are available. To see if your language is supported, visit http://www.mozilla.org/products/thunderbird/all.html for a list of official builds that are distributed by mozilla.org.

# FAQ

Following are some common questions before installing:

### Can I migrate my profile from Mozilla email clients?

Yes. Auto migration is available for Mozilla 1.x or Netscape 6.x and 7.x profiles.

### Will I be able to import messages from other email programs? What about exporting messages?

Yes. You can import by going to Tools | Import. Thunderbird's "mbox" format should allow you to export mail messages as well. If you are looking for an easy way to import mbox files, there is an extension available that allows you to do this. You can find it at http://nic-nac-project.de/~kaosmos/mboximport-en.html. For more information concerning how to install extensions in Thunderbird, see Chapter 13.

### I use AOL. Can I use Thunderbird to send and read my mail?

Yes. You need to set up an IMAP account in Thunderbird (see Chapter 10) and use the following settings:

- Incoming Server Type: imap.aol.com
- Port Number: 587
- User Name: Your AOL screen name
- Outgoing Server (SMTP): smtp.aol.com

### Can I use Gmail, Hotmail, or Yahoo! Mail with Thunderbird?

Yes. Follow these links to learn how you can accomplish this:

- Gmail: http://gmail.google.com/support/bin/answer.py?answer=13285?ctx=search
- Hotmail: Blue HttpMail : http://bhttpmail.sourceforge.net/
  Hotmail Popper: http://boolean.ca/hotpop/
  hotwayd/hotsmtpd: http://hotwayd.sourceforge.net/news.php
- Yahoo! Mail: YPOPs! http://yahoopops.sourceforge.net/
- Mr. Postman: http://2mod2.com/mohot/
- Yosucker: http://yosucker.sourceforge.net/

### Can Thunderbird help my horrible spelling?

Yes, thanks to http://spellchecker.mozdev.org/.

### Can I sync my address book in Thunderbird with my Palm?

Yes, if you use Windows. Go to
http://kb.mozillazine.org/index.phtml?title=Thunderbird_:_FAQs_:_PalmSync
to find out how to do this.

### I would like some kind of notification that I have new mail. Can Thunderbird do this?

The Windows version of Thunderbird serves up mail notification in the system tray while Thunderbird is running. An extension discussed in the "Getting and Sending Messages" section of Chapter 13 might be of some help in this area. On the Mac side, you can configure Thunderbird to animate the dock icon to notify you when you have new mail.

## Installing Thunderbird

### Windows: Installer

1. Click the **Download Now** icon.
2. Save the `thunderbird.exe` file to your hard drive or launch the .exe (if you have your system configured to automatically open `.exe` files).
3. If you have saved the file, double-click the Thunderbird `setup.exe` icon.
4. The file extracts and you are taken to the Thunderbird Setup Wizard, as shown in Figure 9-2.
5. The wizard guides you through the remainder of the installation.

**Figure 9-2**

*Mozilla
Thunderbird
Setup Wizard.*

## Mac OS X: Compressed Disk Image

1. To uncompress and mount the disk image, double-click the **Thunderbird 1.0.dmg.dz** Disk Image (this may already have been done for you depending on your configuration).

2. Double-click the **Thunderbird Disk Image** to open it, and drag the Thunderbird application to a location on your hard disk.

   **Don't run Thunderbird from the disk image!**

3. *Do not* double-click the icon in the disk image! Instead, be sure to drag the Thunderbird application out of the disk image and onto your hard disk before you run the application. If you do this accidentally and find that the Thunderbird icon bounces and disappears and reappears in the dock, you will have to kill the process by opening a terminal and typing **killall thunderbird-bin** and then pressing Enter.

4. To place Thunderbird in the dock, drag the icon there. You have to set the "Keep in Dock" parameter if you want Thunderbird to continue to be present in the dock after the application has been closed.

## Linux: GTK2 + XF (No Installer Available)

1. Download the **thunderbird-1.0.tar.gz** file.

2. Make sure you are logged in as a root user.

3. Save the file to the place where it will be used.

4. Extract the file by issuing the command tar **zxvf tbird-1.0.tar.gz**.

5. cd into the Thunderbird folder.

6. Start the program by typing ./thunderbird

---

**Need Thunderbird in Your Hip Pocket?**

Go to http://portablethunderbird.mozdev.org and download a version of Thunderbird that is optimized for use on a USB key drive. The author of this version claims that it also works from zip drives, external hard drives, flash RAM cards, and some MP3 players. At the time of this writing, it is available only on the Windows platform.

Interestingly enough, the author states that the whole idea of having a portable version of Thunderbird originated from a MozillaZine forum topic—yet another way that forums can be useful in ideas regarding the development of open source products.

---

## Uninstalling Thunderbird

### Windows

1. Navigate to Control Panel.

2. Select **Add or Remove Programs**.

3. Highlight Mozilla Thunderbird.

4. Select **Change/Remove**.

5. Answer **Yes** to the dialog.

6. If you receive a prompt indicating that "Not all files were uninstalled from the install directory—do you want to completely delete this directory?", answer Yes.

### Mac OS X

Drag and drop the Thunderbird application into the Trash.

### Linux

Remove the Thunderbird folder that was created when you decompressed the tar file by running this command: `rm -rf thunderbird/`.

**What happens to my profile when I uninstall Thunderbird?**

When you uninstall Thunderbird following these instructions, your profile is left untouched in the event you decide to install Thunderbird again at a later date. To remove your profile folder, you need to delete the location described in Table 9-1.

**Are You Absolutely Certain That You Want to Delete Your Profile?**

If you decide to delete your profile, you will permanently lose all your email, address book data, settings, themes and extensions, junk mail configuration, and so on. In the event that you elect to use Thunderbird again, you will need to start from scratch with a fresh profile. A better approach would be to rename your profile rather than permanently deleting it.

**Table 9-1  Mozilla Thunderbird Profile locations by platform**

| | |
|---|---|
| Windows 2000, XP | Documents and Settings\<UserName>\ Application Data\Mozilla Thunderbird |
| Windows NT | WINNT\Profiles\<UserName>\Application Data\ Mozilla Thunderbird |
| Windows 98, Me Thunderbird | Windows\Application Data\Mozilla |
| Mac OS X | ~/Library/Thunderbird |
| Linux and Unix systems | ~/.thunderbird |

# Accessing Mozilla Thunderbird Help

As of this writing, Thunderbird does not have a built-in Help Viewer. Navigating to Help | Mozilla Thunderbird Help routes you to http:// mozilla.org/support/thunderbird, which is the online help site for the Mozilla Thunderbird mail client. If this site doesn't address your specific question, there are a number of other places to go to get help.

### Forums

One great resource is the MozillaZine Thunderbird Support forum, located at http://forums.mozillazine.org/viewforum.php?f=39.

These forums require you to register, but after you post your questions, responses usually come fairly rapidly (sometimes within 24 hours). Because mail configurations can be rather complex, it is helpful to include as much information as you can in your post. This will definitely help the many forum watchers who are around troubleshoot your problem and get a solution posted much more quickly.

MozillaZine (http://www.mozillazine.org) also hosts several Thunderbird developer forums (http://forums.mozillazine.org/index.php?c=8) that may contain useful information, but the support forum listed previously is the better first stop. These forums are categorized into sections that cover Thunderbird builds, general topics, features, and bugs.

## IRC

If you want to visit IRC (moznet, or irc.mozilla.org) and try to get some live help, you can visit the #thunderbird forum, but you are probably better off going to #mozillazine if you have Thunderbird questions.

## Release Notes

You can also consult the Release Notes, which can be accessed from the Help | Release Notes menu option. The Release Notes may save you some frustration if something is not working as expected and you can't figure out why. Just like any software that is continuously under development, Thunderbird will have bugs, so don't expect perfection. But do expect a very active development community that is monitoring the Bugzilla bug database and is continually working to make the product better.

## Third-Party Support Options

Remember that Thunderbird is distributed as a free product, and the Mozilla Foundation does not offer end-user support. There are a few options for paid support if you cannot get your questions answered in the forums or on IRC. For a list of these options, visit http://www.mozilla.org/support.

## Other Online Resources

There are also a number of other online resources that you can consult for helpful information:

- Introduction to Mozilla Thunderbird (a wonderful introduction with loads of screenshots to walk you through step by step): http://www.nidelven-it.no/articles/introduction_to_thunderbird
- MozillaZine Knowledge Base: http://kb.mozillazine.org/index.phtml?title-Thunderbird
- Mozilla Thunderbird Help: http://www.mozilla.org/support/thunderbird/

- Thunderbird Tips and Tricks (for advanced users): http://www.texturizer.net/thunderbird/tips.html

- Mozilla Thunderbird Tips, Tricks, and Secrets: http://email.about.com/od/mozillathunderbirdtips/

- Mozilla Tips: http://www.moztips.com/wiki/index.pcgi?page=ThunderbirdFaq

**FAQ**

**How is the default email check done in Thunderbird?**

The default email check performed by Thunderbird occurs on a per-computer account basis, not a per-profile basis.

# Making Mozilla Thunderbird Your Default Email Client

Launching Thunderbird on Windows or Linux for the first time should generate a prompt asking you if you want Thunderbird to be your default email client. If you happen to answer "No" and you want to go back later and make Thunderbird the default, follow these steps:

## Windows

1. Go to Tools | Options.
2. Click **General**.
3. As shown in Figure 9-3, check the box under General Settings that says "Use Thunderbird as the default mail application."
4. In the event that you are using Thunderbird as your default news reader, you should check that box as well.

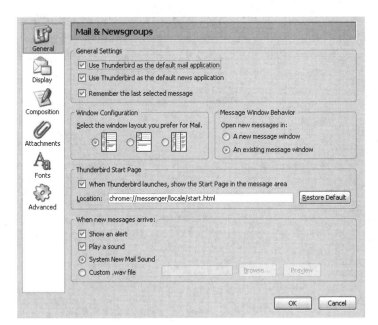

**Figure 9-3**

*The Thunderbird General Settings with Thunderbird set as default on Windows.*

## Linux

- The unofficial Thunderbird FAQ at http://texturizer.net/thunderbird/faq.html covers how to do this for GNOME and KDE 3.

- http://www.linuxquestions.org/ is a good resource if you are having any issues with making Thunderbird your default.

If at some point you switch to another email client and you want to go back to using Thunderbird, the next time you launch Thunderbird you should get a dialog box asking you if you want to make Thunderbird the default. At the time of this writing this is not supported on the Mac due to the way Apple manages the default email choice through `mail.app`. To set Thunderbird as your default, you actually have to set up a `mail.app` account first and then go into mail.app Preferences to make Thunderbird your default email client.

> **Opening URLs from Thunderbird with a Mac**
>
> If you want to click URL links in Thunderbird and have them launch in Firefox, you will have to go into Safari and set Firefox as your default browser. Those tricky Apple developers sure don't make it easy!

If you encounter problems with `mailto:` links not launching when you're using Windows, you might have to go to Start | Settings | Control Panel and open the **Internet Options** tab. Go to **Programs** and select Thunderbird from the dropdown list under E-Mail.

You've taken the first step and downloaded Thunderbird. An exciting world of mail management awaits you. Let's move on to the next chapter and show you how to set up your mail, RSS, and news accounts in Thunderbird. You'll quickly see how Thunderbird will allow you to soar to new heights!

# 10

# Setting Up Your Mail, RSS, and Newsgroup Accounts Using Mozilla Thunderbird

Now that we've got Thunderbird up and running, it is time to move to the next stage. Just like your first car, Thunderbird looks really shiny sitting in the garage, but the open road beckons. It's time for a test drive. Get ready: you're about to learn how to set up your mail, RSS, and newsgroup accounts using Thunderbird. This includes showing you how to migrate email settings from other email clients, set up new accounts, and configure your account settings.

You'll also learn how you can manage multiple email accounts using Thunderbird, send and receive messages, use the address book, and configure offline settings.

Because readers may be in different situations regarding their email, this chapter is divided into a few different sections. The experience of setting up Thunderbird will be slightly different depending on whether you have used other mail clients on your machine.

Email is important to all of us, so it is important to read this section to avoid some of the pitfalls you could encounter.

# Scenario 1: Migrating from Another Mail Client Used on Your Machine

Consult the "Migration" section of this chapter to learn how to set up your account in Thunderbird and bring in your settings from another mail client.

## Important Considerations

You should not uninstall any of the clients you are migrating from until you have completed migrating to Thunderbird and have thoroughly tested your new setup. If you do this, you will not be able to bring any of the information and settings into Thunderbird.

The "Migration" section of this chapter is written assuming that Thunderbird has never been installed on the machine you are using. If it has, the Migration Wizard will not run. In order for the Migration wizard to run, Thunderbird must detect that no existing Thunderbird profile is present on the machine (if there is, Thunderbird launches with that profile). Even if you have uninstalled Thunderbird, a Thunderbird profile remains on your system. To resolve this problem, you have to remove or rename the existing Thunderbird profile folder (see Table 9-1 in Chapter 9, "Getting Started with Mozilla Thunderbird," for profile locations). After that is done, the Thunderbird Migration Wizard should launch, and you can begin importing your mail and account settings.

# Scenario 2: Setting Up Thunderbird for the First Time, No Previous Mail Client Used on Your Machine

Consult the "New Account Setup" section to learn how to set up your account in Thunderbird.

## Information You Should Have on Hand

If you are setting up Thunderbird for the first time, you need a base set of information to set up your account. Examples of the format are shown in Table 10-1. If you don't have this information, you need to contact your Internet service provider (ISP).

Table 10-1   **Information Needed to Set Up a Mail Account.**

| INFORMATION | SAMPLE FORMATS |
|---|---|
| Email address: | domain@generic.com, domain@generic.org |
| Name of Incoming Mail Server | popdomain.generic.com |
| Name of Outgoing Mail Server | smtp.generic.com (could also be the same as incoming) |
| Type of Server (IMAP or POP) | IMAP or POP (see "A Pop and IMAP Primer" below for an explanation of these protocols) |
| User or Login Name | marcia |

## A POP and IMAP Primer

You may have seen this terminology but might not understand what the acronyms stand for or which mail protocol is the better one for your needs. Now is as good a time as any to demystify POP and IMAP so you can decide which one would better suit your needs. (Many of you will not be able to use IMAP because it is more commonly used in the corporate world, but some of you may have the ability to use both.) Much of the decision to use POP or IMAP will also be determined by the speed of the connection you may have (dial-up versus broadband) as well as how many locations you check mail from.

IMAP stands for *Internet Message Access Protocol*. In the IMAP world, the server manages all your mail. When you download new messages from your mail server, it only sends a list of the headers to your email application. When you are ready to read the message, the message body gets downloaded from the server. If you decide to delete the message, it is deleted from the server. The great thing about IMAP is that you can store messages locally as well, but the primary function of IMAP is to use the server to house your mail. The downside? Users all over the country have a tendency to think servers can handle saving all of their mail, and thus may go over quota. So if you think you want to be a mail pack rat, IMAP is perfect for you as long as your Internet service provider offers that option and your server can handle your mail quota.

POP stands for *Post Office Protocol*. The POP strategy employs your local computer as your mail manager, rather than a server. If your account is set up with POP, your mail is downloaded from the server and then deleted. POP is configured to recognize only an Inbox on the server and won't recognize other mailboxes unless you set them up locally. POP does afford you the opportunity to leave your mail on the server, but this may result in more confusion than it is worth if you check mail from multiple locations, because each location may have a different variation of your inbox if you are using POP at these locations.

If you have the choice, which protocol is best for you? It really depends on your appetite. What do you plan on cookin' up with your protocol? Here are some different scenarios of when it might be beneficial to use IMAP and POP or just POP. OK, everyone, grab your aprons, and let's see what's cookin':

### IMAP Recipe: Hobo IMAP

Ingredients:

    1 generous helping of broadband

    1 computer that allows you to install software

    Imagine you are a hobo, always finding yourself at different locations, but always within reach of a broadband connection. You have a computer that allows you to install software so that you can configure a mail client.

    You might have a situation where you need to check your mail from more than one location (say office and home), but the primary location you check it is the office. You decide that you want to see only new mail at your home location. In this scenario, it might be wise to use POP at your office and IMAP at home.

### POP Recipes

Here are some recipes for POP that you might find helpful:

### Stay-at-Home POP

Ingredients:

    1 computer that you never lose sight of

    In this scenario, you primarily use one computer to manage your mail. In this case, POP might be the better choice for you.

### Split-Personality POP

Ingredients:

    2 locations

    All your Inbox messages

    You like to work from both office and home, and you want both locations to contain all your Inbox messages. Both machines need to have the "leave mail on server" preference turned on.

## Important Considerations

Using POP? Thunderbird checks the default account for mail on startup, even if you uncheck the box in the Account Setup Wizard that says "Download Messages Now." If you are using POP as your default account, it might be wise not to be connected to the Internet when you are setting up Thunderbird. That way, you prevent mail from being deleted from your server and then having to go back and import these messages to your previous mail application in the event that you decide to forgo using Thunderbird.

# Migration

If you are migrating from another email client, such as Outlook or Eudora, the first time you run Thunderbird you should get the Import Wizard (see Figure 10-1).

**Figure 10-1**

*The Thunderbird Import Wizard.*

Here is the current list of mail clients that you can migrate from. Remember that it is possible that support for other clients may be added in the future:

- Netscape Communicator 4.x
- Netscape 6.x and 7.x
- Mozilla 1.x
- Outlook
- Outlook Express
- Eudora

Follow these instructions to migrate:

1. Click the radio button of the mail client you want to import.
2. The wizard continues and you begin to see information being imported.

**Note:**

At the time of this writing, migrating from Eudora is not supported on the Mac.

**What if I have an older version of Thunderbird installed on my system?**

The best way to proceed in this case is to uninstall the older version and download and install the latest version from www.mozilla.org/products/thunderbird/.

# Manual Migration: Importing Mail the Old-Fashioned Way

Thunderbird also allows you to import mail, address books, and preference settings from other email clients. To accomplish this task, navigate to Tools | Options. The Import Wizard should launch and present a series of radio buttons asking you what you want to import (Address Books, Mail, or Settings). Follow the wizard, and your mail, address books, or preferences should be imported from the directory you specified into Thunderbird.

# New Account Setup

After launching Thunderbird, you first arrive at the New Account Setup Wizard, as shown in Figure 10-2. A series of radio buttons allows you to choose to set up an email account, RSS account, or newsgroup account.

**Figure 10-2**

*New Account screen with radio button selections.*

## Setting Up a Mail Account

As shown in Figure 10-3, you need to fill in your Identity Information: "From" Name, as well as your email address. Click Next.

Select the type of server you are using, POP or IMAP. Figures 10-4 and 10-5 show the server screens for POP and IMAP. See the "A POP and IMAP Primer" sidebar for more information if you are unsure which type of server you use.

If you choose POP, you need to decide whether to use the Global Inbox feature. The Global Inbox preference is *on by default*, so you have to uncheck the box if you don't want to use it. Proceed directly to the "Global Inbox" section of this chapter if you are in doubt, because it is easier to set this preference from the outset than to go back and change your accounts to use Global Inbox (although this is certainly possible).

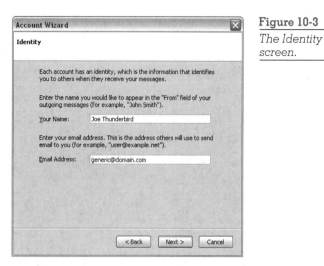

**Figure 10-3**

*The Identity screen.*

**Tip**

If you are using POP, one setting that you might want to consider setting right after you set up your account is the Leave Messages on Server setting, which is located under Server Settings. If your account is set up with POP, your mail will be downloaded from the server and then deleted. This setting allows you to keep the messages on the server for the number of days that you specify.

**Figure 10-4**

*The Server screen for POP.*

Fill in the name of your incoming server as well as your outgoing (SMTP) server. If you don't have this information, contact your ISP. Click Next.

**Figure 10-5**

*The Server screen for IMAP.*

Fill in your user names (incoming and outgoing names), as shown in Figure 10-6.

**Figure 10-6**

*The User Names screen.*

Done. Now that you have finished setting up your account, you probably want to get your new mail.

If you need to change any of your mail settings, please consult the "Mail Account Settings" section of this chapter to learn how to make the changes. Before you begin sending and receiving mail, it is a good idea to review the "Account Settings" section to make sure that you have the mail client configured with the settings that will make it easiest for you to manage your mail.

### Setting Your Outgoing Mail Server for Multiple Accounts

If you envision creating multiple mail accounts, you might want to consider setting *different SMTP servers* for your various accounts. Thunderbird uses the outgoing server of the account that was first created as your default account for your outbound messages. Be aware that because some mail servers may verify where the mail is coming from (the headers), you might not be able to send an email from an @netscape.com address through another SMTP server, such as @aol.com.

To set your outgoing mail server for multiple accounts, go to Tools | Account Settings and click Outgoing Server. Clicking the Advanced button leads you down the primrose path to "Advanced Outgoing Server (SMTP) Settings." In this area, you can configure to your heart's desire, but I will warn you (and the dialog box does, too) that this is an area for more advanced users. Monkeying around in this area could lead to problems, but if configured properly it could make your life that much easier.

## Getting New Mail

Thunderbird offers you two ways to retrieve your mail: automatically or manually. If you wish to check automatically, you can configure how often Thunderbird checks for new mail by tweaking a preference.

## Automatically

When you launch Thunderbird, it automatically checks for new messages every *10 minutes*. To change this setting, go to Tools | Account Settings | Server Settings to adjust how frequently Thunderbird checks for new mail.

## Manually

To get new mail, you can either click the **Get Mail** icon or go to File | Get New Messages For and either specify the particular account you want to get mail from or get all your new messages. When you download messages, the mail progress meter on the lower-right portion of the screen should show signs of life as mail is downloaded into your account.

> **Using Global Inbox and Retrieving Mail**
>
> If the account you are retrieving mail from is set up with Global Inbox or set up under another account's folder directory, and you have not set the preference in Advanced Account Settings to "Include this server when getting new mail," you will not be able to use "Get All New Messages" for that account. Instead, you need to click "Get Mail" and select that account specifically.

## Setting Up an RSS Account

Really Simple Syndication (RSS) is a content-delivery mechanism that allows news and web content to be shared in the online space. The RSS format allows this content to be aggregated and then delivered to the user when changes are made. For a more in-depth explanation of RSS, see the FAQ in this chapter.

You can manage your news content in Thunderbird by creating an RSS account.

>  FAQ
>
> **What is RSS?**
>
> Fortunately, here is everything you need to know about RSS but were afraid to ask.
>
> RSS stands for Really Simple Syndication (or Rich Site Summary, depending on who you ask) and has become a widely used format for syndicating news and other online content. If the motto for the *New York Times* is "All the news that's fit to print," the motto for RSS might be "All the news whenever and wherever you want it" because RSS serves as a powerful mechanism for gathering and sharing news and other content. Distilled to its most basic element, RSS lets you know when content on a website has been updated or changed.

As the Internet increasingly becomes a thoroughfare full of "information overload," web developers are beginning to rethink ways that information needs to be organized in order to be useful. RSS is a way that this information can be streamlined so that it is much easier for the user to handle (and saves lots of time, too). In years gone by, users would have to visit many websites and join mailing lists to get information. Now they can sit back and let an RSS program do the work for them. By the way, RSS isn't a totally new format, having been originated by UserLand back in 1997 and then used by Netscape in its Netcenter division. It just seems as if its time may have come, especially when blogging is starting its starry-eyed descent into the mainstream.

### RSS Feeds

If you surf the Internet today, you might have noticed that many websites have now added RSS "feeds" to their sites. Typically these feeds are designated by a link or a button that says "RSS," "XML," or "Syndicate this site." Think of an RSS feed as a shining beacon (a lighthouse of sorts) that flashes and alerts subscribers when information on the website has been updated.

### Subscribing to an RSS Feed

After you have located some feeds, it's time to subscribe. You need the URL link for the RSS feed you want. These typically look like web addresses and may end in either .rdf or .xml. All you have to do is add that link to Thunderbird (by dragging or dropping or through the Subscriptions Manager) and you can begin downloading your feeds.

### Cool Things RSS Feeds Can Do for You

RSS feeds are now being used to let Firefox and Thunderbird users know when there are new extensions and updates. Other sites are using them as notification mechanisms. As far as I can tell, RSS feeds will continue to grow in popularity because they operate on the one thing that people value most—time. So if you want to hitch your wagon to a star, go get some RSS feeds and get started!

## Creating an RSS Account

To create an RSS account, follow these steps:

1 Click the **RSS News and Blogs** radio button.

2. Name your account.

3. The account is created and added to the folder pane.

## Managing Your RSS Account

After your account has been created, there are a few ways to manage your feed subscriptions.

You can either do this:

1. Drag and drop the XML link from the browser directly onto the account.
2. Thunderbird should begin downloading messages to your account.

Or you can do this:

1. Right-click the account to launch the RSS Subscriptions Manager.
2. Click Add.
3. Enter the Feed URL as well as where to store the Feed articles.
4. Click OK.
5. Thunderbird should begin downloading messages to your account.

If this doesn't happen, click **Get all new messages** or right-click and select **Get all new messages for the account** and the messages should download.

**Feeds Not Updating?**

Make sure to check the default setting in your RSS Account Settings - Check for new articles every XX minutes. Thunderbird sets it to 100 minutes by default, but you might want to make it less because some RSS feeds are updated rather frequently. If you don't check the box Check for new articles at startup, you need to check for new messages manually.

If you need to change any of your RSS settings (and you might, because sometimes feed URLs do change), consult the "RSS Account Settings" section of this chapter to learn how to make the changes.

**Adding Feeds the Right Way**

RSS feeds may be distributed in a variety of ways. When you add a feed, make certain that you enter the actual feed file and not a link to the site that may be hosting the file. Websites often display these files with words such as RSS, XML, or Atom.

## Setting Up a Newsgroup Account

Thunderbird also lets you set up newsgroup accounts to manage your life in the Usenet world. To create a new newsgroup account, follow these steps:

1. Select the **Newsgroup Account** radio button.
2. Enter your identity information.

3. Enter the name of your newsgroup server.

4. Enter the name of the account.

5. The account is created and added to the folder pane.

## Adding Newsgroups

Right-clicking **Subscribe** leads you to a dialog box (shown in Figure 10-7) that allows you to subscribe to, unsubscribe from, and refresh your newsgroups.

If you need to change any of your newsgroup settings, consult the "Mail Account Settings" section of this chapter to learn how to make the changes.

**Figure 10-7**

*The Newsgroup Subscribe dialog box.*

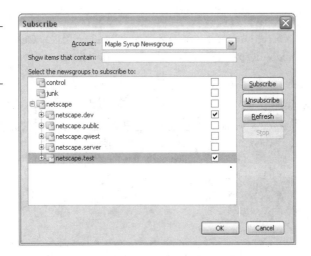

**Forumzilla, an Extension That Can Help You Manage RSS Feeds in Thunderbird**

*Forumzilla* is way cool. It's an extension that lets you read RSS and Atom feeds in Thunderbird. Thunderbird's native feed-reading feature is based on *Forumzilla*, but *Forumzilla* includes extra features that make it easier to manage feeds and download them into different folders (including IMAP folders).

To get *Forumzilla*, go to http://forumzilla.mozdev.org/ and follow the instructions for downloading and installing it. To use it, select Edit | Feed Subscriptions and the Feed Subscriptions window appears. Click the Add button to subscribe to a feed, and enter the URL of the feed when prompted.

*Forumzilla* adds the feed to your subscriptions list, checks for new stories periodically, and downloads new stories into one of your mail folders. By default, *Forumzilla* checks for new stories every 30 minutes and downloads them into the Feeds folder within the Local Folders account, but you can change the settings for existing subscriptions by clicking the Advanced button, and you can change the defaults for new subscriptions in *Forumzilla's* preferences.

# A POP Un-Birthday Gift: Global Inbox

Do you have multiple POP accounts and need a neat and tidy way to manage them by using a single inbox? It just must be your lucky day, because Thunderbird's Global Inbox feature does exactly that. The great thing about Global Inbox is that you don't necessarily have to use it for all your POP accounts. Here's the deal:

- Use Global Inbox for POP accounts—Folders are not displayed in the folders pane—Local Folders shows a single set of folders. All POP mail for those accounts is stored and managed in one folder directory structure, as shown in Figure 10-8.

**Figure 10-8**

*Thunderbird with Global Inbox turned on.*

- Do not use Global Inbox for POP accounts—Inbox and a set of folders is displayed in the folders pane for each POP account, as shown in Figure 10-9.

A good companion for Global Inbox is the Managing multiple identities feature, which is discussed in the next section.

**Figure 10-9**

*Thunderbird with Global Inbox turned off.*

## Changing to Global Inbox After You Have Already Set Up Your Account

It is possible to modify an existing POP account to use the Global Inbox feature. To do this, go to Tools | Account Settings | Server settings and click the Advanced button. Click **Global Inbox** and then click OK. Restart Thunderbird, and you should no longer see the non-Global Inbox listed in the Folders pane. The next time you retrieve your mail, the mail from the prior account should be channeled into the Local Folders Inbox.

## Storage Considerations for Global Inbox

If you set up your POP account to use Global Inbox, you can manage where your mail is stored by going to Tools | Account Settings | Server Settings and clicking Advanced. A dialog box launches that allows you to define where you want to store the mail. If you don't want the account you are setting up to use Global Inbox, you must select either **Inbox for this server's account** or **Inbox for different account**.

- If you want an account to have its own folder directory, select **Inbox for this server's account**.
- To group an account under another account folder's directory, select **Inbox for different account**.

The final preference applies only if you are using the shared folder directory. If you check the box that says "Include this server when getting new mail," Thunderbird checks that account for new mail when you click the **Get Mail** button.

Here are some other factors you might want to consider when changing Inbox Account Settings:

- Check your Copies and Folders settings—Tools | Account Settings | Copies and Folders.
- Check your Junk Mail filtering settings—Tools | Junk Mail Controls.
- Check your filters—Tools | Message filters. If you are using filters that funnel messages into any of the folders for that account, and you change an account to Global Inbox, you should either disable or delete the filters or change the location of the filter destination folder.
- Check your Saved Search folders.

> **Tip: Restart Thunderbird When You Change Global Inbox Account Settings**
>
> If you change account settings for Global Inbox, it is good practice to restart Thunderbird before downloading any new mail. Why? If you fail to do this, these messages might be routed to their old location, such as the inbox of the individual account rather than the Global Inbox.

## Changing a Global Inbox Account Back to a POP Account

At some point you might decide that you want to change your Global Inbox account back to a POP account. To do this, go to Tools | Account Settings | Server settings and click the Advanced button. Select the dialog that says "Inbox for this server's account" and then click OK. After Thunderbird is restarted, a separate POP account should display in the folder pane. Any messages sent to that account should no longer be directed to the Local Folders but should be routed to that account.

# Creating and Managing Multiple Identities

One of Thunderbird's unique features is that you can easily manage multiple email accounts. Using Thunderbird's Manage Identities feature, you can manipulate your "From" address when composing or replying to mail by just selecting the address you want to use from the drop-down list, as shown in Figure 10-10. This can be done on a per-account basis, so you can actually create a unique identity for each of your accounts.

To create or edit a mail identity for an account, do the following:

1. Go to Tools | Account Settings.
2. Create or edit your default identity.
3. Click **Manage Identities**.
4. Add a new identity for that account.

Remember, you can create different identities for each email account, something even Dr. Jekyll would have enjoyed.

Figure 10-10

Figure 10-10

*Thunderbird's Multiple Identity drop-down list.*

# Composing, Sending, and Reading Mail

Now it's time to get to the fun part, composing and sending mail. You might want to configure a few options before you begin sending mail. Most of these configuration options are located in Tools | Options in Windows:

| | |
|---|---|
| Forwarding Messages | Tools \| Options \| Composition |
| Address Autocompletion | Tools \| Options \| Composition |
| Saving Attachments | Tools \| Options \| Attachments |
| Enable the spellchecker | Tools \| Options \| Composition |
| Adjust your font sizes | Tools \| Options \| Fonts |
| Customize your toolbar | Right-click the toolbar to get the customize menu, and drag and drop items to the toolbar. |

**FRIDGE**

*Buttons!* (http://www.chuonthis.com/extensions/buttons.php) is a cool extension that allows you to add buttons to your toolbar. My favorite? The Delete Junk button. It makes me feel like I don't have to take out the trash for another week.

# Composing Mail

Thunderbird gives you a few different ways to compose mail. You can click the Write Icon on the toolbar, choose File | Message | New Message, or press Ctrl+M to compose a mail message.

Here is a message I just composed. You will see a few things that you can do to the message before and after it is sent.

```
To: Alice
From: Chase
Re: Quality of our Maple Syrup


It has come to my attention that our current Maple
Syrup production is not up to our usual standards - can
you please investigate? You know how important it is
for our company to generate high-quality Vermont Maple
Syrup.

Also, please set up a meeting with myself and Elaine to
discuss how we can further commodify our Maple Syrup. I
have some ideas about getting into the ice cream/gelato
business.

By the way, I hear you are going up to Maine this week-
end. If you would be so kind as to pick me up some wild
blueberries, I would greatly appreciate it.
```

**FAQ**

**What if I want to...**

**Resend it?**
Select the message, choose Message | Edit Message as New, and click Send.

**Add a cc or bcc?**
Click the dropdown widget on the left side of the Compose window to access the options for the various addresses.

**Save as a draft?**
File | Save as draft.

**Get a return receipt?**

Options | Return Receipt.

**Send with the highest priority?**

In the Compose window, click Options | Priority | Highest.

**Have it look like it came from an alternate email address?**

Set up the address in the account you are using by going to Tools | Account Settings | Manage Identities. Then select it from the dropdown list when you compose the email from that account.

**Flag the message so I can read it offline?**

Message | Mark | Flag. To read it offline: File | Offline | Get Flagged Messages.

## Sending Mail

To send this message, I can click the **Send** icon or File | Send Now or File | Send Later. But because everyone seems to be in a rush these days, I usually opt for the former.

## Reading Mail

The two options you should configure for reading mail are the mail window option and the message window behavior, which are both located in Tools | Options | General.

**Advice From a Starry-Eyed Reader: What to Do If Your Headers Are Out of Control**

If you don't want to see all those headers when reading mail (especially when you want to print emails), you can toggle the Headers preference by going to View | Headers and selecting Normal instead of All. Phew.

## Account Settings

After you initially set up your mail, if you need to change any account settings for an existing account, you can go to Tools | Account Settings. To change settings for an account, you need to select that account. Within each account, a number of settings can be adjusted. The screenshots shown next pertain to a POP account, but the screens for an IMAP account are almost identical, with only a few slight variations. I will note the variations in the relevant sections.

## Mail Account Settings

Figure 10-11 shows the Main Account Settings screen, which is the area where you manage the creation and removal of your accounts. This screen also allows you to name your email account as well as configure your default identity, which is the information that people see when they read the messages you have sent.

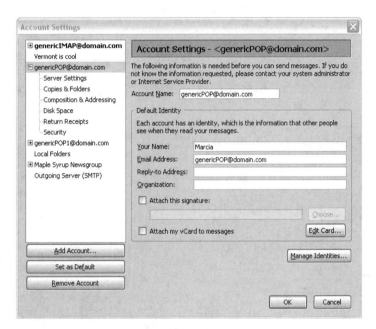

**Figure 10-11**

*Main Mail screen with a default identity.*

## Adding and Removing Accounts, Default Account

Click **Add Account** if you want to create a new email, RSS, or news account.

Click **Remove Account** to remove any of your existing accounts. You will receive a confirmation dialog box asking if you are sure you want to do this.

**TOOL KIT**

### Oops, I Accidentally Deleted My Account

Did you have a bad click day and delete your mail account when you didn't mean to? Thunderbird does throw up a warning dialog box asking you if you are sure you want to delete it, but heck, even I might hit the wrong button if I was having a bad mail day.

Actually, you may be in luck, because your mail has not been deleted from your profile folder. Assuming that you are not using Global Inbox, that mail is housed in your profile folder. If you are using Global Inbox, it is being stored locally. Refer to Chapter 9 to learn where your profile folder is stored in Thunderbird.

Here are the steps to recover from this seeming disaster:

1. Navigate to your profile folder to confirm mail still is there. See Chapter 9 for Thunderbird's profile locations.
2. To be extra safe, make a backup copy of your profile in case something goes awry. See the "Moving Thunderbird to a New Computer" Toolkit in this chapter to learn how to do this.
3. Fire up Thunderbird and create a new mail account. It is **important** that you use the same settings as the account that was accidentally deleted.
4. Close Thunderbird and go to your profile folder. A new folder should have been created.
5. Locate the folder for the deleted account and copy its contents, pasting them into the newly created profile folder.
6. Restart Thunderbird. You should see your new mail, and it should be a joyous day. Callooh! Callay!

# Main Account Settings

## Default Identity

In this section, you can make adjustments to your default identity:

- Name
- Email address
- Reply-to address
- Organization
- Attach a signature or vCard to your outbound emails (see Chapter 13, "Customizing the Look and Feel of Mozilla Thunderbird," for a cool extension you can install to help you add signatures).
- Manage Identities allows you to configure multiple names for your outbound mail. That way, when you go to compose a message, you can choose what account it is actually being sent from. This is a really handy feature if you are managing multiple accounts. Consult the "Creating and Managing Multiple Identities" section of this chapter for more about how you can use this feature to its fullest potential.

## Server Settings

The Server Settings (see Figure 10-12) include the following:

- Server Name
- User Name
- Port
- Authentication preferences

- Check for New Messages at Startup
- Check for New Messages every *X* minutes
- What to do when you delete a message

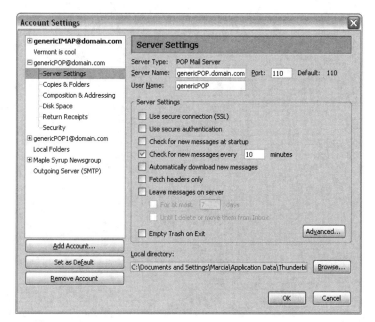

**Figure 10-12**

*The Server Settings.*

Probably the most important settings here are how often you want to check messages, whether you want Thunderbird to check mail on startup, and how you want to deal with trash.

Clicking the **Advanced** button leads you to a place where you manage the SMTP and IMAP parameters. Finally, this screen also lets you change the location of your local mail folders. If you click the **Browse** button, you can modify the local directory where your mail is stored.

**Note**

If you are using IMAP, you will not see the following three selections on the Server Settings screen because they are relevant for POP only:

- **Automatically download new messages**
- **Fetch headers only**
- **Leave messages on server**

**Thunderbird Profiles**

Thunderbird stores your mail in a profile folder along with all the other information related to your account. For more about profiles, see Chapter 9.

## Copies and Folders

In Copies & Folders (see Figure 10-13), you can manage a number of preferences, including where you want copies of your "Sent" mail to be placed. You can also identify where you want copies of your draft messages and templates to be housed.

**Figure 10-13**

*The Copies & Folders screen.*

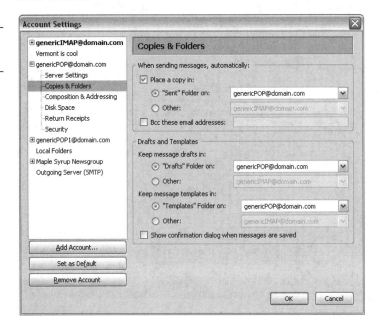

## Composition and Addressing

The Composition & Addressing section (see Figure 10-14) allows you to set preferences as to how you want your emails to be composed and where you want your text to start when you are replying to a message, (my one pet peeve—I always forget where this preference is, and I prefer to have my text appear above instead of below, which is the default). If you are using LDAP, there is also an option to select where you want Thunderbird to look for addresses.

### What is LDAP?

LDAP stands for Lightweight Directory Access Protocol. It is an Internet protocol that email programs such as Thunderbird use to look up address information from a server. LDAP is more commonly used in corporate settings where you might need to send someone mail who has never sent you mail (in this case your personal address book would be of little value), but LDAP servers can also be configured for smaller workgroups.

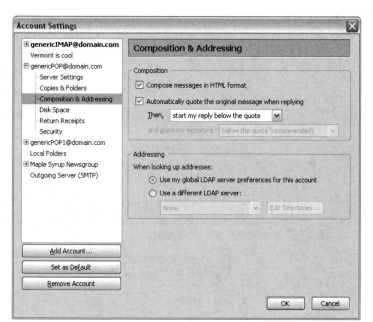

**Figure 10-14**

*The Composition & Addressing screen of Account Settings.*

## Offline and Disk Space

If you need to use Thunderbird in offline mode, you can manage your offline settings in the Disk Space area (see Figure 10-15). You can also set how large messages should be before they are downloaded for offline use.

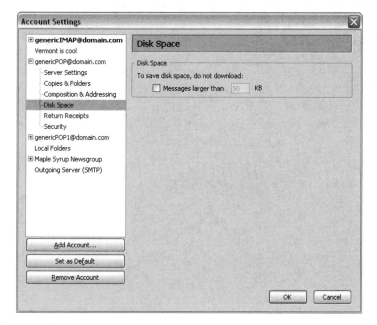

**Figure 10-15**

*The Disk Space area of Account Settings.*

## Return Receipts

If you like to know that people have actually read the email you have sent, you can manage all your return receipt options on the Return Receipt screen shown in figure 10-16.

**Figure 10-16**

*The Return Receipts area of Account Settings.*

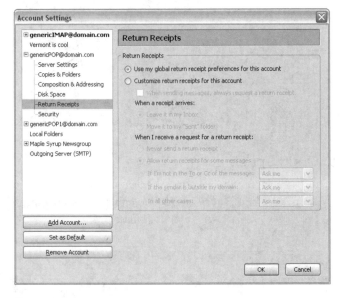

## Security

Figure 10-17 shows where you can manage your certificates as well as identify what kinds of encryption you want to use. There is also a certificate and security device manager. See Appendix F, "Security, Certificates, and Validation," to learn more about how to use certificates in Thunderbird.

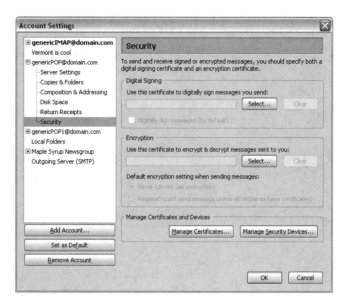

**Figure 10-17**
*The Security
area of
Account
Settings.*

## RSS Account Settings

If you have an RSS Account, you can change the name and also specify how often you want to check for new articles. There is also a button for subscription management. By default, Thunderbird displays the entire web page. If you find you just want to see the article summary instead, make sure to check the preference in this area.

## Newsgroup Account Settings

Your newsgroup account has many of the same options as your mail account:

- Server Settings
- Copies and Folder
- Composition and Addressing
- Offline and Disk Space

Reference the "Mail Account Settings" section to understand how to use these settings.

### A Quick Way to Access Account Settings

You don't necessarily have to go to the File menu to access the Account Settings section. If you right-click any of your mail accounts and select "Properties," you are taken to the Account Settings.

# Address Book

I can't remember names and numbers very well, so my Address Book is my lifeline. Clicking the **Address Book** icon or going to Tools | Address Book puts you in the address book, where you can manage your contacts in a number of ways. Preserving the data in this area may be important to you. At some point you may want to back up, import, or move your address book information to another location. Thunderbird's address book allows you to import addresses from another location as well as export your addresses as an LDIF file.

## Exporting Your Addresses

To export your addresses to an LDIF file, follow these steps:

1. Click **Address Book**.
2. Select the Address Book you want to export.
3. Click Tools | Export.
4. Supply a name for the address book. Make sure the file is saved in LDIF format.
5. Save the file to a location on your computer. It is probably a good idea to burn this file to a CD so that you have a backup on a location other than your computer.

> **Mac OS X: Using the Address Book Exporter to move your addresses to Thunderbird**
>
> Mac OS X users can use the Address Book Exporter application to convert their address book to a plain text file and then import it into Thunderbird using Tools | Import (http://gwenhiver.net/applications/addressbookexporter/index.php).

## Importing Your Addresses

To import addresses, follow these steps:

1. Click **Address Book**.
2. Click on Tools | Import.
3. Select the **Address Books** radio button. Click Next.
4. Select the program you would like to import from.

## Sending an Instant Message

If you have an Instant Message client running, it is possible to add an Instant Message icon to the toolbar and actually launch a chat session with someone listed in your address book.

## Quicksearch

The address book also has a handy quicksearch feature that allows you to type in a name or email address to quickly locate the person you are looking for. You can search by either name or email address.

> **Importing AOL Addresses into Thunderbird**
>
> It is possible to import your AOL addresses into Thunderbird, but you have to use one of the third-party utilities listed at http://www.emailman.com/conversion/.

**TOOL KIT**

**The Contacts Sidebar—A Handy Address Book Extension for Thunderbird**

The *Contacts Sidebar* (http://jpeters.no-ip.com/extensions/?page=tb_cs) is a great extension to add to Thunderbird if you are looking for a way to display your address book in a sidebar in the bottom portion of the three-pane window. This extension does a few helpful things. First, it allows you to double-click a name in your address book to launch an instant compose window. The other thing I like about this extension is that you can use the F4 key to quickly toggle this feature on or off, thereby quickly freeing up space if you need to look at your long list of mail folders (or maybe I mean *my* long list of mail folders).

## Creating a Mailing List

You can also create mailing lists here by clicking the **Create List** icon. You have three choices of how to enter names into the list (you will have to create the list first):

- **Supersonic Method**—Make sure that you have the autocomplete feature (Tools | Options | Composition) turned on—start to type the first few letters of the name, and it should automatically complete.

- **Subsonic Method**—Drag and drop address cards from the address book to the list (you need to locate the list in the Address Books pane on the left side).

- **Mavis Beacon Method**—Type the email addresses the old-fashioned way—by hand.

**FRIDGE**

Supersonic transport (SST) came into vogue in the 1960s when the Concorde commercial airliner took to the skies. With its stylized delta wing, slender fuselage, and four Olympus engines powering it to speeds of Mach 2.04 and a cruise altitude of 58,000 feet, it was an engineering marvel that cut flight times in half. However, in many ways the SST was a victim of bad timing, since the onset of the 1960s brought a surge of heightened environmental awareness. Thus, 1960s environmentalists condemned supersonic transport, citing concerns over possible ozone damage and the threat of sonic booms disrupting people's lives. The Concorde was banned from many U.S. airports, and eventually the entire Concorde fleet was grounded on November 26, 2003. Alas, if they had only had the benefit of computer-aided design, history might have been quite different, and the Concorde would still be flying today.

# Offline Settings

After a long day at work, there is nothing I like better than downloading another set of messages to read when I get home. (Actually, this is pretty handy for reading Bugzilla bugmail if you don't happen to have a broadband connection available, or if you just want to have your mail and newsgroup messages available offline to consult if you expect a long plane ride.) Thunderbird has a number of ways to manage your offline experience.

If you would like to make your messages available locally when you work offline, you need to set the preference in Tools | Account Settings. Clicking the **Select Folders for offline use** button launches a window with checkboxes so that you can mark the folders you want to download for offline use. I never used this feature much until I started writing this book, but now I probably couldn't live without it.

## How Do I Go Offline?

To go offline, toggle the **Online/Offline** button at the bottom left of the mail window or select File | Offline | Work Offline.

## Composing Mail Offline

It is possible to compose mail messages while in offline mode and then send them when you go back online. To do this, click the **Write** icon and compose your message. When you are finished, click the **Send Later** icon. When you go back online, Thunderbird launches a dialog box asking if you want to send these unsent messages. See the next section if you want to configure your unsent messages settings.

## Managing Your Offline Settings

In addition to the settings that are available in Account Settings, File | Offline | Offline Settings allows a few other configuration options for your offline settings:

- Start Up options—whether you want to be offline or online when starting the client
- Whether to send unsent messages when going back online
- Whether you want a confirmation prompt for downloading messages

### Download/Sync Now

If you have already selected folders for offline use, Download/Sync now allows you to download/sync mail and newsgroup messages. Selecting **Download/sync now** launches a dialog box that allows you to select mail messages and/or newsgroup messages. You can also select a checkbox to send your unsent messages. The last preference allows you to continue working offline when the download/sync is complete.

### Flagging and Selecting Your Messages

You also have the opportunity to flag your messages as you are reading them and then later download just those messages for offline use. There is also a way to download messages that you have selected. To flag your messages:

1. Flag the messages first (Message | Mark | Flag) while you are in online mode.
2. Go to File | Offline | Get Flagged Messages.

To select your messages:

1. Select the messages first by highlighting the ones you want to download while you are in online mode.
2. Go to File | Offline | Get Selected Messages.

After completing these operations, messages that you have flagged or selected will be available when you go into offline mode.

**TOOL KIT**

## Moving Thunderbird to a New Computer

Let's face it—the way technology is moving today, you might find yourself in a situation where you get a new computer and want to move Thunderbird to your new system. Just installing the program on your new computer won't help, because you will need to bring your Thunderbird profile over from your old computer so you can access all your mail, address books, and account settings that are stored in the profile folder. (Note: If you are using IMAP, your mail will be stored on a server, but you should still bring your Thunderbird profile over from your old machine to capture your address book and other settings.) There are a few different ways to accomplish this. I suggest consulting the MozillaZine FAQ on Backup and Restoring (http://kb.mozillazine.org/index.phtml?title=Thunderbird_:_FAQs_:_Backing_Up_ and_Restoring) because it provides a good overview of all the ins and outs of back-ups and restoring.

### Using a Backup Utility

The other option you have is to use a utility to back up your Thunderbird profile. An example of one such utility is MozBackup (http://mozbackup.jasnapaka.com/), which is a Windows-only utility that backs up your Thunderbird profile into a single file (with the extension *.pcv, which is really a zip file format). That file can then be restored on the same Windows machine you are working on or a new machine.

### Using MozBackup to Back Up Your Profile

1. Make sure Thunderbird is not running.
2. Download and install MozBackup.
3. Launch MozBackup and select the "Back up a profile" option.
4. Select the profile you would like to back up in addition to the location where you want the file to be saved.
5. Select the details you would like to back up by checking the appropriate boxes.
6. Move through the rest of the screens until the backup is complete.

### Using MozBackup to Restore Your Profile

1. Make sure that Thunderbird is on your computer and has been used at least once.
2. Launch MozBackup and select the "Restore a profile" option.
3. Select the profile you would like to restore and then the backup file you want to restore from. Be aware that the profile you select will be overwritten by the file you are restoring from. MozBackup does allow you to create a new profile if you don't want to do this.
4. Move through the rest of the screens until the profile restoration is complete.
5. Fire up Thunderbird. You should now be able to use the profile you backed up.

   Note that MozBackup is an example of one utility that can help you with backups. Go to http://www.fileguru.com/backup-tools/backup-tools.asp to see a list of other programs that you may be able to use for backup.

Phew. That was a lot to digest. Because of the multitude of server configurations and mail providers, there can be a lot of different permutations when setting up mail. If you happen to encounter a setup issue that was not covered in this chapter, head to the Thunderbird forums and newsgroups and post your question there. The "Accessing Mozilla Thunderbird Help" section in Chapter 9 gives a summary of all the places you can go to get help for Thunderbird.

# Protecting Your Privacy and Blocking Spam

**DO OR DIE:**

>> Confront spam head on (you won't need a helmet)

>> Block loading of remote images in mail messages

>> Can I get a SPAM and cheese to go?

Ahh, spam. It's everywhere. Check out this 2004 quote from Bill Gates at the World Economic Forum: "Two years from now, spam will be solved." Well, he certainly took a rather optimistic view of how many inroads we would be able to make in the fight against spam. Instead of winning the war on spam, in many ways, we are continuing to fight a seemingly never-ending battle. Spam continues to flow into inboxes all over the world at an alarming rate. Companies scramble to implement server-side spam filters while consumers troll the web trying to find solutions to keeping spam out of their inbox and to keep themselves free of viruses, Trojan horses, and worms. Spam isn't only an annoyance—it carries a host of other threats that can be damaging to both you and your livelihood. It's also a very popular luncheon meat.

In many ways, this might be the most important chapter that you read in the Thunderbird section. First, you are probably concerned about protecting your privacy, especially when it comes to sending and receiving email. Second, you are most likely painfully aware of how precious time is and how annoying it can be to have to deal with large volumes of spam as well as the threat of viruses arriving via email messages. The takeaways from this chapter will be significant. You should come away with a better understanding of ways Thunderbird helps protect your privacy and keep you safe. You will confront spam head on by configuring Thunderbird's powerful junk mail controls so that spam will be a thing of the past, thus leaving you more time to focus on the mail that is really important to you. You will learn how to accept content from trusted sources by blocking remote images. Finally, your odyssey will take you into the brave new world of password and privacy options as you learn about ways you can use digital signatures to protect your privacy and security.

### SPAM: Five Billion Cans and Still Going Strong

Monty Python has lampooned it, soldiers have feasted on it, and Nikita Kruschev claimed in his autobiography that it helped keep his army alive. What is it about this mystery pink meat encased in a blue tin that has enthralled people throughout the years?

Maybe it is because SPAM is so versatile. You can do just about anything with it—recipes abound on the Internet for various ways you can prepare this intriguing product. You can doctor it up so that it seems as if you are eating baked ham (you might try the original recipe for Baked SPAM that is on the side of the can and see if you can fool your grandmother). It also lasts a long time, so if you are one of those people who like to stockpile canned goods, SPAM might be your luncheon meat of choice. Hawaiians seem to prefer SPAM as their luncheon meat—they are currently the largest consumers of the product in the United States.

Finally, probably the most interesting question—how did SPAM originate? According to the www.hormel.com website, the story begins in 1936 when the Foods division created the recipe. Determined to find a unique name for the product, Jay C. Hormel offered a $100 prize to whoever could generate the best name for this new creation. However, there was a little nepotism involved when the finalist was selected, because Kenneth Daigneau, who was the brother of then-President Ralph Daigneau, was declared the winner. Daigneau created the unique brand name by using a combination of the "sp" from spiced ham with the "am" from ham. So if you are tired of the same old bologna, try some SPAM. I won't be trying any, though, because I'm a vegetarian.

## How Thunderbird Protects Your Privacy and Security

Thunderbird does a few things that will immediately put your mind at ease:

- Thunderbird does not allow any scripts to run by default.
- Thunderbird's remote image blocking feature allows you to control remote content that is embedded in email messages.
- Thunderbird's junk mail controls offer a powerful way to filter out unwanted mail.

Why are these things important? Scripts can carry executable files that can cause irreparable damage to your email as well as to your computer. If you save your email locally to your hard drive, there are scripts that can run on your computer that can erase your hard drive—thus taking away all your saved mail in one fell swoop. Thunderbird puts you in control by not allowing these scripts to run by default.

Many spammers have now harnessed the power of remote content and are using it to harvest email addresses to propagate more spam. Thunderbird puts you in the driver's seat by allowing you to control who can send you messages and content.

Finally, fighting spam is an almost endless battle. Spammers can bring corporate mail servers to their knees and waste valuable resources. Even server-side spam filters can't catch every piece of spam. When trained, Thunderbird's junk mail controls helps keep your inbox spam-free.

Let's forge ahead and see some of these concepts in action. Pass the ham, and please hold the spam.

## How to Train Thunderbird's Junk Mail Filter

Junk, junk, and more junk—it seems that some days I get more spam email than I do legitimate email. At least I don't get as much as Bill Gates, who reportedly receives four million emails a day, most of which are spam.[1] If you put your email address out in the Internet space, it is likely at some point that your address will be harvested by spammers and you will become a victim of spam email. Ready to enter a contest that has a prize that looks too good to be true? It just might be that the contest you are entering will lead you down the primrose path to an inbox full of spam (not surprisingly, the entry form probably only asked for your email address). Luckily, Thunderbird has an excellent way to keep spam in check.

Thunderbird uses Bayesian filtering to classify junk mail, which is a system that requires some degree of user intervention and training (see the FAQ on the next page for an explanation of how Bayesian filtering works). In order to train Thunderbird to weed out spam, you have to manually mark messages as Junk by either clicking the Junk icon or going to File | Message | Mark | As Junk. But the important factor to remember here is that you also need to mark your "good" messages by going to Message | Mark | As Not Junk (note that no icon is

---

[1] Steve Ballmer, the CEO of Microsoft, was quoted in the same story as saying that an entire department at Microsoft is devoted to doing nothing more than ensuring that nothing unwanted gets into Gates' inbox.

available for this in the toolbar). That way, you train the filter on both ends and ensure that a better percentage of spam will be captured.

---

### Tip: In the Early Phase of Training, Check Your Junk Mail Folder

In the early days of training your filter, you will probably want to check your "Junk" mail folder just to make sure that mail has not been classified incorrectly. If it has, you will have the chance to mark it correctly so the next message that comes through will not be marked as spam.

---

### Easy Way to Mark All Your "Good" Mail

In case you want to mark all your "Good" mail in one fell swoop, the best way to do this is to go to the View dropdown list and select Not Junk, and then go to the File menu and mark the messages as not junk. Going to the File menu and selecting View | Sort by | Junk Status is another way you can accomplish this.

---

**Figure 11-1**
*The Junk icon.*

Thunderbird marks junk mail with a junk icon (see Figure 11-1). Note that if you change Thunderbird's theme (see Chapter 13), the Junk icon will likely not look the same as it does in Thunderbird's default theme.

---

### What Is Bayesian Filtering?

Bayesian filtering first came into vogue when Paul Graham covered it in his seminal paper "A Plan for Spam" (http://www.paulgraham.com/spam.html), even though Graham himself admits that Bayesian text classification methods have been used for years. Although Bayesian filtering is a technique that can be used to classify many types of data (it has been applied in a number of other disciplines, including the scientific realm, and has been applied in the machine learning environment in AI), programs such as Mozilla Thunderbird use it to distinguish spam email (junk) from ham email (non-junk).

The essence of Bayesian filtering boils down to examining probabilities and focuses on the probabilities of certain words appearing in ham or spam email. For example, a word such as "Rolex" might appear more frequently in your spam email, but not in your ham email (unless, of course, you are a watch dealer). Even though the filter isn't savvy enough to figure this out at first, it can be trained by the user over time.

When it is trained, a computation is made (using Bayes' theorem) regarding the probability of an email belonging to either the ham or spam category. This assessment is done by looking over all the words (or combinations of words) contained in the email. After the assessment is complete, if the total exceeds a particular threshold, the filter then identifies the email as spam. Mozilla Thunderbird has a handy feature that can automatically move these messages to a "Junk" folder.

The user-centric nature of Bayesian filtering does have some distinct advantages over systems that use other rule filter methodology or point value systems, such as Mailshield. This is largely due to the fact that we all get different types of spam and ham, and the Bayesian system allows the user the flexibility to make corrections over time in the event that email is classified incorrectly (one person's ham may look like spam to another). However, the downside of the Bayesian system is that it will not perform well if it is not trained (you must mark both the spam and ham email in the training phase), and it does need some degree of training data (a past collection of email messages is helpful in this regard).

Despite the fact that Bayesian filtering does a good job of nipping spam in the bud after it is trained, spammers are constantly developing new techniques to get mail into your inbox. Recently, I have started to see emails that have my coworkers' names inserted in the subject line. In this instance, they are attempting to defeat the Bayesian system by using familiar name patterns. While Bayesian filtering isn't perfect, it is just one method that is being used to fight the seemingly never-ending battle against spam.

# Configuring Junk Mail Controls

Junk mail controls are configured by going to Tools | Junk Mail Controls, which displays the screen shown in Figure 11-2. You should first make sure that you select the account that you want the controls to apply to in the drop-down list. It is possible to define different controls for different accounts.

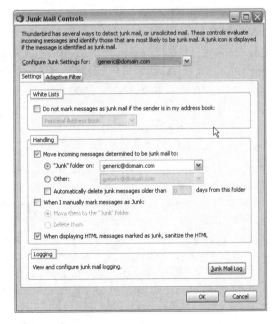

**Figure 11-2**

*The Junk Mail Controls screen.*

## White Lists

Thunderbird allows you to identify your trusted senders by setting this preference. If you enable the checkbox, Thunderbird honors the address book choice from the drop-down menu and does not mark messages as junk if the sender is in the selected address book. The default setting for this preference is Personal Address Book.

## Handling

In this section, you can define where you want junk mail to be routed. I prefer to select Thunderbird's Junk folder, but you can also define another place where you want junk mail to be housed. You can also define where you want junk messages to go when you delete them manually. Finally, there is a preference you can enable to have Thunderbird sanitize the HTML when messages are marked as junk.

What does sanitizing HTML mean, and how can it help protect you? By checking this preference in Thunderbird, you effectively strip out all remote requests, images, JavaScript, cookies, and tables from messages that have been identified as junk. This is another feature that protects you from HTML that may come through embedded with potentially harmful scripts or tags. This preference is on by default, and you should leave it on for the fullest level of protection.

## Logging

The junk mail log allows you to keep track of the operations that are made on junk mail. To turn on the log option, click the Junk Mail Log button and then check the box that says "Enable the Junk Mail log."

## Adaptive Filter

The Adaptive Filter tab (shown in Figure 11-3) allows you to manage your junk mail settings. This preference is enabled by default. It is probably a good idea to keep this checked unless you are planning to possibly use regular filters to manage your junk mail. There is also a button to reset your training data, but you probably should never have to use this button unless you want to start your filter training from scratch. Thunderbird stores your training data in a file called `training.dat` that is stored in your Profile folder. Remember, if for some reason your profile folder gets deleted, you will lose your training data and will have to retrain Thunderbird to identify junk mail (yet another reason it is a good idea to back up your Profile folder—see the Toolkit in Chapter 10, "Setting Up Your Email, RSS, and Newsgroup Accounts Using Mozilla Thunderbird," for some ideas on how to do this).

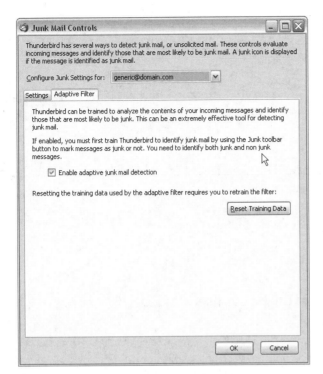

**Figure 11-3**

*The Junk Mail Controls screen with the Adaptive Filter options displayed.*

Thunderbird also gives you the ability to run junk mail controls on individual folders and delete mail marked as junk that resides in a folder. To do this, highlight the folder you want to run the controls on and then go to Tools | Run Junk Mail Controls on Folder or Tools | Delete Mail Marked as Junk in Folder.

# Blocking Remote Images

Thunderbird's remote image blocking feature is a good way to protect yourself from possible contamination from viruses as well as protect you from spammers who are trying to capture your email address. This preference is on by default in Thunderbird and is set to allow the display of remote images from people in your personal address book. You can change this option by going to Tools | Options | Advanced, where you see a dropdown box that allows you to select the address book you want to use to manage who can send you remote content.

As shown in Figure 11-4, Thunderbird lets you know when it has blocked images by issuing an alert at the top of the mail message (similar to the alert Firefox uses to warn you about popups that have been blocked). If you view the email message and decide you want to see the content, you can simply click

**Show Images** to see the images that have been blocked. Note that after you click this option, there is no way to undo this action, so be certain that you really want to see the images before you click **Show Images**.

**Figure 11-4**

*Thunderbird's remote image blocking feature in action.*

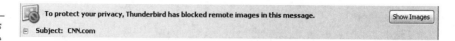

# Other Ways You Can Protect Yourself

There is another setting available in Thunderbird that you can configure to help protect your privacy and security: Return Receipt settings. You can also choose to digitally sign and encrypt your mail for an extra layer of protection, or use certificates and security devices. This section provides some other avenues to explore to get maximum protection.

## Return Receipt Settings (Tools | Options | Advanced)

It is probably a good idea to configure your settings so that Thunderbird prompts you when you receive a request for a return receipt. That way, you will prevent spammers from even knowing that your account exists. (I do not recommend checking the "Always Send" box in this area—either "Ask me" or "Never send" are better choices to protect your privacy.) Figure 11-5 shows one way you can configure your settings.

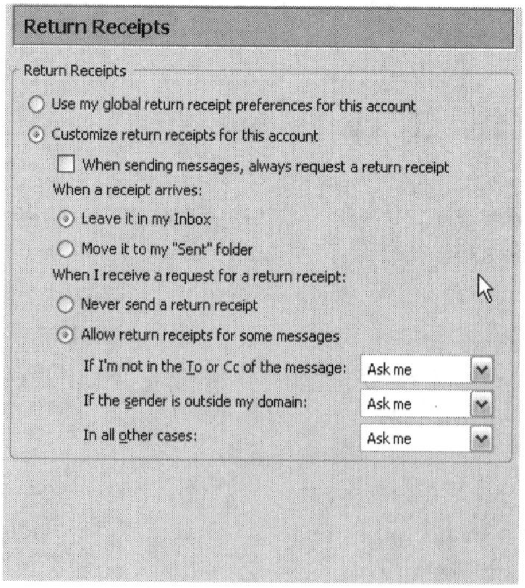

**Figure 11-5**

*A good way to configure your Return Receipts options for maximum protection.*

**Return Receipts**

Return Receipts

○ Use my global return receipt preferences for this account
⦿ Customize return receipts for this account
☐ When sending messages, always request a return receipt
When a receipt arrives:
⦿ Leave it in my Inbox
○ Move it to my "Sent" folder
When I receive a request for a return receipt:
○ Never send a return receipt
⦿ Allow return receipts for some messages
If I'm not in the To or Cc of the message: [Ask me ▼]
If the sender is outside my domain: [Ask me ▼]
In all other cases: [Ask me ▼]

## Anti-Virus Programs

It is important that you have an anti-virus program installed on your computer. A number of anti-virus programs are compatible with Thunderbird. See the sidebar for some tips on programs that play well with Thunderbird.

## Signing and Encrypting Your Email

Signing and encrypting your email are simple but effective ways to maintain your privacy while ensuring that no one is masquerading as you online.

### Digitally Signing Your Email

Signing your mail is a good thing, especially because it is often difficult to discern by looking at the email header who actually sent the mail. If more people began signing their mail, spam would probably be nipped in the bud considerably because it would be possible to configure Thunderbird to not accept mail from unsigned senders.

By using specialized cryptographic techniques such as S/MIME, you can actually include a signature that lets you stamp your outgoing messages with a signature that proves you are the person who sent the mail. For a good overview of how to use digital signing, go to http://www.cs.washington.edu/lab/services/email/EmailSigningHowTo/.

### Encrypting Your Email

Encrypting your email adds an extra layer of security beyond a digital signature because the encrypted email appears as garbage data unless the recipient has the key necessary to decrypt the information. If you want to take a deeper dive into learning about how to encrypt your mail in Thunderbird, a tutorial available at http://www.uk-dave.com/tutorials/misc/enigmail.shtml explains how to encrypt your email with Thunderbird, Enigmail, and GnuPG. Enigmail is an extension that allows you to encrypt/sign sent mail, as well as decrypt/authenticate incoming mail. Go to http://enigmail.mozdev.org/ to learn more about this program and how it can help you with encryption.

## Certificates/Security Devices

The certificate and security device management procedures are the same in Thunderbird as they are in Firefox. See Appendix F, "Security, Certificates, and Validation," for more information about using certificates and security devices.

# Passwords

The Password Management section of Thunderbird can be accessed by going to Tools | Options | Advanced. Under the Saved Passwords section, you can manage your Stored Mail password settings as well as set a Master Password for your account. Note that the Password Manager functionality in Thunderbird is based on the same principles as those in Firefox, so there will be some overlap here between what is discussed in Chapter 2, "Protecting Your Security and Privacy." I have elected to go into a little more depth discussing the Master Password settings than what was covered in Chapter 2.

## Managing Your Stored Mail Passwords

Clicking **View Saved Passwords** allows you to manage your stored passwords. See Chapter 2 for more information about the Password Manager functionality as well as some screenshots.

## What Is a Master Password?

A master password is a mechanism that can be used to protect different types of devices (both software and hardware devices). Both Thunderbird and Firefox have built-in Software Security devices, so you are able to use a master password to manage the information that is stored on the device (literally, the software).

If you work in an office, someone probably has the master key to the office (and, if you are like me, you are usually trying to find that person when the alarm in the Riser Room is going off for no apparent reason...and Sparky is whining—well, that's another story...). While the Master Password is not actually the *Master Key* in this instance, it does protect the Master Key, which is the mechanism used to protect potentially sensitive data—things such as your email password or certificates, for example.

## Why Would You Want to Set a Master Password?

You might be using a machine that other people have access to, and you don't want them to be able to download any new messages or send any messages from your account. If you have saved passwords and then set a Master Password, Thunderbird protects the saved passwords by prompting you for the Master Password when you click **View Saved Passwords**.

When you click **Show Password** in the Password Manager dialog box, Thunderbird prompts you for the Master Password before you are allowed to see the saved password information.

## Setting a Master Password

In addition to being able to store your saved passwords, Thunderbird allows you to set a Master Password for your mail accounts. Follow these steps to set your Master Password:

1. Go to Tools | Options | Advanced.

2. Click the **Master Password** button.

3. As shown in Figure 11-6, make sure to check the box that says "Use a master password to encrypt stored passwords."

4. Click **Change Password**.

5. Make sure that "Software Security Device" shows in the dropdown menu.

6. Type your password twice and click OK.

**Figure 11-6**

*The Master Password options screen.*

## An Extra Layer of Security—Encrypting Versus Obscuring

"Encrypting" data and "obscuring" data are two very different animals. If you elect to save your mail passwords by using the Password Manager functionality built into Thunderbird, this information is stored locally on your computer in a file that is fairly difficult to crack (but it can be done). If you enable the check box in the first section that says "Use a master password to encrypt stored passwords," this file is then encrypted, making it extremely difficult for someone to open or view it.

### Change Master Password

As shown in Figure 11-7, clicking **Change Master Password** launches a screen that allows you to change or set your Master Password. *Make certain to pick a password that you will remember*—if you forget your Master Password and have to reset it, you will lose all of your stored passwords. It also helps you to rely on the *password quality meter* when selecting a password—using combinations of numbers, letters (uppercase and lowercase), and symbols is always a good idea. Remember, if someone gets the master password to your account, he can easily masquerade as you in a number of ways.

**Figure 11-7**

*The Thunderbird Change Master Password screen.*

**Don't Want Other People to See Your Messages?**

Okay, I can't be the only one who detests people hovering over my computer and reading my mail. If you are an IMAP user, there is a way you can configure Thunderbird so that the message pane (which shows the subject, and so on, of your mail) renders as blank until you log in and enter a password. Sound cool? Head over to Appendix E, "Hacking Configuration Files," to learn how to create a user.js file, and then add these two lines to the file:

```
// Password protect the message list pane
   user_pref("mail.password_protect_local_cache", true);
```

The other option is to change the about:config line item from false to true. See Appendix E for more information on how to do this.

### Master Password Timeout

You can use these settings to manage how often you want to be prompted for a Master Password. To be extra cautious, it might be wise to set the preference to "Every time it is needed."

### Reset Master Password

Resetting your Master Password causes you to lose all your stored passwords as well as any certificates or keys.

---

#### Using Anti-Virus Programs with Thunderbird

Depending on which type of anti-virus program you have installed, you might want to consider performing scans on incoming email messages as well as outbound messages (to make sure that you are not transmitting a virus).

Email can be a little trickier to scan, depending on how and where your email program stores your email. Some anti-virus programs can't tell the difference between when a single email is infected or when an entire inbox or folder may be infected.

To make sure that you have a good anti-virus experience, you should make sure that you have an anti-virus program that is compatible with Thunderbird. For a list of programs that are compatible with Thunderbird, go to http://kb.mozillazine.org/Thunderbird_:_FAQs_:_Anti-virus_Software.

I have personally used the free version of AVG's Anti Virus (http://free.grisoft.com/doc/1) to scan incoming and outbound mail with Thunderbird 1.0 and experienced no problems.

---

**TOOL KIT**

#### Thunderbird Extension for Sender Verification: An Extension to Protect Yourself Against Phishing

The Thunderbird Extension for Sender Verification plugs into Thunderbird to help prevent the practice known as "phishing," which has become a widespread problem on the Internet. Phishing is a practice whereby you may get an email, purportedly from Citibank or AOL (these are two examples; there are countless others), that is not really sent by them and asks for your credit card number, password, or other sensitive information. These emails are often so cleverly designed that it is difficult to tell that they are fraudulent.

Note: If you are looking for the Firefox equivalent of this extension, see Chapter 7, "Customizing Firefox with Third-Party Extensions and Themes," for a discussion of *Spoofstick*.

This extension helps identify whether the sender of the email that appears in the "From" portion of the header was actually the domain sender of the email. It does this by attempting to verify the domain of the sending entity. For example, if generic@domain.com sends an email, the extension can report whether the email is coming from an @domain.com email domain. Note that this extension cannot check whether a generic or any other @domain.com user was actually the person who sent the email. Remember, this extension is one way to help you recognize suspicious emails, but just because you get a positive verification on an email doesn't mean that it is necessarily a legitimate email.

Because this extension performs verification, the author does caution that information is sent to his web server in order to complete the verification. If you are not comfortable with this, you have a few choices of other ways that this can be done. Go to http://taubz.for.net/code/spf/ to read the FAQ that explains other information regarding the extension. As this book goes to press, the Thunderbird development team is working on integrating phishing support directly into the application, so there is a good chance there will be another alternative available to try to combat this problem down the road. Note that banks and financial institutions will never ask you to reconfirm user account data via email, so be wary anytime you receive an email like this, even if it looks legitimate.

---

Although Thunderbird contains features that can help protect your privacy and security, there are no magic bullets for trying to eliminate practices such as phishing. Spyware, worms, and viruses may be transmitted via email messages, but you can also unknowingly download them from a website, and when installed on your computer they can affect your email that may be stored locally. Remote image blocking and configuring your spam controls are two ways Thunderbird can help, but the onus is still on you to err on the side of caution when an email just doesn't "look right." One of the best ways to protect yourself is to make sure to use a good anti-virus program to scan your inbound and outbound email and to always keep your virus definitions up to date. Be cautious, watch your step, take your vitamins, and always remember to use real maple syrup on your pancakes.

# BLOG

## Phishing

**Y**ou probably won't get taken in by most spam. Let's face it: emails offering Vioxx, Viagra, or other meds, that low mortgage, get-rich-quick schemes, or mail-order brides waiting for you are all messages that don't pass the "Do I have 'born to pay retail' tattooed on my forehead?" test. Even the venerable "419" scam (where someone is the widow of some high official in Nigeria or some other war-ravaged country who has tens of millions of dollars to move out of the country and all she needs is your bank info and a small wire transfer fee) is getting so well known that entire websites like http://www.419eater.com are devoted to scamming the scammers.

Unfortunately, con artists are always looking for a new way to finagle money out of their victims. The latest version is known as *phishing*. Phishing is where you receive an email that's supposedly from some organization that you might be doing business with that hands you some variation on the following:

- Your account doesn't exist
- Your account has been suspended
- Someone's using your account fraudulently
- Your name/account number/credit card/other information has expired

These emails look official: they have the real company logos and everything. The underlying theme of all these is that something dire will happen unless you click the official-looking web address near the bottom of the email and enter some account information so they can correct whatever little problem you're being informed of. On the off chance that you actually do so, you'll see an even more official-looking website (again, with company logos and graphics) that asks you for account numbers, passwords, and credit card or Social Security numbers.

Therein lies the problem: The emails are bogus. The websites you go to are bogus. These are bad people who will take your credit card and account information and do whatever they can with it, up to and including grand larceny and identity theft. You won't like any of it.

How can you avoid this kind of scam? The first few times you get a message like this, you may not know that it's really a scam, and it might raise your anxiety level to the point you go look at it. First and foremost, *never trust an email notification that ultimately requires you to give confidential information over the Internet.* Always check it out through several independent sources and, even then, if you aren't completely sure, don't give any information at all. (It's best to not even go to the website listed; if nothing else, phishers can often identify that it's you with the specific web address you went to and can target you for future scams. For the same reason, you should never click the "unsubscribe" options in email; these are fake and only serve to verify that your email address is live, which makes it more valuable to spammers.)

If you've just gotten email from someone, such as Citibank, MBNA, PayPal, SouthTrust, SunTrust, Washington Mutual, or eBay (among the dozens of companies currently popular with phishers), the first thing to do is to check on the company's website to see if there's something about phishing scams. If there's nothing on the main page, look in the website's "security" or "announcements" section, or just use the site search feature to look for "phishing," "scams," or "fraud." You can also check Snopes (http://www.snopes.com), the Internet Urban Legend websites, for information on the latest phishing scams.

If there are spelling errors in the text of the message, that's pretty suspicious. Most companies are very careful about spell checking their broadcast announcements, although once in a while things escape. Also, no matter how official the web address looks in the email, the actual address that you're routed to is something different. Sometimes the real address uses the website's IP address, sometimes it looks a bit like the real address, sometimes it is completely different, but it is never the same as what you think you're clicking.

Phishers send out emails by the millions. There's no reason not to expect that phishers will use other mechanisms to get you to fill in information, including credit card applications, "You've won a lottery!" announcements, and so on. (In the half-hour or so it took me to write this, I got three phishing emails supposedly from PayPal and another from some miscellaneous company promising me a free cell phone if I'd fill out a long web form.) Be careful.

One thing you can do when you get a phishing email is to send it to the company by using "spoof" as the username, such as `spoof@paypal.com`, `spoof@wamu.com`, or `spoof@ebay.com`. This helps the companies involved track down and stop phishers. You'll usually get an acknowledgment from the company about this that gives you a little information on what to do with future bogus emails.

# 12

# Organizing Your Email Topics

**DO OR DIE:**

>> There's more than one way to save a search

>> Grouped by Sort (at the touch of a key!)

>> Keeping your head above the water with filters

>> Searching up a storm

>> Looking for the elusive soluble fish

Thunderbird offers a number of roads you can take to manage and organize your mail. When I began using Mozilla-based email clients, I really started to appreciate what a good email client can do for you from an organizational and efficiency perspective. Building on its Mozilla roots, Thunderbird has taken all the great features of Mozilla email and added some other exciting features, such as Saved Searches and Grouped by Sort—the result is a powerful email client that makes it a breeze to organize and manage your email. This chapter exposes you to these great features, including managing your email, sorting and viewing your mail, and searching your mail. So let's learn about ways Thunderbird can help you get organized—the open road beckons!

## Managing Your Mail

Everyone organizes things in different ways. The important thing is that you can find things quickly when you are looking for them and organize them in such a way that makes sense to you. By using labels, saved searches, and filters in Thunderbird, you can accomplish great things. Let's see how by looking at Thunderbird's excellent mail management features.

## Creating Folders and Subfolders

At some point, you might need to create some additional folders to house different categories of email. To create a new folder, go to File | New Folder and give the folder a name. You can also designate whether you want the newly created folder to be a subfolder of an existing folder. Folders can be moved around, so it is a good idea to store your mail in a folder if you anticipate having to move it (to a local folder, for example) at some later time.

**Note**

If you are using IMAP to manage your email, you might not be able to create subfolders.

## Labeling and Marking Your Mail

Labeling and marking your mail allows you to quickly categorize email messages that you want to follow up on. When you need to find these categories quickly, Thunderbird offers you numerous ways to search your mail to find the messages you have labeled or marked.

## Labeling Your Mail

Thunderbird allows you to label your mail into five categories:

- Important
- Work
- Personal
- To Do
- Later

To label a message, go to Message | Label and select the category you want (you can also highlight a group of messages and mark them all at once). Thunderbird uses a default set of colors to highlight the messages after you mark them. These colors can be changed by going to Tools | Options | Display and clicking the box that shows the default color. You can also restore the default colors at any time by clicking Restore defaults.

After you have labeled your mail into the various categories, you can use the View feature described next to see messages in the various categories.

## Marking Your Mail

To mark a message, go to Message | Mark and select the category you want. You can mark a message in the following categories:

- As Read
- Thread as Read

- As Read by Date
- All Read
- Flag
- As Junk
- As Not Junk

## Creating Saved Searches

Thunderbird's Saved Search feature creates a "virtual folder" in a place you designate according to a set of search criteria you define. As shown in Figure 12-1, the search criteria can be constructed using Boolean logic, and you can formulate the search using attributes such as subject, sender, junk status, and so on.

**For Outlook Users**

Microsoft Outlook's Search Folders feature is the same as Thunderbird's Saved Search feature.

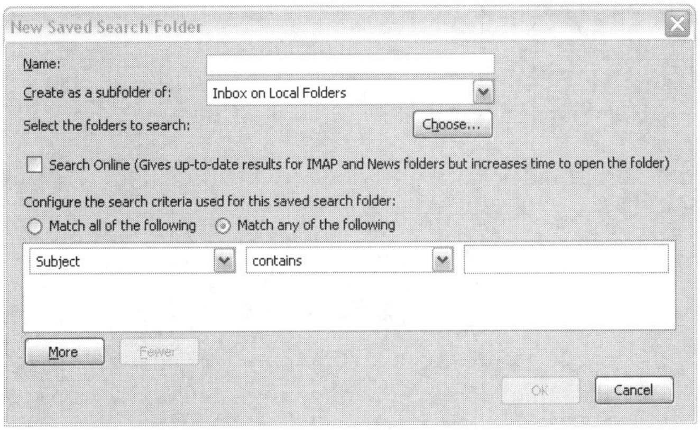

**Figure 12-1**

*The New Saved Search Folder creation screen.*

**Note**

A Saved Search folder is identified with a different icon than the one for a regular folder (as shown in Figure 12-2), so you can easily distinguish the difference between the two.

 Saved Search

**Figure 12-2**

*The Saved Search icon.*

When you create a saved search, the messages do not actually get removed from the original location but are actually stored there in a virtual state. However, here are two *essential* things to remember when you are working with Saved Searches:

- Individual messages deleted from a saved search are removed from their original location.
- Deleting an entire saved search folder does not result in the loss of any messages, because you are operating on the saved search, not the individual messages within the search.

## Ways to Create a Saved Search

Thunderbird gives you four different ways to create saved searches:

1. File Menu—File | New | Saved Search
2. File Menu—Edit | Find | Search Messages
3. View Menu
4. Quicksearch

To create a saved search, follow these instructions:

1. Name the search.
2. Designate where the folder will be stored.
3. Select the folders to be searched by checking the appropriate boxes.
4. If you are using IMAP, enable the checkbox to search online.
5. Construct your search criteria by entering your search terms in the box. Clicking the **More** button allows you to build a more complex search, as shown in Figure 12-3.

**Figure 12-3**

*A Saved Search with the More option enabled.*

## Using the View Menu to Create a Saved Search

If you want to use the View menu to create a saved search, you first need to select the category that you want to view (such as "Recent Mail"). After Thunderbird sorts that view, click the View drop-down list and select **Save Search as a Folder**. You will get the same screen as in Figure 12-1, but it will be filled in with criteria since "Recent Mail" is defined as "Age in Days" is less than 1. Remember that you can change the criteria for this saved search to be anything you want.

## Using Quicksearch to Create a Saved Search

If you want to use Quicksearch to create a saved search, you must select the category you want to search, such as "Sender" (see the "Searching Your Mail" section for an explanation of the Quicksearch feature). After Thunderbird retrieves that search and returns a set of results, you can click Save **Search as a Folder** and you will get the same screen as shown in Figure 12-1, filled in with the search criteria you have defined. If you want to change the search in some way, you have the opportunity to do that.

## Changing Criteria on an Existing Saved Search

After you have created a saved search, it is easy to change the criteria at any time. Right-click the saved search you have created, select **Properties**, and then adjust the criteria you want.

Remember that if you have conducted a saved search and then change the criteria of the messages (like changing messages from one state to another), those messages will no longer appear in the Saved Search folder when you open it. Thunderbird refreshes the screen after you have changed criteria, so you should see an immediate change when you click back to the folder.

If you find you need to rename or delete an existing saved search, you can accomplish this by selecting the saved search and then right-clicking to bring up the context menu.

# Creating and Using Filters

Filters are a powerful mechanism that you can use to channel your mail to a variety of locations within your mail client. Here is a summary of a few essential components of filters:

- They can be applied automatically or run manually.
- They are set up and operate per-account—there is no option to apply filters globally.
- They are stored in your profile folder in a file called `msgFilterRules.dat`.

Alice, Tobias, and Christine are planning a class reunion. Each of them will be responsible for one aspect of planning the reunion. Alice will handle the food, Tobias will manage the entertainment, and Christine will be responsible for the wine. Each of them decides it would be best to use email filters (as well as some of Thunderbird's other great features) to filter all the relevant email regarding the reunion into various locations where they can get quick and easy access to it.

## Filtering by Sender

Alice starts the process by deciding that she wants all email from both Tobias and Christine to go into a Reunion folder, which she has created as a sub-folder of her inbox.

Alice navigates to Tools | Message Filters to begin constructing her filters. She clicks **New** to construct a filter that channels all of the email from Tobias and Christine to her Reunion folder. Figure 12-4 shows Alice's filter criteria. Note that Alice needs to select the radio button that says "Match any of the following" in order for email to be properly filtered to her Reunion folder.

With this filter in place, all the email from Tobias and Christine will be funneled into the Reunion folder Alice has designated.

**Figure 12-4**

*Filtering email by sender.*

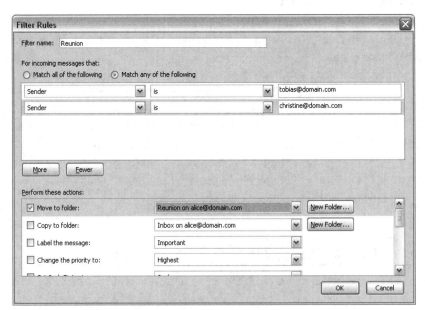

## Filtering Email into Folders

Tobias envisions a slightly more complicated scenario for managing his Reunion email. He wants to first create a folder that will house all the email he gets from prospective entertainers. He names this folder Entertainment and creates it as a subfolder under his inbox. When he receives an email that contains the subject "Reunion Entertainment," it will be routed to the folder named Entertainment.

Because Alice and Christine can't seem to keep their noses out of the entertainment portion of the reunion, they are continually sending Tobias email regarding suggestions that they have for entertainment options. So Tobias decides to create an email filter that filters their suggestions *directly* to his Entertainment folder. Figure 12-5 shows the criteria Tobias uses.

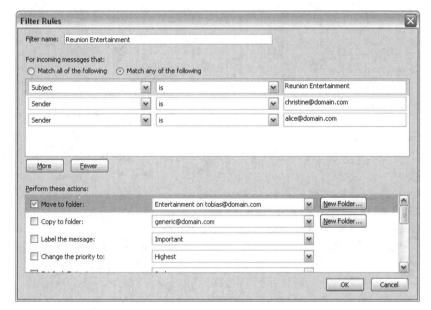

**Figure 12-5**

*Filtering Tobias's email into a folder.*

But later, it seems as if Alice and Christine both have a penchant for making good suggestions, so Tobias decides to adjust his filter criteria so that the email that comes in from Alice and Christine regarding Entertainment is actually labeled "Important" and then filtered to a new folder labeled "Important Stuff." Figure 12-6 shows the new criteria for that filter.

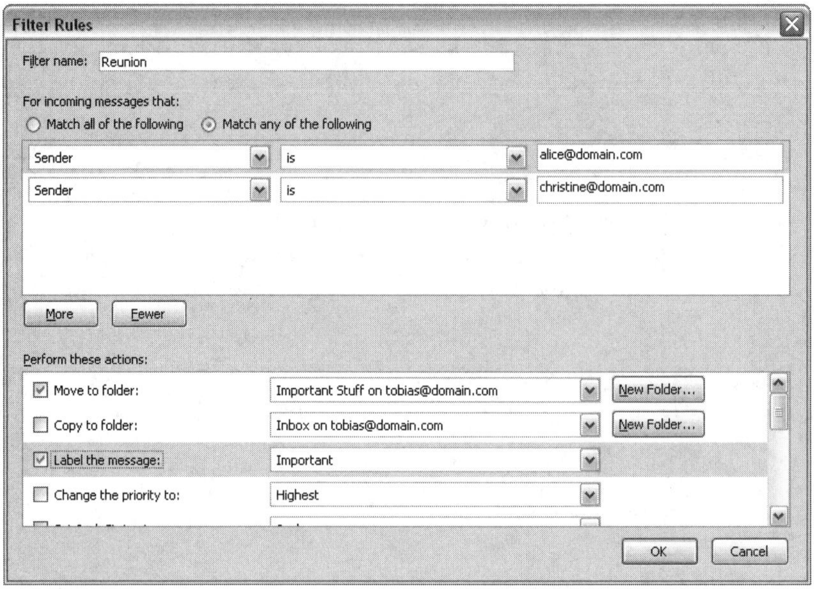

**Figure 12-6**

*Tobias's new
filter criteria
with
Important
invoked.*

## Creating a New Filter from Any Message

Christine really has her act together. She is so organized that she already knows who the wine merchant will be. The first time she contacted the vendor and got a reply, she right-clicked the "From" hyperlink in the email she received and selected **Create Filter from Message**. When the Filter Rules dialog box displayed, she also checked the **Label the Message** box and then selected "To Do" from the dropdown box. That way, whenever she gets an email from the wine merchant, it will be automatically labeled as a "To Do" and she will be able to sort all the email by using the View drop-down list.

## Manually Running Filters on a Folder

Christine likes to live in an automated world, but there are still times when she prefers to do things manually. She finally decides that she wants to have Merlot and Chardonnay for the reunion, so now she needs to construct a filter that will allow her to extract all the Merlot and Chardonnay choices from the set of emails sent to her by the wine merchant. Figure 12-7 shows her criteria.

In Figure 12-8, you can see that she has multiple filters for this category. Filters will be run in the order that they are listed in the Message Filters dialog box. If Christine decides she wants to change the order in which they are run, she can move them up or down accordingly.

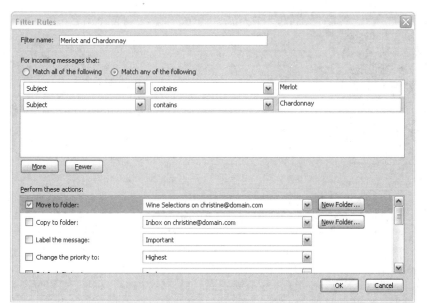

**Figure 12-7**
*Using filters to narrow down the wine list.*

**Figure 12-8**
*Multiple message filters.*

To manually run the filters on the folder, she will have to first highlight the folder she wants to run the filter on and then go to Tools | Run Filters on Folder.

### Sorry, No Global Filters

Filters cannot act globally in Thunderbird. If you are using Global Inbox, you can use filters for Local Folders. But these filters will not be able to automatically run on any incoming mail received—you must do so by using the manual option. If you want, you can create filters for specific POP accounts, but you must make sure to select that account from the drop-down list when you are setting up the filter. In this instance, the filters will operate on an automatic basis on the account you have designated.

**Note**

There is a logging feature present in Junk Mail Controls that has the same functionality as the Filter Log. See Chapter 11, "Protecting Your Privacy and Blocking Spam," for more information about the Junk Mail Log.

## The Filter Log

Tobias is in a hurry most of the time, but he has taken a moment to enable the Filter Log by going to Tools | Message filters and clicking the **Filter Log** button. Checking the box that says **Enable the Filter log** causes Thunderbird to keep a running log that documents the filters he has run. When Tobias tires of all that logging, he can clear the log periodically by clicking the **Clear Log** button.

# Sorting and Viewing Your Email

Let's face it—if Tweedledum and Tweedledee had email accounts, they would likely manage their email quite differently (or contrarily). Luckily, Thunderbird allows you some degree of flexibility in how you can view and sort your email, which will please even the most discriminating email connoisseur. The View menu drop-down list and Grouped by Sort are two handy ways you can rapidly sort your mail in a variety of configurations.

## Views

Thunderbird has a "View" drop-down list that allows you to sort your email into various categories, including the "Unread" category, which is particularly useful if you are like me and skip through messages from previous days and then need to go back and find them quickly. You can view mail that you have labeled in the five categories that are set forth in the "Labeling and Marking Your Mail" section, as well as a few other default categories, including People I know, Recent Mail, Last 5 Days, Not Junk, and Has Attachments. Perhaps the

**Figure 12-9**
*The Customize Message Views dialog box.*

best feature in this section is the ability to customize these existing views as well as create new ones. If you click the Customize button, you see the dialog box shown in Figure 12-9, which shows you the existing views that you can operate on.

Clicking **New** generates a Message View Setup screen that allows you to construct a new custom view according to criteria you set.

## Grouped by Sort

How would you like to press one key and immediately have your mail sort by a particular category? That is exactly what the Grouped by Sort feature can do for you, as demonstrated in Figure 12-10. Pressing the "G" key while you are in your inbox or in a folder triggers Thunderbird to sort the mail according to the default set in the File menu—View | Sort By (if you have never configured this before, the default is by date).

**Figure 12-10**
*Grouped by Sort using Date as the default parameter.*

As you can see from the example, sorting by date collapses the mail into a set of categories that makes it easier for you to find mail from two weeks ago, for example. Clicking the widget next to the name expands the set of messages so you can see the mail listed in that category.

Before you use Grouped by Sort, you should sort your mail in columns by the category that you want to sort on (you can do this by simply clicking the column name or by using the View | Sort By option before you press the "G" key). Then you can either press the G key or go to the File menu—View | Sort By, choose which category you want to sort on, and then select **Grouped by Sort**. To move from Grouped by Sort mode back to your original state (either Threaded or Unthreaded), you need to go back to the File menu and select that parameter under View | Sort By.

> **Note**
> Pressing the "G" key again will not undo the sort action. You must go into the File menu to change the sort.

## Other Considerations

The Grouped by Sort feature does not work with all the categories that are shown in the View | Sort By drop-down list. You can operate on the following categories: Date, Priority, Sender, Recipient, Status, Subject, and Label. Also, you *cannot* use the Grouped by Sort feature on saved searches.

Grouped by Sort parameters operate per folder. If you set Grouped by Sort by date in your inbox, it should not be applied to any of your other folders. Also, when you switch back and forth between folders, the Grouped by Sort state that you have set should be retained.

## Threaded Versus Unthreaded

These are two ways you can view your mail. In unthreaded mode, your mail simply shows as a long laundry list, with the messages rendered in the mail thread pane in the order they were received or sent. If you elect to show your mail in threaded mode, the messages are arranged by subject and sender (similar to who has responded to whom so that you can follow the flow of a conversation, or thread).

The File menu option View | Thread allows you to expand or collapse your threads, as well as some other options, to tweak your mail threading preferences. Happy threading!

# Searching Your Mail

Thunderbird gives you a variety of ways to search your email messages. If you need a "quick fix," you can use Quicksearch to blaze a search trail through your email collection. If you want to perform a more refined search, you can do so by using Thunderbird's search messages feature.

## Quicksearch

Quicksearch allows you to search your messages by Subject, Sender, Subject Or Sender, or Entire Message. The Quicksearch bar is shown in Figure 12-11.

**Figure 12-11**

*The Quicksearch bar.*

There is also a mechanism for highlighting words in messages (similar to the Find functionality in Firefox). If you type some text in Quicksearch and you want to clear the text for a new search, you can click the "X" to the right of the Quicksearch box and the text will be cleared, and you will be ready for takeoff on your next search.

## Power Searching Using Edit | Find | Search Messages

Edit | Find | Search Messages is another way to search your messages. It allows you to construct powerful queries that can find terms you are looking for in your email messages. The Search Messages dialog box also affords you the opportunity to operate on your search results in a number of ways.

After you have entered criteria in the screen and Thunderbird returns a set of results, you can then choose from a number of options using the buttons at the bottom of the screen, as shown in Figure 12-12. For example, you might want to search through your mail and find a set of messages, and then move them to another folder. You can do this by highlighting the group of messages and then using the File drop-down menu to relocate them to another folder. There is also an option here to create a Saved Search using the criteria you have set.

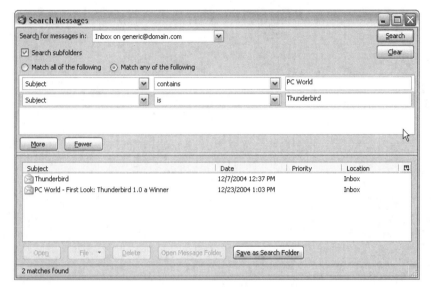

**Figure 12-12**

*The Search Messages screen after a search has been performed.*

As you can see, Thunderbird gives you a number of ways to organize and manage your mail. We have explored many avenues in this chapter—labels, saved searches, and filters are just some of the features you can use to save time and effort when you are managing your email. Next, you will learn how you can customize the look and feel of Thunderbird by using extensions and themes and customizing the toolbar. Our journey continues, and there is still more to learn about the many faces of Thunderbird.

# BLOG

## My Email Tirade of the Day

I tell you everything that is really nothing, and nothing of what is everything, do not be fooled by what I am saying. Please listen carefully and try to hear what I am not saying.
—Charles C. Finn

This quote by Charles Finn certainly provides some food for thought because I am often puzzled by the state of email communication at the time of this writing. Email is certainly a great method of communication, but it seems people do not always use this method of communication in the best way. Instead of my friends telling me interesting things that happened to them during the course of their week, my inbox is filled with an onslaught of silly jokes and urban legends. Perhaps I might get more information in emails if everyone wasn't blogging away their lives in online journals.

There are a number of things I dislike about the way people use email; here are my top choices:

1. Joke forwarding—Probably the single biggest waste of anyone's time, as well as bandwidth. I cringe when I see subject lines such as "This really works!" or "This is really funny." Not only do I get the same jokes from everyone, many of the jokes are not that funny at all. Anytime our country goes to war, the tone of the email jokes changes to back-slapping anti-everyone-but-American jokes that seem to have been generated from somewhere deep within the Redneck Riveria. Luckily, Thunderbird has a

good filtering system, and I can easily filter these types of messages into my Black Hole filter. By the way, I have asked some of my relatives to remove me from their joke lists, but apparently they haven't complied with my request.

2. Spam—Spam is like being sick and never getting better. Weeding through spam and training your spam filter isn't much fun. If we could track down a lot of these spammers, we should arrest them and sentence them to spam-monitoring Bill Gates' inbox, which allegedly gets four million pieces of spam per day. We could also make them read all the spam and then give them a quiz, if we really wanted to punish them further. Or perhaps we could sentence them to the same facility as Martha Stewart and have them work on developing SPAM recipes in their spare time.

3. Avoidance—Email allows people the opportunity to "pass" on things that they don't want to deal with. People say "I'll send you an email," but I never get one. I may ask a series of questions in an email, but in the reply message I rarely get all the answers to the questions I posed. Even being direct in email sometimes doesn't work. When all else fails, you may need to use the telephone, or turn on Thunderbird's return receipt option to see if people are even reading your mail.

4. Difficulty discerning tone—When people communicate on the phone or in person, it is often easier to tell when they are upset about something. In email mode it is often difficult to read tone, and certainly that leads to many more misinterpretations than if we just picked up the phone and asked the question or addressed the issue in person. If you are going to compose an email that has an underlying questionable tone, make sure that you think it through carefully before you send it.

5. Proliferation of smiley faces—Too many of these have invaded our shores; in my book, there should just be two categories, a happy face and a sad face. Anything purely in-between doesn't make sense. I don't want people I am communicating with to know my every mood. I would much rather be purposely vague.

6. "Thank you" replies—Another waste. I definitely don't need any more of these thank-yous filling up my inbox. If you asked me for something and I provided it, I don't require a thank-you; I deserve a raise.

7. Using CC and BCC options, and using Reply All unnecessarily—There are reasons that email clients have To CC and BCC options. Use them. Also, don't "Reply All" to an email if you don't want to include the other parties in what you are saying. Sometimes I get emails that go on wild tangents because someone "replied all" to an email and started a completely different thread that is of no interest to me. Think before you click "Reply All."

Despite the fact that people don't seem to always use email in the most useful ways, there are a lot of things to *love* about email—here are some of my favorites:

- Across the miles—Email is a good way to communicate with people when they live far away and it is tough to connect via phone. If you like to travel to faraway places, email has overtaken the fax machine as the preferred method of communicating with hotels regarding reservations and confirmations. Most airlines can now send you an email confirmation. There are many ways that email has improved our efficiency as it relates to global communication.

- Sharing information and links to websites—I don't often have time to surf the information highway, so I appreciate when someone takes the time to forward an article that they think might be of interest to me. I also enjoy when my friends send pictures of their kids frolicking in the snow, or sprawled on the beach with an ice cream cone in hand. One caveat—if you are going to send twenty pictures of your kids frolicking in the snow, consider putting them in an online album instead of attaching them to the email message you send me. Why? Large attachments (especially images) can cause very slow download times.

- The "reveal"—Sometimes information is "revealed" that might not be otherwise. Sometimes you are added to a thread and happen upon some interesting information that may be useful. This usually happens in corporate settings.

- Bill reminders—This is so much better than a Palm Pilot alert or tracking these things manually using a calendar. I use Thunderbird's "To Do" feature for my bill reminders and then periodically go back and check to see which ones I have to follow up on.

All in all, email is a great method of communication. I hope I have given you some food for thought. If you want to forward some jokes, please be selective about what you send. Take a moment and forward a picture of the splendid New England foliage to your friends who are marooned in the desert. Think about learning about the features that are present in Thunderbird and using them to their fullest advantage. There is a lot to be said for getting the most out of your email experience. You have the opportunity to use Thunderbird; don't underestimate its power! Finally, remember to have fun with both Thunderbird and your email—in the end, that is what it is all about!

# 13

# Customizing the Look and Feel of Mozilla Thunderbird

Way back in Chapter 7, "Customizing Firefox with Third-Party Extensions and Themes," you were introduced to some of the cool things you can do to enhance the look and feel of Firefox by using extensions and themes. You can do the same thing with Thunderbird thanks to its support of extensions and themes. No sense in wasting any time—let's get right to it and show you how you can personalize Thunderbird in a number of interesting ways. Our journey continues, and now it's time to have some fun!

**DO OR DIE:**

>> Is it me or my virtual identity?

>> Playing hide and seek with your preferences

>> There's a Throbber in the house!

>> Birds of a feather find themes together

## Thunderbird Extensions

Chapter 7 covers extension and theme management in Firefox. Because both products share a common Extension and Theme Manager, you will occasionally need to reference that chapter for some of what you need to know to install and manage extensions and themes. Chapter 7 also contains a good explanation of what extensions are and why they are created.

# How Thunderbird Extensions Can Help You

Many times there are features that don't make it into the milestone releases or may be planned for some time down the road. Thunderbird's extension support allows developers to create extensions that will plug into Thunderbird to extend its already powerful capabilities. An example is an extension, such as *Allow Empty Subject*, which basically allows you to bypass the warning dialog box when you send a message with an empty subject (obviously someone felt passionate enough about this feature or creating extensions in general to spend the time to design such an extension). There are extensions that run as applications within Thunderbird, such as *Mozilla Calendar* and *Forumzilla*. There are even extensions that mimic behavior in Outlook, such as the *Purge* extension. If you look hard enough, there is probably an extension out there that you can use to enhance your use of Thunderbird.

# Locating Extensions on the Web

Your recommended first stop for extensions is the official Mozilla repository, *addons.update.mozilla.org (UMO)*, which can be accessed directly from the "Get more Extensions" link on the right side of the Thunderbird extension manager. *UMO* contains a categorized list of extensions that are updated frequently and can be sorted by platform and version number. *UMO* also breaks down extensions into several categories, including top-rated, most popular, and newest.

In addition to *UMO*, there are a number of other places on the web where you can find extensions for Thunderbird.

# Installing Extensions

Although Thunderbird and Firefox share the same Extension Manager architecture, there is one important difference—extension files are installed differently in Thunderbird from the way they are in Firefox. In Firefox, you can click the `.xpi` file directly and have it installed into the Extension Manager (note that there is no "Install" button in the Firefox Extension Manager, but there is in Thunderbird, as shown in Figure 13-1).

**Figure 13-1**
*Thunderbird
Extension
Manager.*

In Thunderbird, you must right-click the file and save it to a location on your computer, and then install it through the Extension Manager interface (the same procedure applies when it comes to themes). To install an extension in Thunderbird, simply do the following:

1. Locate the relevant extension, either at UMO or at another site.

2. Right-click the **Download** link for the extension (or the file itself) and save the file to a location on your computer.

3. Click the **Install** button and highlight the extension file you want to install.

4. A dialog box appears that requests your permission to install the extension. This measure is built into Thunderbird to protect you from possibly installing malicious software by confirming that you actually want to install the file.

5. After a brief delay, the Install button becomes active. Click this button. This delay is intentional. It was installed as a security measure to protect users from accidentally installing an extension.

6. The `.xpi` file installs in Extension Manager. A progress meter shows the progress until the extension installation is complete.

After installation, you **must** restart Thunderbird in order to enable the extension.

## Extension Development and Version Numbers

Remember that extensions are constantly under development and may contain different features by the time this book goes to press. Make sure when you download an extension that it is compatible with the version of Thunderbird you are running.

For information on managing, disabling, and uninstalling extensions, refer to Chapter 7.

# Updating Your Extensions

**Upgrading to a New Version of Thunderbird?**

If you have an older version of Thunderbird and you upgrade to a newer version, this check is done automatically upon installation. If Thunderbird finds extensions that are not compatible with the version you have installed, it identifies the extensions.

Extension developers frequently offer updates to their extensions. Thunderbird provides two ways to check whether your extensions have been updated. You can click the Update button in the Extension Manager or go to Tools | Options | Advanced and click the box under Software Update that is labeled **Check Now** to update your extensions and themes. If Thunderbird is unable to find any updates, it lets you know and provides a Details button you can click to see any errors that might have been encountered when the check was performed.

# Featured Extensions

Now that you have gained an appreciation for how extensions can help you in Thunderbird, let's take a look at some ways you can customize Thunderbird. The extensions are divided into the following categories:

- Getting and sending messages
- Who am I?
- Productivity
- Configuration
- Privacy and security
- RSS
- Applications
- Simple is better
- Living in a Windows world
- Fun
- Great companion extensions

Each of these extensions was installed in Thunderbird 1.0. Remember, it is important to make sure the extension you are installing is compatible with the version of Thunderbird you are using.

## Getting and Sending Messages

### MagicSLR (http://www.thunderbird-mail.de/extensions/magicslr/index-en.php)

If you find yourself needing more flexibility to get and send messages, *MagicSLR* is truly a great extension (see Figure 13-2). It provides a set of five buttons that you can add to the toolbar that allow you options to Get/Send, Get All, Send All, Syncro, and Send Later. Two of the buttons (Get/Send and Get All) can be configured by using the *MagicSLR* preferences. If you think you don't need a Send Later option when Thunderbird already has it in offline mode, you are wrong. The button in this extension actually allows you to send mail later when you are working *online* as well. This is a well-designed extension that will benefit anyone who needs these sending and receiving preferences. It also is helpful for users who like to work in offline mode.

**Figure 13-2**
*Thunderbird customized with MagicSLR Toolbar buttons.*

### Yet Another Mail Biff (http://extensionroom.mozdev.org/more-info/yamb)

They say patience is the greatest virtue, but this might not apply when it comes to checking your email. This extension allows you to define when you get new mail notifications (in seconds) as well as configure Thunderbird to launch an external notifier. You actually have to go into the Account Settings to manage the number of seconds between new mail notifications, but the rest of the extension parameters can be set by using the Options button in Extension Manager.

## Who Am I?

### Virtual Identity Extension (http://www.absorb.it/hacked/thunderbird/v_identity.html)

Sometimes you just don't feel like yourself. That is when you might want to use the *Virtual Identity* extension (see Figure 13-3), which allows you to change your sending identity when composing an individual message. This extension creates a small button that appears directly to the right of the From label in your email compose window. After you click this button, you see a screen that allows you to change your full name, email address, and SMTP settings. Whatever information you enter here becomes your virtual identity until you change it from the dropdown list, which you do before you send the message by collapsing the button and then selecting the identity you want from the dropdown list. The virtual identity you select also appears as the last entry in this list.

**Figure 13-3**

*Thunderbird Compose window with Virtual Identity invoked.*

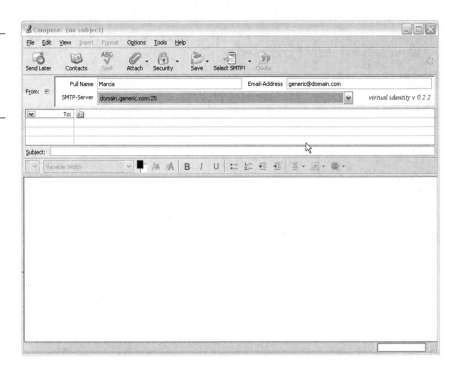

If you want to manage copy and folder settings, you must go into Extension Manager, highlight the extension, and click **Options**.

## Signature (http://www.grim-world.com/miek/)

*Signature* (see Figure 13-4) is a fairly simple extension that gives you the ability to insert custom signatures by right-clicking in the Compose window. This is a great companion extension to *Virtual Identity* because both of them allow a great deal of flexibility in configuring your identity in Thunderbird.

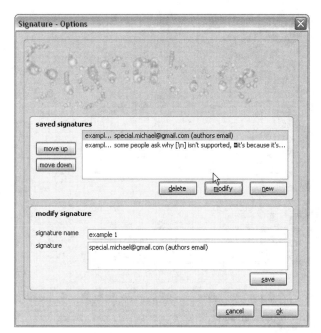

**Figure 13-4**

*The Signature configuration screen.*

## Show SMTP Username (http://www.chuonthis.com/extensions/ssun.php)

This is a great little extension that gives you SMTP nickname support by modifying how the SMTP servers are displayed. You also have the option to display the username that is affiliated with the SMTP server.

## Productivity

## DictionarySearch (http://dictionarysearch.mozdev.org/)

My Italian relatives have a habit of sending me emails half in Italian and half in English, so I was looking for a tool that would help me translate some of the words I could not understand. I had to look no further than *Dictionary Search* (see Figure 13-5), which is an extension that allows me to both look up and translate words contained in my email with a simple right-click (this launches a browser window or tab that opens with the meaning of the word you have highlighted). The great part about this extension is that you use four dictionaries, and there are possibilities to add dictionaries in other languages by accessing the *Dictionaries* page at http://dictionarysearch.mozdev.org/dictionaries.html.

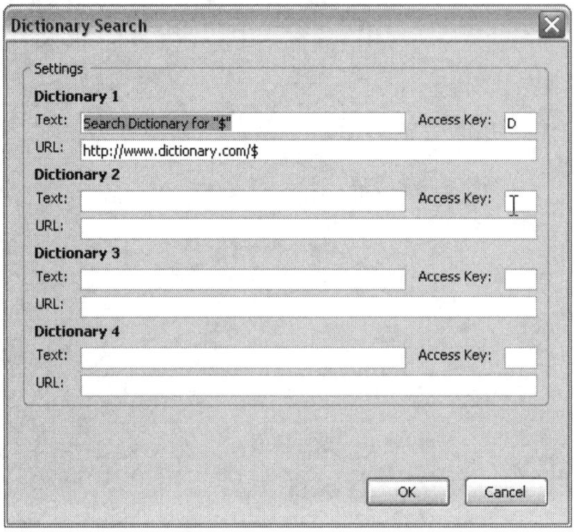

**Figure 13-5**

*Dictionary Search Settings configuration screen.*

Configuring this extension is relatively easy; you just have to make sure that you include a "$" sign at the end of the URL.

## Quick File (http://www.paultomlin.com/projects/mozilla/ thunderbird/quickfile/)

This extension leverages the power of the AutoComplete feature (also known as type-ahead-find) to help you locate message folder names so that you can quickly and efficiently file messages. You define the hot key combination you want, and that launches a dialog box that permits you to start typing the folder name, and presto!—the folder you want to channel messages to can be selected, and the messages are moved. You could drag and drop messages or use the File menu to accomplish this, but *Quick File* gives you the flexibility to complete this operation in a different way.

## Thunderbird Attachment Tools (http://www.supportware.net/mozilla/)

Have you ever just wanted to "zap" an attachment? This extension allows you to do this plus a whole lot more—you will be able to master manipulating any message that has attachments. Here are some of the things you can do under the Tools menu:

- Delete all attachments in a selected message

- Zap all attachments (leaves zero trace of attachments)

- Control the movement of attachments that you have deleted or zapped

*Thunderbird Attachment Tools* also contains a series of six menu popup items that are launched when you click on the attachment pane. When you are done using this extension, you might qualify for a Master of Attachments Degree (I wonder what that acronym would be…).

# Configuration

## Hidden Prefs (https://nic-nac-project.de/ kaosmos/hiddenprefs-FF-en.html)

This extension allows you to access some of Thunderbird's hidden preferences that are usually accessible only by hacking the `user.js` file or `about:config`. See Appendix E, "Hacking Configuration Files," to learn more about `about:config` and `user.js`.

*Hidden Prefs* allows you to configure some of Thunderbird's settings, including things like hiding the progress bar when mail is being sent. It also has an area where you can define how attachments are handled, as well as configure preferences related to personalizing the reply header. There are a number of settings here that can be tweaked that might be of use, so this extension is definitely worth checking out, especially if you don't want to take a deeper dive into uncovering the mysteries of about:config and `user.js`, which can be accomplished by installing the *About:Config* extension described next.

## About:Config (http://aboutconfig.mozdev.org/)

What is `about:config` all about? Go to Appendix E to learn more about it. Because this functionality isn't as easily accessible as it is in Firefox, this extension makes it easy to access the `about:config` preferences for Thunderbird. After you read Appendix E to understand the functionality, you can use it to alter your preferences. A stern warning—before you venture into this area, be careful! You can make changes in `about:config` that can cause issues with Thunderbird.

## Privacy and Security

### Enigmail (http://enigmail.mozdev.org/)

*Enigmail* is an extension that allows users to encrypt and sign email on the outbound end and decrypt/authenticate on the receiving end. When installed, the extension adds a menu item to the File menu. *Enigmail* supports encryption and signing per account, as well as handling per-recipient rules for automated key selection, and enabling/disabling encryption and signing.

*Enigmail* also supports Thunderbird's Multiple Identities feature. If you have questions about this extension, a mailing list on the homepage can help you get an answer.

## RSS

See Chapter 10, "Setting Up Your Mail, RSS, and Newsgroup Accounts Using Mozilla Thunderbird," for a description of *Forumzilla*, an extension that can help you manage your RSS feeds (http://forumzilla.mozdev.org/).

## Applications

See Chapter 7 for a discussion of *Mozilla Calendar*, a XUL-based calendar that you can plug into both Firefox and Thunderbird. In many ways, it might be more useful in Thunderbird because you might need to reference dates more frequently when you are trying to arrange meetings.

**From the Funny Calendar Story Department**

I had to check the calendar of a consultant with whom I was trying to arrange a meeting. He had several calendar entries that simply said "Meeting with the Clouds." It was only after I gave it a little thought (and expanded the calendar entry) that I realized this was an entry for his outbound and inbound flights. Now why didn't I think of that?

## Simple Is Better

### Allow Empty Subject
### (http://jpeters.no-ip.com/extensions/index.php?page=tb_aes)

Sometimes, simple is better (except, of course, when it comes to potato chips). This extension does one thing and does it well—it disables the warning dialog box that displays when you send a message without a subject. As the author of the extension points out, his intent was not to promote the wanton sending of empty messages. Rather, this is just another example of the great things you do to customize Thunderbird to help you be more efficient in your everyday work.

### Timestamp
### (http://jpeters.no-ip.com/extensions/index.php?page=tb_ts)

Can't remember what time it is? This extension provides a means to add a time-stamp to your outbound messages by using five predefined formats that can be set in the Options menu. When you are composing a message, all you have to do is right-click in the message body and select "Insert timestamp," or go to the File menu and choose Options | Insert timestamp, or press Ctrl+Shift+T.

**FRIDGE**

Right about now is a good time to head over to www.taquitos.net to see how truly complex potato chips can be. This site bills itself as the "World of Potato Chips and Snack Food" and includes reviews of hundreds of varieties of potato chips and snacks. My favorite is Humpty Dumpty Grilled Cheese and Ketchup Chips—someone in that company definitely knows how to spot a truly sublime combination.

## Living in a Windows World

### Minimize to Tray (http://minimizetotray.mozdev.org/)

Where would we be without the system tray? If you are like me and have tons of windows open at a time, the system tray is a good way to be able to quickly find a program and relaunch it, or simply manage the program while it is still minimized. Thanks to this extension (which packs a lot of punch), you can now minimize Thunderbird, but you can also do a whole lot more that that. Here are a few of the cool things you can do with this extension:

- Right-click the Thunderbird icon while it is in the system tray to get new messages, compose a message, check your address book, and restore or close Thunderbird.
- Right-click the Minimize button to send Thunderbird to the system tray.
- Right-click the Minimize button in the Thunderbird message compose window to minimize that window to the system tray.
- Force the application to always minimize to the system tray (instead of the taskbar) by configuring the extension's options.

## Purge (http://extensionroom.mozdev.org/more-info/purge)

The *Purge* extension is nothing more than a shortcut for compacting your folders (and something that former Outlook IMAP users might miss). Instead of right-clicking the folder and selecting **Compact this Folder**, this extension creates a toolbar button that you can add for one-click purging.

**TOOL KIT**

### IMAP Users: Why You Should Compact Your Folders

You should get in the habit of compacting your folders on a regular basis. When you delete a message, Thunderbird actually only marks it for deletion and places it in a "hidden" state. When you empty the trash, you are still not really completely ridding yourself of these hidden emails, because they technically are still contained within the folder. They actually remains there until you run the Compact Folders command.

Some strange things can happen if you fail to compact your IMAP folders. Suddenly, you may see email that you thought you deleted mysteriously reappear. So, do the right thing, and remember to compact your folders.

## Fun

### MessageFaces (http://tecwizards.de/mozilla/messagefaces/)

This extension allows you to add "face" images to email and newsgroup postings. You first need to find the image you want to use and scale it to 48×48 pixels. After saving it in the PNG (portable network graphic) format, you may have to tweak things a little—the homepage for this extension explains how. You can then add your identity by going to Tools | Extensions and clicking the Options button for the MessageFaces extension.

## Great Companion Extensions

### Linky (http://gemal.dk/mozilla/linky.html) and Launchy (http://gemal.dk/mozilla/launchy.html)

I couldn't resist including both of these extensions. After all, they both start with "L" and are written by the same author. Seriously, these two extensions are great companions.

*Launchy* allows you to open links and `mail:to` with a host of external applications, including browsers, FTP clients, and even download managers. If you use Windows, *Launchy* can autodetect 63 applications at the time of this writing. *Launchy* also has a cool feature where you can actually add an `.xml` file to your user chrome directory that allows you to add your own applications to *Launchy*. You can even tweak a preference that allows you to debug in the JavaScript console. (Warning: this is not for the faint of heart.)

Its companion extension, *Linky*, allows you much greater control over how you can handle links in Thunderbird (and Firefox too). See Chapter 7 for more about this extension.

**TOOL KIT** | **The JavaScript Console**

You might have noticed this menu item in the Tools dropdown list and wondered what it does. The JavaScript Console is a reporting tool that is present in most Mozilla-based applications (Firefox included). The console provides useful information for developers when there are errors in the application *chrome* and when an end user opens a web page. The *chrome* is that part of the Thunderbird application window that lies outside the confines of a window's content area. Examples of elements that are usually part of the chrome are toolbars, progress bars, menu bars, and window title bars.

As an end user, you will probably not have much use for the JavaScript console. But if for some reason you report a bug, you might be asked to see if any errors appear in the console.

## Themes

If you want to add a splash of color and some great iconography to Thunderbird, you can install some themes. Think of themes as "skin" for the Thunderbird application, allowing you to change everything from the colors and icons of Thunderbird to almost every piece of the UI, including things like the icons and the Throbber.

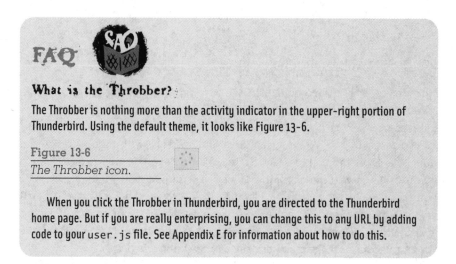

**FAQ**

**What is the Throbber?**

The Throbber is nothing more than the activity indicator in the upper-right portion of Thunderbird. Using the default theme, it looks like Figure 13-6.

**Figure 13-6**

*The Throbber icon.*

When you click the Throbber in Thunderbird, you are directed to the Thunderbird home page. But if you are really enterprising, you can change this to any URL by adding code to your user.js file. See Appendix E for information about how to do this.

Figures 13-7 and 13-8 are examples of how themes can be used to make Thunderbird unique.

**Figure 13-7**

*The Atlas theme installed in Thunderbird.*

**Figure 13-8**

*The Mostly Crystal Theme, Windows flavor.*

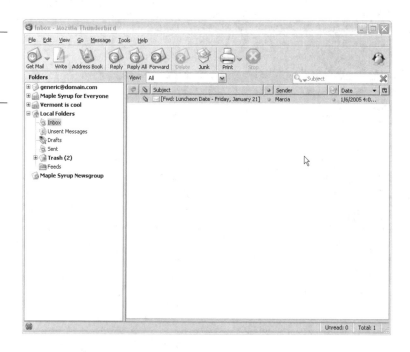

**FRIDGE**

The Mostly Crystal theme (http://www.tom-cat.com/mozilla/thunderbird.html) is a cool theme for Thunderbird.

I use this theme on my Mac—it is well designed, well supported, and easy on the eyes. The author provides matching menu item and program window icons. A companion theme is also available for Firefox. A truly beautiful theme to gaze at while you are composing an email.

## Locating Themes on the Web

Your recommended first stop for themes is the official Mozilla repository, *addons.update.mozilla.org (UMO)*, which can be accessed directly from the "Get more Themes" link on the right side of the Thunderbird Extension Manager. *UMO* contains a categorized list of themes that are updated frequently and can be sorted by platform.

In addition to *UMO*, there a number of other places on the web where you can find themes for Thunderbird.

## Installing Themes

Thunderbird provides a Theme Manager that makes installing themes very easy. Here are the steps:

1. Locate the relevant theme, either at *UMO* or at another site.

2. Right-click the **Download** link for the theme (or the file itself) and save the file to a location on your computer.

3. Click the **Install** button and highlight the extension file you want to install.

4. A dialog box launches that requests your permission to install the extension. This measure is built into Thunderbird to protect you from possibly installing malicious software by confirming that you actually want to install the file. Click OK.

5. The `.jar` file installs in Extension Manager. A progress meter shows the progress until the theme installation is complete.

6. Click the theme you want to use, and then click the button that says Use Theme.

After installation, you **must** restart Thunderbird in order to enable the theme.

**FRIDGE**

Some theme authors go to great lengths to make the icon set really stand out in Thunderbird. The Atlas theme author has "themed" the toolbar icons of several of the most popular extensions, including Mozilla Calendar, Chatzilla, and the Googlebar. Go to http://www.spuler.us/atlas/index.html to see a more comprehensive list of the other extensions that are supported. Ultra cool!

## Switching Themes

To switch to a new theme, follow these steps:

1. Highlight the new theme you want to use.
2. Click the **Use Theme** button at the bottom of the Theme Manager. You may also right-click the theme and select Use Theme from the context menu.
3. After selecting **Use Theme**, you should see a message under the theme name that indicates that you must restart Thunderbird to use the new theme.
4. Restart Thunderbird, and *voila!* Your new theme should now appear.

## Uninstalling Themes

To uninstall a theme you have been using, follow these steps:

1. Highlight the theme you want to uninstall.
2. Click the **Uninstall Theme** button at the bottom of the Theme Manager. You may also right-click the theme and select Uninstall from the context menu.
3. After clicking **Uninstall Theme**, you should see a message under the theme name that indicates that you must restart Thunderbird to use the new theme.
4. Restart Thunderbird, and *voila!* Your theme should no longer be present.

## Updating Themes

To check for theme updates, you can always click the **Update** button in Theme Manager. You can also highlight the relevant theme and right-click to get the Update option. The Update Wizard will launch and guide you seamlessly through the update process.

# Customizing the Toolbar

Customizing the toolbar in Thunderbird is a snap. You simply right-click the toolbar, highlight the **Customize** button, and then drag and drop the icons you want to use to the toolbar area. If you want to get rid of an existing icon in the toolbar, all you have to do is drag it back to the Toolbar window.

If you are looking for some new icons to add to your toolbar, these extensions provide some great options:

- *Buttons!* (http://www.chuonthis.com/extensions/buttons.php)
- *Extension Manager Buttons* (http://moonwolf.mozdev.org/#embtb)
- *MoreButtonsPlus* (http://forums.mozillazine.org/viewtopic.php?t=77129)
- *MagicSLR* (http://www.thunderbird-mail.de/extensions/magicslr/index-en.php)

---

This has been a long and fruitful journey. Our journey has taken us along the highways and byways of Thunderbird, demonstrating how you can use Thunderbird to manage your email, how to protect your privacy and security, and how to customize the program using extensions and themes. With Thunderbird, there are many roads to take and many roads to further explore as development continues on this product. Remember, the development community and all the open source contributors continue to make Thunderbird the best it can be.

I conclude with a quote from Lewis Carroll, from his seminal work *Alice in Wonderland*: "Begin at the beginning and go on till you come to the end; then stop." You can stop reading now, but don't stop having fun experimenting with Thunderbird and what it can do for you.

# Keyboard and Mouse Shortcuts for Firefox

his appendix is for people who want to be as proficient as possible in their use of Firefox. You'll see how to use keyboard and mouse shortcuts instead of menu commands. (Some of these things can't even be done through the menus, so you're getting some inside stuff here!)

The keyboard shortcuts are broken out by operating system and include keyboard shortcuts for Firefox, Internet Explorer, and Opera. (Netscape Navigator keyboard shortcuts are the same as in Firefox.) When you see a command such as Ctrl+B or Shift+Backspace, it means that you should press and hold down the first key in the combination and then press the second key. Ctrl is the Control key on Windows and Linux computers. Cmd is the Command key on Macintosh computers.

## Keyboard and Mouse Shortcuts for Windows

These are the keyboard and mouse shortcuts for Windows.

### Keyboard Shortcuts for Windows

The following tables show the various keyboard shortcuts for Windows. Where there is no equivalent keyboard shortcut, the field contains a dash. If there is no corresponding feature in the browser, the field is labeled "Feature not available."

## General

| Shortcut | Windows Firefox | Internet Explorer | Opera |
|---|---|---|---|
| Copy | Ctrl+C | Ctrl+C | Ctrl+C |
| Cut | Ctrl+X | Ctrl+X | Ctrl+X |
| Paste | Ctrl+V | Ctrl+V | Ctrl+V |
| Select all | Ctrl+A | Ctrl+A | Ctrl+A |
| Delete | Delete | Delete | Delete |
| Redo | Ctrl+Shift+Z Ctrl+Y | Ctrl+Y | Ctrl+Shift+Z Ctrl+Y |
| Undo | Ctrl+Z | Ctrl+Z | Ctrl+Z |
| Help | F1 | F1 | F1 |

## Moving Around the Screen

| Shortcut | Windows Firefox | Internet Explorer | Opera |
|---|---|---|---|
| Go down one line | Down | Down | Down |
| Go up one line | Up | Up | Up |
| Go down one page | PageDown | PageDown | PageDown |
| Go up one page | PageUp | PageUp | PageUp |
| Go to the bottom of a page | End | End | End |
| Go to the top of a page | Home | Home | Home |
| Go to the next field or link | Tab | Tab | Tab |
| Go to the previous field or link | Shift+Tab | Shift+Tab | Shift+Tab |

## Browsing

| SHORTCUT | WINDOWS FIREFOX | INTERNET EXPLORER | OPERA |
|---|---|---|---|
| Back | Backspace<br>Alt+← | Backspace<br>Alt+← | Backspace<br>Alt+←<br>Ctrl+←<br>Z |
| Forward | Shift+Backspace<br>Alt+→ | Shift+Backspace<br>Alt+→ | Shift+Backspace<br>Alt+→<br>Ctrl+→<br>X |
| Bookmark the current web page | Ctrl+D | Ctrl+D | Ctrl+T |
| View bookmarks in sidebar | Ctrl+B<br>Ctrl+I | Ctrl+I | F4<br>Ctrl+Alt+B<br>Ctrl+1 |
| View history in sidebar | Ctrl+H | Ctrl+H | Ctrl+Alt+H<br>Ctrl+4 |
| Go to a web address | Ctrl+L<br>Alt+D | Alt+D<br>F4<br>Ctrl+Tab | F8 |
| Complete an address with .com. This shortcut works only in the address bar. | Ctrl+Enter | Ctrl+Enter | Enter |
| Complete an address with .net. This shortcut works only in the address bar. | Shift+Enter | Feature not available | Feature not available |
| Complete an address with .org. This shortcut works only in the address bar. | Ctrl+Shift+Enter | Feature not available | Feature not available |
| Print the current web page | Ctrl+P | Ctrl+P | Ctrl+P |
| Stop loading the web page | Esc | Esc | Esc |

| Shortcut | Windows Firefox | Internet Explorer | Opera |
|---|---|---|---|
| Reload the web page from the cache | F5<br>Ctrl+R | F5<br>Ctrl+R | F5<br>Ctrl+R |
| Reload the web page directly from the server (override information in the cache) | Ctrl+F5<br>Ctrl+Shift+R | Ctrl+F5 | — |
| Downloads | Ctrl+J | Feature not available | Ctrl+Alt+T<br>Ctrl+5 |
| Start a new mail message | Ctrl+M | — | — |
| Caret browsing | F7 | Feature not available | Feature not available |
| Save page as | Ctrl+S | — | Ctrl+S |
| Save link target as | Alt+Enter | — | — |
| Delete individual form auto-complete entry | Shift+Delete | Delete | — |
| Select next autocomplete entry in text field | Down | — | — |
| Select previous autocomplete entry in text field | Up | — | — |

| **Searching** | | | |
|---|---|---|---|
| Shortcut | Windows Firefox | Internet Explorer | Opera |
| Find in this page | Ctrl+F | Ctrl+F | Ctrl+F |
| Find again | Ctrl+G<br>F3 | | F3 |
| Find as you type link | ' | Feature not available | '<br>Shift+/ |
| Find as you type text | / | Feature not available | /<br>. |

| Shortcut | Windows Firefox | Internet Explorer | Opera |
|---|---|---|---|
| Find previous | Ctrl+Shift+G<br>Shift+F3 | — | Shift+F3 |
| Select next search engine in search bar | Ctrl+Down | — | — |
| Select previous search engine in search bar | Ctrl+Up | — | — |
| Web search. Web search moves the cursor to the Search bar and works only if the Search Bar is visible. If the Search Bar is hidden, this keyboard shortcut has no effect. | Ctrl+K | — | Shift+F8 |
| DOM Inspector | Ctrl+Shift+I | Feature not available | Feature not available |

### Window Manipulation

| Shortcut | Windows Firefox | Internet Explorer | Opera |
|---|---|---|---|
| Open new window | Ctrl+N | Ctrl+N | Ctrl+Alt+N |
| Close window | Ctrl+Shift+W<br>Alt+F4 | Ctrl+W<br>Alt+F4 | Ctrl+W<br>Alt+F4 |
| Open new tab | Ctrl+T | Feature not available | Ctrl+N |
| Close tab | Ctrl+W<br>Ctrl+F4 | Feature not available | Ctrl+W<br>Ctrl+F4 |
| Go to tab [1 to 9] | Ctrl+[1 to 9] | Feature not available | — |
| Open file | Ctrl+O | Ctrl+O | Ctrl+O |
| Open link | Enter | Enter | Enter |

| SHORTCUT | WINDOWS FIREFOX | INTERNET EXPLORER | OPERA |
|---|---|---|---|
| Open link in new tab | Ctrl+Enter | Feature not available | — |
| Open link in new window | Shift+Enter | Shift+Enter | Shift+Enter |
| Open address in new tab. This shortcut works only in the address bar. | Alt+Enter | Feature not available | Shift+Enter |
| Toggle full-screen mode | F11 | F11 | F11 |
| Go to the home page | Alt+Home | Alt+Home | Alt+Home |
| Move to the next frame | F6 | — | — |
| Move to the previous frame | Shift+F6 | — | — |
| Zoom in text | Ctrl++ | — | 0 |
| Zoom out text | Ctrl+0 | — | 6 |
| Go to the next tab | Ctrl+Tab | Feature not available | Ctrl+Tab Ctrl+PageDown Alt+PageDown Ctrl+F6 2 |
| Go to the previous tab | Ctrl+Shift+Tab Ctrl+PageUp | Feature not available | Ctrl+Shift+Tab Alt+PageUp Ctrl+Shift+F6 1 |
| View the page source | Ctrl+U | Ctrl+F3 | Ctrl+F3 |

# Mouse Shortcuts for Windows

The following table shows you the mouse shortcuts for Windows.

| SHORTCUT | WINDOWS FIREFOX | INTERNET EXPLORER | OPERA |
|---|---|---|---|
| Back | Shift+Scroll down | Shift+Scroll down | Shift+Scroll down |
| Forward | Shift+Scroll up | Shift+Scroll up | Shift+Scroll up |
| Scroll line by line | Alt+Scroll | — | — |
| Open new tab | Double-click tab bar | Feature not available | Double-click tab bar |
| Close tab | Middle-click tab | Feature not available | Shift+Left-click |
| Open in background tab | Ctrl+Left-click Middle-click | Feature not available | Ctrl+Shift+ Left-click Middle-click |
| Open in foreground tab | Ctrl+Shift+Left-click Shift+Middle-click | Feature not available | Shift+Left-click Shift+Left-click |
| Open in new window | Shift+Left-click | Shift+Left-click | — |
| Zoom in text | Ctrl+Scroll down | Ctrl+Scroll down | Ctrl+Scroll down |
| Zoom out text | Ctrl+Scroll up | Ctrl+Scroll up | Ctrl+Scroll up |
| Reload the web page directly from the server (override information in the cache) | Shift+Reload button | Shift+Reload button | — |
| Save page as | Alt+Left-click | — | — |

Clicking a link while holding down Ctrl (Ctrl+Left-click) opens the link in a background tab. This is useful for quickly opening several links that will take time to load from a main page without having to jump back and forth each time you create a new tab. Clicking a link while holding down Shift and Ctrl (Shift+Ctrl+Left-click) opens the link in a foreground tab. You can reverse the way these two shortcuts work by going to Tools | Options | Advanced and clicking the **Select new tabs opened from links** checkbox under Tabbed Browsing.

# Keyboard and Mouse Shortcuts for Linux

These are the keyboard and mouse shortcuts for Linux.

## Keyboard Shortcuts for Linux

The following tables show the various keyboard shortcuts for Linux. Where there is no equivalent keyboard shortcut, the field contains a dash. If there is no corresponding feature in the browser, the field is labeled "Feature not available."

| | General | | |
|---|---|---|---|
| SHORTCUT | LINUX FIREFOX | INTERNET EXPLORER | OPERA |
| Copy | Ctrl+C | Ctrl+C | Ctrl+C |
| Cut | Ctrl+X | Ctrl+X | Ctrl+X |
| Paste | Ctrl+V | Ctrl+V | Ctrl+V |
| Select all | Ctrl+A | Ctrl+A | Ctrl+A |
| Delete | Delete | Delete | Delete |
| Redo | Ctrl+Shift+Z Ctrl+Y | Ctrl+Y | Ctrl+Shift+Z Ctrl+Y |
| Undo | Ctrl+Z | Ctrl+Z | Ctrl+Z |
| Help | F1 | F1 | F1 |
| | Moving Around the Screen | | |
| SHORTCUT | LINUX FIREFOX | INTERNET EXPLORER | OPERA |
| Go down one line | Down | Down | Down |
| Go up one line | Up | Up | Up |
| Go down one page | PageDown | PageDown | PageDown |
| Go up one page | PageUp | PageUp | PageUp |
| Go to the bottom of a page | End | End | End |
| Go to the top of a page | Home | Home | Home |

| SHORTCUT | LINUX FIREFOX | INTERNET EXPLORER | OPERA |
|---|---|---|---|
| Go to the next field or link | Tab | Tab | Tab |
| Go to the previous field or link | Shift+Tab | Shift+Tab | Shift+Tab |

**Browsing**

| SHORTCUT | LINUX FIREFOX | INTERNET EXPLORER | OPERA |
|---|---|---|---|
| Back | Backspace<br>Alt+← | Backspace<br>Alt+← | Backspace<br>Alt+←<br>Ctrl+←<br>Z |
| Forward | Shift+Backspace<br>Alt+→ | Shift+Backspace<br>Alt+→ | Shift+Backspace<br>Alt+→<br>Ctrl+→<br>X |
| Bookmark the current web page | Ctrl+D | Ctrl+D | Ctrl+T |
| View bookmarks in sidebar | Ctrl+B<br>Ctrl+I | Ctrl+I | F4<br>Ctrl+Alt+B<br>Ctrl+1 |
| View history in sidebar | Ctrl+H | Ctrl+H | Ctrl+Alt+H<br>Ctrl+4 |
| Go to a web address | Ctrl+L<br>Alt+D | Alt+D<br>F4<br>Ctrl+Tab | F8 |
| Complete an address with .com. This shortcut works only in the address bar. | Ctrl+Enter | Ctrl+Enter | Enter |
| Complete an address with .net. This shortcut works only in the address bar. | Shift+Enter | Feature not available | Feature not available |

| Shortcut | Linux Firefox | Internet Explorer | Opera |
|---|---|---|---|
| Complete an address with .org. This shortcut works only in the address bar. | Ctrl+Shift+Enter | Feature not available | Feature not available |
| Print the current web page | Ctrl+P | Ctrl+P | Ctrl+P |
| Stop loading the web page | Esc | Esc | Esc |
| Reload the web page from the cache | F5 Ctrl+R | F5 Ctrl+R | F5 Ctrl+R |
| Reload the web page directly from the server (override information in the cache) | Ctrl+F5 Ctrl+Shift+R | Ctrl+F5 | — |
| Downloads | Ctrl+Y | Feature not available | Ctrl+Alt+T Ctrl+5 |
| Start a new mail message | Ctrl+M | — | — |
| Caret browsing | F7 | Feature not available | Feature not available |
| Save page as | Ctrl+S | — | Ctrl+S |
| Save link target as | Alt+Enter | — | — |
| Delete individual form auto-complete entry | Shift+Delete | Delete | — |
| Select next autocomplete entry in text field | Down | — | — |
| Select previous autocomplete entry in text field | Up | — | — |

## Searching

| Shortcut | Linux Firefox | Internet Explorer | Opera |
|---|---|---|---|
| Find in this page | Ctrl+F | Ctrl+F | Ctrl+F |
| Find again | Ctrl+G<br>F3 | — | F3 |
| Find as you type link | ' | Feature not available | ,<br>Shift+/ |
| Find as you type text | / | Feature not available | /<br>. |
| Find previous | Ctrl+Shift+G<br>Shift+F3 | — | Shift+F3 |
| Select next search engine in search bar | Ctrl+Down | — | — |
| Select previous search engine in search bar | Ctrl+Up | — | — |
| Web search. Web search moves the cursor to the Search bar and works only if the Search Bar is visible. If the Search Bar is hidden, this keyboard shortcut has no effect. | Ctrl+K<br>Ctrl+J | — | Shift+F8 |
| DOM Inspector | Ctrl+Shift+I | Feature not available | Feature not available |

## Window Manipulation

| Shortcut | Linux Firefox | Internet Explorer | Opera |
|---|---|---|---|
| Open new window | Ctrl+N | Ctrl+N | Ctrl+Alt+N |
| Close window | Ctrl+Shift+W<br>Alt+F4 | Ctrl+W<br>Alt+F4 | Ctrl+W<br>Alt+F4 |

| SHORTCUT | LINUX FIREFOX | INTERNET EXPLORER | OPERA |
|---|---|---|---|
| Open new tab | Ctrl+T | Feature not available | Ctrl+N |
| Close tab | Ctrl+W<br>Ctrl+F4 | Feature not available | Ctrl+W<br>Ctrl+F4 |
| Go to tab [1 to 9] | Alt+[1 to 9] | Feature not available | — |
| Open file | Ctrl+O | Ctrl+O | Ctrl+O |
| Open link | Enter | Enter | Enter |
| Open link in new tab | Ctrl+Enter | Feature not available | — |
| Open link in new window | Shift+Enter | Shift+Enter | Shift+Enter |
| Open address in new tab. This shortcut works only in the address bar. | Alt+Enter | Feature not available | Shift+Enter |
| Toggle full-screen mode | F11 | F11 | F11 |
| Go to the home page | Alt+Home | Alt+Home | Alt+Home |
| Move to the next frame | F6 | — | — |
| Move to the previous frame | Shift+F6 | — | — |
| Zoom in text | Ctrl++ | — | 0 |
| Zoom out text | Ctrl+0 | — | 6 |
| Go to the next tab | Ctrl+Tab<br>Ctrl+PageDown | Feature not available | Ctrl+Tab<br>Alt+PageDown<br>Ctrl+F6<br>2 |
| Go to the previous tab | Ctrl+Shift+Tab<br>Ctrl+PageUp | Feature not available | Ctrl+Shift+Tab<br>Alt+PageUp<br>Ctrl+Shift+F6<br>1 |
| Get page info | Ctrl+I | — | Ctrl+8 |
| View the page source | Ctrl+U | Ctrl+F3 | Ctrl+F3 |

# Mouse Shortcuts for Linux

The following table shows you the mouse shortcuts for Linux.

| SHORTCUT | LINUX FIREFOX | INTERNET EXPLORER | OPERA |
|---|---|---|---|
| Back | Shift+Scroll down | Shift+Scroll down | Shift+Scroll down |
| Forward | Shift+Scroll up | Shift+Scroll up | Shift+Scroll up |
| Scroll line by line | Alt+Scroll | — | — |
| Open new tab | Double-click tab bar | Feature not available | Double-click tab bar |
| Paste URL and go | Middle-click tab | Feature not available | Feature not available |
| Open in background tab | Ctrl+Left-click Middle-click | Feature not available | Ctrl+Shift+ Left-click Middle-click |
| Open in foreground tab | Ctrl+Shift+Left-click Shift+Middle-click | Feature not available | Shift+Left-click |
| Open in new window | Shift+Left-click | Shift+Left-click | — |
| Zoom in text | Ctrl+Scroll down | Ctrl+Scroll down | Ctrl+Scroll down |
| Zoom out text | Ctrl+Scroll up | Ctrl+Scroll up | Ctrl+Scroll up |
| Reload the web page directly from the server (override information in the cache) | Shift+Reload button | Shift+Reload button | — |
| Save page as | Alt+Left-click | — | — |

Clicking a link while holding down Ctrl (Ctrl+Left-click) opens the link in a background tab. This is useful for quickly opening several links that will take time to load from a main page without having to jump back and forth each time you create a new tab. Clicking a link while holding down Shift and Ctrl (Shift+Ctrl+Left-click) opens the link in a foreground tab. You can reverse the way these two shortcuts work by going to Tools | Options | Advanced and clicking the **Select new tabs opened from links** checkbox under Tabbed Browsing.

# Keyboard and Mouse Shortcuts for the Mac

These are the keyboard and mouse shortcuts for the Mac.

## Keyboard Shortcuts for the Mac

The following tables show the various keyboard shortcuts for Mac. Where there is no equivalent keyboard shortcut, the field contains a dash. If there is no corresponding feature in the browser, the field is labeled "Feature not available."

| General | | | |
|---|---|---|---|
| SHORTCUT | MAC FIREFOX | INTERNET EXPLORER | OPERA |
| Copy | Cmd+C | Cmd+C | Cmd+C |
| Cut | Cmd+X | Cmd+X | Cmd+X |
| Paste | Cmd+V | Cmd+V | Cmd+V |
| Select all | Cmd+A | Cmd+A | Cmd+A |
| Delete | Delete | Delete | Delete |
| Redo | Cmd+Shift+Z | Cmd+Y | Cmd+Shift+Z Cmd+Y |
| Undo | Cmd+Z | Cmd+Z | Cmd+Z |

| Moving Around the Screen | | | |
|---|---|---|---|
| SHORTCUT | MAC FIREFOX | INTERNET EXPLORER | OPERA |
| Go down one line | Down | Down | Down |
| Go up one line | Up | Up | Up |
| Go down one page | PageDown | PageDown | PageDown |
| Go up one page | PageUp | PageUp | PageUp |
| Go to the bottom of a page | End | End | End |
| Go to the top of a page | Home | Home | Home |
| Go to the next field or link | Tab | Tab | Tab |

| SHORTCUT | MAC FIREFOX | INTERNET EXPLORER | OPERA |
|---|---|---|---|
| Go to the previous field or link | Shift+Tab | Shift+Tab | Shift+Tab |

## Browsing

| SHORTCUT | MAC FIREFOX | INTERNET EXPLORER | OPERA |
|---|---|---|---|
| Shortcut | Mac Firefox | Internet Explorer | Opera |
| Back | Cmd+← | Backspace<br>Option+← | Backspace<br>Option+←<br>Cmd+←<br>Z |
| Forward | Shift+Backspace<br>Option+→ | Shift+Backspace<br>Option+→ | Shift+Backspace<br>Option+→<br>Cmd+→<br>X |
| Bookmark the current web page | Cmd+D | Cmd+D | Cmd+T |
| View bookmarks in sidebar | Cmd+B | Cmd+I | Cmd+Option+B<br>Cmd+1 |
| View history in sidebar | Cmd+H | Cmd+H | Cmd+Option+H<br>Cmd+4 |
| Go to a web address | Cmd+L | Option+D<br>Cmd+Tab | — |
| Complete an address with .net. This shortcut works only in the address bar. | Shift+Return | Feature not available | Feature not available |
| Print the current web page | Cmd+P | Cmd+P | Cmd+P |
| Stop loading the web page | Esc | Esc | Esc |
| Reload the web page from the cache | Cmd+R | Cmd+R | Cmd+R |

| SHORTCUT | MAC FIREFOX | INTERNET EXPLORER | OPERA |
|---|---|---|---|
| Reload the web page directly from the server (override information in the cache) | Cmd+F5 Cmd+Shift+R | — | — |
| Downloads | Cmd+J | Feature not available | Cmd+Option+T Cmd+5 |
| Start a new mail message | Cmd+M | — | — |
| Save page as | Cmd+S | — | Cmd+S |
| Save link target as | Option+Return | — | — |
| Delete individual form auto-complete entry | Shift+Delete | Delete | — |
| Select next autocomplete entry in text field | Down | — | — |
| Select previous autocomplete entry in text field | Up | — | — |

**Searching**

| SHORTCUT | MAC FIREFOX | INTERNET EXPLORER | OPERA |
|---|---|---|---|
| Find in this page | Cmd+F | Cmd+F | Cmd+F |
| Find again | Cmd+G | — | — |
| Find as you type link | ' | Feature not available | , Shift+/ |
| Find as you type text | / | Feature not available | / . |
| Find previous | Cmd+Shift+G | — | — |
| Select next search engine in search bar | Cmd+Down | — | — |
| Select previous search engine in search bar | Cmd+Up | — | — |

| Shortcut | Mac Firefox | Internet Explorer | Opera |
|---|---|---|---|
| Web search. Web search moves the cursor to the Search Bar and works only if the Search Bar is visible. If the Search Bar is hidden, this keyboard shortcut has no effect. | Cmd+K | — | — |
| **Window Manipulation** | | | |
| Shortcut | Mac Firefox | Internet Explorer | Opera |
| Open new window | Cmd+N | Cmd+N | Cmd+Option+N |
| Close window | Cmd+Shift+W | Cmd+W | Cmd+W |
| Open new tab | Cmd+T | Feature not available | Cmd+N |
| Close tab | Cmd+W | Feature not available | Cmd+W |
| Go to tab [1 to 9] | Cmd+[1 to 9] | Feature not available | — |
| Open file | Cmd+O | Cmd+O | Cmd+O |
| Open link | Return | Return | Return |
| Open link in new tab | Cmd+Return | Feature not available | — |
| Open link in new window | Shift+Return | Shift+Return | Shift+Return |
| Open address in new tab. This shortcut works only in the address bar. | Option+Return | Feature not available | Shift+Return |
| Go to the home page | Option+Home | Option+Home | Option+Home |
| Zoom in text | Cmd++ | — | 0 |

| Shortcut | Mac Firefox | Internet Explorer | Opera |
|---|---|---|---|
| Zoom out text | Cmd+0 | — | 6 |
| Go to the next tab | Cmd+Tab<br>Cmd+PageDown | Feature not available | Cmd+Tab<br>Option+<br>PageDown<br>2 |
| Go to the previous tab | Cmd+Shift+Tab<br>Cmd+PageUp | Feature not available | Cmd+Shift+Tab<br>Option+<br>PageUp<br>1 |
| Get page info | Cmd+I | — | Cmd+8 |
| View the page source | Cmd+U | — | — |

## Mouse Shortcuts for the Mac

The following table shows the mouse shortcuts for the Mac.

| Shortcut | Mac Firefox | Internet Explorer | Opera |
|---|---|---|---|
| Back | Shift+Scroll down | Shift+Scroll down | Shift+Scroll down |
| Forward | Shift+Scroll up | Shift+Scroll up | Shift+Scroll up |
| Scroll line by line | Alt+Scroll | — | — |
| Open new tab | Double-click tab bar | Feature not available | Double-click tab bar |
| Close tab | Middle-click tab | Feature not available | Shift+Left-click |
| Open in background tab | Ctrl+Left-click<br>Middle-click | Feature not available | Ctrl+Shift+<br>Left-click<br>Middle-click |
| Open in foreground tab | Ctrl+Shift+Left-click<br>Shift+Middle-click | Feature not available | Shift+Left-click |
| Open in new window | Shift+Left-click | Shift+Left-click | — |
| Zoom in text | Ctrl+Scroll down | Ctrl+Scroll down | Ctrl+Scroll down |

| Shortcut | Mac Firefox | Internet Explorer | Opera |
|---|---|---|---|
| Zoom out text | Ctrl+Scroll up | Ctrl+Scroll up | Ctrl+Scroll up |
| Reload the web page directly from the server (override information in the cache) | Shift+Reload button | Shift+Reload button | — |
| Save page as | Alt+Left-click | — | — |

# Keyboard and Mouse Shortcuts for Mozilla Thunderbird

This appendix is for people who want to be as proficient as possible in their use of Thunderbird. You'll see how to use keyboard and mouse shortcuts instead of menu commands. (Some of these things can't even be done through the menus, so you're getting some inside stuff here!)

The keyboard shortcuts are broken out by operating system and include keyboard shortcuts for Thunderbird and Outlook Express. When you see a command such as Ctrl+B or Shift+Backspace, it means that you should press and hold down the first key in the combination and then press the second key. Ctrl is the Control key on Windows and Linux computers. Cmd is the Command key on Macintosh computers.

## Keyboard and Mouse Shortcuts for Windows

These are the keyboard and mouse shortcuts for Windows.

### Keyboard Shortcuts for Windows

The following tables show the various keyboard shortcuts for Windows. Where there is no equivalent keyboard shortcut, the field contains dashes. If there is no corresponding feature in the mail client, the field is labeled "Feature not available."

## Text Commands

| SHORTCUT | THUNDERBIRD | OUTLOOK EXPRESS |
|---|---|---|
| Copy | Ctrl+C | Ctrl+C |
| Cut | Ctrl+X | Ctrl+X |
| Paste | Ctrl+V | Ctrl+V |
| Select all | Ctrl+A | Ctrl+A |
| Delete | Delete | Delete |
| Redo | Ctrl+Shift+Z<br>Ctrl+Y | Ctrl+Y |
| Undo | Ctrl+U | Ctrl+U |

## Getting, Sending, and Replying to Messages

| SHORTCUT | THUNDERBIRD | OUTLOOK EXPRESS |
|---|---|---|
| New message | Ctrl+N/Ctrl+M | Ctrl+N |
| Edit as new | Ctrl+E | Feature not available |
| Open message in new window | Ctrl+O | Ctrl+O |
| Get new messages for current account | Ctrl+T | — |
| Get new messages for all accounts | Ctrl+Shift+T | Ctrl+M |
| Toggle message pane | F8 | — |
| Send message now | Ctrl+Enter | Ctrl+Enter+Alt+S |
| Send message later | Ctrl+Shift+Enter | — |
| Send and receive all messages | Ctrl+T | F5 |
| Reply to message (only to sender) | Ctrl+R | Ctrl+R |
| Reply to message (all recipients) | Ctrl+Shift+R | Ctrl+Shift+R |
| Save message as file | Ctrl+S | — |

## Reading Messages

| SHORTCUT | THUNDERBIRD | OUTLOOK EXPRESS |
|---|---|---|
| Go to next message | F | Ctrl+> |
| Go to next unread message | N | Ctrl+U |
| Go to next unread thread | T | Ctrl+Shift+U |
| Go to previous message | B | Ctrl+< |
| Go to previous unread message | P | Feature not available |
| Increase text size | Ctrl++ | — |
| Decrease text size | Ctrl+- | — |
| Restore text size | Ctrl+0 | — |
| Expand all threads | * | Feature not available |
| Collapse all threads | \ | Feature not available |
| Print | Ctrl+P | Ctrl+P |
| Grouped by Sort | G | Feature not available |
| Move to next mail pane | F6 | Tab |

## Searching

| SHORTCUT | THUNDERBIRD | OUTLOOK EXPRESS |
|---|---|---|
| Find Text in this message | Ctrl+F | Ctrl+F |
| Find again | Ctrl+G<br>F3 | F3 |
| Find Link as you type | ' | Feature not available |
| Find previous | Ctrl+Shift+G<br>Shift+F3 | — |
| Search messages | Ctrl+Shift+F | Ctrl+Shift+F |

## Labeling and Marking Messages

| Shortcut | Thunderbird | Outlook Express |
| --- | --- | --- |
| Label: None | 0 | Feature not available |
| Label: Important | 1 | Feature not available |
| Label: Work | 2 | Feature not available |
| Label: Personal | 3 | Feature not available |
| Label: To Do | 4 | Feature not available |
| Label: Later | 5 | Feature not available |
| Mark message as read/unread | M | Ctrl+Q |
| Mark thread as read | R | Ctrl+T |
| Mark all read | Ctrl+Shift+C | Ctrl+Shift+A |
| Mark all read by date | C | Feature not available |
| Mark as junk | J | Feature not available |
| Mark as not junk | Shift+J | Feature not available |

## Miscellaneous

| Shortcut | Thunderbird | Outlook Express |
| --- | --- | --- |
| Open new window | Ctrl+N, Ctrl+M | Ctrl+N |
| Close window | Ctrl+Shift+W Alt+F4 | Ctrl+W Alt+F4 |
| Toggle message pane | F8 | F11 |
| Move to the next mail pane | Shift+F6 | — |
| View the message source | Ctrl+U | Ctrl+F3 |
| Help | F1 | F1 |
| Caret browsing | F7 | Feature not available |
| Quit | Ctrl+Q | — |
| Stop | Esc | Esc |

## Mouse Shortcuts for Windows

The following table shows you some of the mouse shortcuts for Windows.

| SHORTCUT | THUNDERBIRD |
|---|---|
| New plain text message | Shift+Create a new message |
| Plain text reply | Shift+Reply |
| Plain text reply all | Shift+Reply All |
| Plain text forward | Shift+Forward |
| Increase text size | Ctrl+Scroll down |
| Decrease text size | Ctrl+Scroll up |

# Keyboard and Mouse Shortcuts for Mac

The keyboard and mouse shortcuts for Mac are the same as the Windows short-cuts described previously, except you need to use the Cmd key instead of the Ctrl key. Also, on the Mac keyboard the Return key is the Enter key.

# Keyboard and Mouse Shortcuts for Linux

The keyboard and mouse shortcuts for Linux are the same as the Windows shortcuts described previously.

# C

## Menu Commands for Firefox

This appendix lists the menu commands available in Firefox. You can access the individual commands using the keyboard by pressing Alt or Option + the shortcut characters for the various commands (shortcut characters are underlined in the command).

Firefox has seven standard menus:

| Menu | Description |
|------|-------------|
| File | Contains basic commands for opening and closing windows, tabs, files, and locations; saving, emailing, and printing pages; importing bookmarks; and exiting Firefox. |
| Edit | Contains commands for cutting/copying/pasting/deleting and searching. For non-Windows versions of Firefox, this also contains the Preferences command (used instead of the Tools \| Options command) for setting Firefox preferences and options. |
| View | Contains commands for displaying the toolbars and page source, which page style and character encoding to use, and toggling the full-screen display. |
| Go | Contains some basic navigation commands as well as a list of the most recently visited websites. |
| Bookmarks | Contains commands for bookmarking pages and managing bookmarks, as well as a list of your stored bookmarks. |
| Tools | Contains commands for bookmarking pages and managing bookmarks, as well as a list of your stored bookmarks. |
| Help | Contains commands for displaying help and for getting more information about Firefox. |

**Note**

Some extensions add to or modify the standard Firefox menu commands. In some cases, the extension adds an entire menu of its own. This appendix describes Firefox's default menus and commands.

## The File Menu

The File menu contains basic commands for opening and closing windows, tabs, files, and locations; saving, emailing, and printing pages; importing bookmarks; and exiting Firefox.

| Command | Description |
|---|---|
| New Window | Opens a new instance of the browser. |
| New Tab | Opens a new tab in the current window. |
| Open File | Displays the standard Open File screen so that you can open a file on your hard disk (or your LAN). Firefox can open a number of files by default, such as HTML files, XML files, text and graphics files, many sound files, and so on. Adding plug-ins (such as the Adobe Reader plug-in) enhances Firefox's ability to open other kinds of files. |
| Close Tab | Closes the current tab and switches the focus to the tab immediately to the right of the closed tab. (This menu item appears only if you have more than one tab open.) |
| Close Window/Close | Closes the current instance of the browser. If no tabs are open, the command appears as Close Window. If multiple tabs are open, the command appears simply as Close, and you are asked to confirm that you want to close however many tabs. |
| Save Page As | Saves the web page you are currently viewing. Firefox can save the complete page with corresponding graphics, the HTML page itself with no graphics, or the page as plain text. |
| Send Link | Opens the default email program and creates a new message for you to address and send that contains a link to the current web page. |
| Page Setup | Displays the Page Setup screen, which lets you set page layout, margins, and page headers and footers. |
| Print Preview | Displays the current web page as it will be printed. You can change how the page will appear in print using the File | Page Setup command. |
| Print... | Displays the standard Print screen, which lets you select the printer to use, the number of copies, the printing range, and options specific to the printer you've selected. |
| Import... | Starts the Import Wizard, which steps you through the process to import bookmarks, display options, history, passwords, and other information from other browsers. |
| Work Offline | Lets you view web pages stored in your cache without having a live Internet connection. (You won't be able to refresh the web pages or transmit information back to the website without having a live Internet connection.) |
| Exit | Similar to the Close Window command, but this also stops any downloads in progress. |

# The Edit Menu

The Edit menu contains commands for cutting/copying/pasting/deleting and searching. For non-Windows versions of Firefox, the Edit menu also contains the Preferences command (used instead of the Tools | Options command) for setting Firefox preferences and options.

| COMMAND | DESCRIPTION |
|---------|-------------|
| Undo | Undoes the last action where information has been changed on your local computer: data you entered in a field or a form, changes to a bookmark in the Bookmark Manager, and so on. |
| Redo | Redoes whatever you just undid with the Undo command. |
| Cut | Cuts the selected text and/or graphics from a document or form and stores it in the clipboard. You cannot cut text and graphics from a web page; you must use the Copy command to get the information to the clipboard. |
| Copy | Copies the selected text and/or graphics to the clipboard. You can copy anything you can select (although you may not be able to paste it into something that will be able to interpret it correctly). |
| Delete | Deletes the selected text and/or graphics from a field. |
| Select All | Selects the entire web page. |
| Find in This Page | Displays the Find bar at the bottom of the screen, which lets you search for an item in the current page. |
| Find Again | Searches for the next occurrence of the search item identified in the Find bar. |
| Preferences (only for Linux and Mac) | Displays the Preferences screen, where you can change the preferences in Firefox. (Windows users use the Tools | Options command instead.) |

# The View Menu

The View menu contains commands for displaying the toolbars and page source, which page style and character encoding to use, and toggling the full-screen display.

| Command | Description |
|---|---|
| Toolbars | Displays the Toolbars submenu. |
| -Navigation Toolbar | Toggles the Navigation toolbar, which by default contains some basic navigation buttons, the Location field, and the Search field. |
| -Bookmarks Toolbar | Toggles the Bookmarks toolbar, which displays any bookmarks in the Bookmarks Toolbar Folder. |
| -Customize… | Displays the Customize Toolbar screen, which lets you drag and drop toolbar buttons to and from the various toolbars. |
| Status Bar | Toggles the status bar at the bottom of the screen. The status bar displays information about the web page being displayed as well as RSS and other status icons. |
| Sidebar | Displays the Sidebar submenu. |
| -Bookmarks | Displays the bookmarks in the sidebar. |
| -History | Displays the History sidebar. You can adjust the way in which the history information is sorted by clicking View in the sidebar. This command is the same as Go \| History. |
| Stop | Stops loading the current page. |
| Reload | Refreshes the current web page. |
| Text Size | Displays the Text Size submenu. |
| -Increase Text Size | Increases the size of the text on the web page. (This applies to all pages displayed in this tab or window until you change it.) |
| -Decrease Text Size | Decreases the size of the text on the web page. (This applies to all pages displayed in this tab or window until you change it.) |
| -Normal | Resets the text display size to the default. |
| Page Style | Displays the Page Style submenu. |
| -No style | Removes the style formatting from the web page. |
| -Basic page style | Displays the page with a general style specified by the web page's author. (If additional page styles have been specified in the web page, they appear on this submenu.) |
| Character Encoding | Displays the Character Encoding submenu. |

| -Auto-Detect | Lets you select a character set to auto-detect from a list of character sets. |
| -More Encodings | Lets you select a character set to auto-detect from several different classes of character sets. |
| -Customize List | Displays the Customize Character Encoding so you can select and activate specific character sets. |
| Page Source | Displays the source HTML and JavaScript code for the current document. |
| Full Screen | Toggles the full-screen mode display. |

## The Go Menu

The Go menu contains some basic navigation commands as well as a list of the most recently visited websites.

| COMMAND | DESCRIPTION |
|---------|-------------|
| Back | Displays the preceding web page. |
| Forward | Displays the subsequent web page. |
| Home | Displays the home page. |
| History | Displays the History sidebar. You can adjust the way in which the history information is sorted by clicking View in the sidebar. This command is the same as View \| Sidebar \| History. |

## The Bookmarks Menu

The Bookmarks menu contains commands for bookmarking pages and managing bookmarks, as well as a list of your stored bookmarks.

| COMMAND | DESCRIPTION |
|---------|-------------|
| Bookmark This Page | Adds a bookmark for the current web page. (You must specify which folder to add the bookmark to.) |
| Manage Bookmarks | Starts the Bookmarks Manager. |

# The Tools Menu

The Tools menu contains commands for bookmarking pages and managing bookmarks, as well as a list of your stored bookmarks.

| COMMAND | DESCRIPTION |
|---|---|
| Web Search | Moves the cursor to the search field. (This command does nothing if the search field is not visible on the toolbar.) |
| Read Mail | Starts the default email program. If the default email program is running, Firefox displays the number of unread messages in the Inbox in parentheses. |
| New Message | Starts the default email program (if necessary) and opens a new message window for composing a new message in the program. |
| Downloads | Opens the Download Manager to show the current/ in-process downloads. |
| Extensions | Opens the Extension Manager so you can update, uninstall, and potentially change settings for the extensions you have installed in Firefox. |
| Themes | Opens the Theme Manager so you can change your theme or uninstall themes you are no longer using. |
| JavaScript Console | Starts the JavaScript console, used for debugging JavaScript code embedded in a web page. |
| Page Info | Displays the Page Info screen, which shows you detailed information about the current web page, including the links and media used in the page. |
| Options | Displays the Options screen, where you can change the options in Firefox. (Linux and Mac users use the Edit \| Preferences command instead.) |

# The Help Menu

The Help menu contains commands for displaying help and for getting more information about Firefox.

| COMMAND | DESCRIPTION |
|---|---|
| Help Contents | Opens the Firefox online help. |
| For Internet Explorer Users | Displays a brief page of information for people familiar with Internet Explorer who need a guide. |
| Promote Firefox | Displays the main page of the Spread Firefox website, which is aimed at encouraging people to use Firefox and spread the word about it to others. |
| About Mozilla Firefox | Displays the Firefox version number and some brief technical information. Also displays the contributor credits when you click **Credit**. |

# Menu Commands for Mozilla Thunderbird

his appendix lists the menu commands available in Thunderbird. You can access the individual commands using the keyboard by pressing Alt or Option + the shortcut characters for the various commands (shortcut characters are underlined in the command).

Thunderbird has seven standard menus:

| Menu | Description |
|------|-------------|
| File | Contains basic commands for opening and closing windows, tabs, files, and locations; saving, emailing, and printing pages; importing bookmarks; and exiting Thunderbird. |
| Edit | Contains commands for cutting/copying/pasting/deleting and searching. For non-Windows versions of Thunderbird, this also contains the Preferences command (used instead of the Tools \| Options command) for setting Thunderbird preferences and options. |
| View | Contains commands for displaying the toolbars, mail and message pane layout, sort order categories, message views, threads, headers, message body format, page style, and the character coding to use. |
| Go | Contains some basic navigation commands, such as Next and Previous, and lets you go back to the Mail Start page. |
| Tools | Contains commands for address book, extensions, themes, message filters, junk mail controls, importing, account settings, and options. |
| Help | Contains commands for displaying help and for getting more information about Thunderbird. |

**Note**

Some extensions add to or modify the standard Thunderbird menu commands. In some cases, the extension adds an entire menu of its own. This appendix describes Thunderbird's default menus and commands.

# The File Menu

| Command | Description |
|---|---|
| New | Displays the New submenu, which allows you to open a new message, folder, saved search, account, or address book card. |
| Open Saved Message | Launches a screen that allows you to select the location of a previously saved message. |
| Attachments | Displays the Attachments submenu, which allows you to open, save as, or save all attachments. |
| Close | Closes the current window. |
| Save As | Saves the current message as a file or template. |
| Get New Messages for | Displays the Get Messages submenu, which allows you to retrieve new messages for particular accounts or get all your new messages. |
| Send Unsent Messages | Sends unsent messages that you have saved while working offline. This menu item is enabled when you are working offline. |
| Subscribe | Allows you to show or hide IMAP folders that might not otherwise be shown. |
| Rename Folder | Renames the selected folder. |
| Compact Folder | Deletes hidden emails contained in mail folders. Until you compact your folders, these hidden emails remain in the folder, even if you empty the trash. |
| Empty Trash | Empties the trash. |
| Offline | Displays the Offline submenu, which allows you to work offline, download/sync now, configure your offline settings and disk space, and get flagged and selected messages. |
| Page Setup | Displays the Page Setup screen, which lets you set page layout, margins, and page headers and footers. |
| Print Preview | Displays the current page as it will be printed. You can change the way the page will appear in print using the File | Page Setup command. |
| Print | Displays the standard Print screen, which lets you select the printer to use, the number of copies, the printing range, and options specific to the printer you've selected. |
| Exit | Closes the Thunderbird program. |

# The Edit Menu

| COMMAND | DESCRIPTION |
|---|---|
| Undo Delete Message | Undoes the last action where a message has been deleted. |
| Redo | Redoes whatever you just undid with the Undo command. |
| Cut | Cuts the selected text and/or graphics from a document or form and stores it in the clipboard. You cannot cut text and graphics from a web page; you must use the Copy command to get the information to the clipboard. |
| Copy | Copies the selected text and/or graphics to the clipboard. You can copy anything you can select (although you may not be able to paste it into something that will be able to interpret it correctly). |
| Delete Message | Deletes the selected message. |
| Select | Displays the Select submenu, which allows you to select all messages or a particular thread. |
| Find | Displays the Find submenu, which lets you find in this message, find again, find previous, search messages, and perform an advanced Address Book search. |
| Folder Properties | Displays general information for the selected folder and allows you to select a folder for offline use and manage sharing and quotas. |

# The View Menu

| COMMAND | DESCRIPTION |
|---|---|
| Toolbars | Displays the Toolbars submenu. |
| -Mail Toolbar | Toggles the Mail toolbar with icons. |
| -Search Bar | Toggles the View and Quickview Search bars. |
| -Status Bar | Toggles the Status bar located at the bottom of the screen. The status bar displays unread/read mail count and the offline icon. |
| -Customize | Lets you customize the mail toolbar by dragging and dropping icons. |
| Layout | Displays the layout submenu. |

| COMMAND | DESCRIPTION |
|---|---|
| -Classic View | Selects classic view, which is the folder pane rendered in full on the left side of the screen, message pane and below. |
| -Wide View | Selects wide view, which increases the message pane to the full width of the screen. |
| -Vertical | Selects a vertical three-pane view, folder pane, thread pane, and message pane. |
| Message Pane | Toggles to open or close the message pane. |
| Sort By | Displays a submenu that allows you to display the categories that you can sort by, including Date, Flag, Order Received, Priority, Sender, Recipient, Size, Status, Subject, Read, Label, Junk Status, and Attachments. You can also sort by Ascending, Descending, Threaded, Unthreaded, and Grouped by Sort. |
| Messages | Displays a submenu that allows you to show message categories and labels, including All, Unread, Important, Work, Personal, To Do, Later, People I Know, Recent Mail, Last 5 Days, Not Junk, Has Attachments, and a Customize feature to create your own message categories and labels. |
| Threads | Displays a submenu that allows you to show thread information, including All, Unread, Threads with Unread, Watch Threads with Unread, Allows you to toggle Ignored Threads, and Allows you to Expand and collapse all threads. |
| Headers | Displays a submenu that allows you to select All or Normal headers. |
| Message Body As | Displays a submenu which allows you to display the message body in Plain HTML, Simple HTML, or Plain Text. |
| Display Attachments Inline | Toggles between showing attachments inline or as attachments. |
| Text Size | Displays the text size submenu. |
| -Increase Text Size | Increases the size of the text in the mail pane. |
| -Decrease Text Size | Decreases the size of the text in the mail pane. |
| -Normal | Resets the text display size to the default. |

| COMMAND | DESCRIPTION |
|---|---|
| Character Encoding | Displays the character encoding submenu. |
| -Auto-Detect | Lets you select a character set to auto-detect from a list of character sets. |
| -More Encodings | Lets you select a character set to auto-detect from several different classes of character sets. |
| -Customize List | Displays the Customize Character Encoding so you can select and activate specific character sets. |
| Message Source | Displays the source HTML and JavaScript code for the current document. |
| Message Security Info | Displays information related to whether the message included a digital signature and whether it was encrypted. |

## The Go Menu

| COMMAND | DESCRIPTION |
|---|---|
| Next | Displays a submenu that allows you to move to the next message, the next unread message, the next flagged message, or the next unread thread. |
| Previous | Displays a submenu that allows you to move to the previous message, the previous unread message, or the previous flagged message. |
| Mail Start Page | Loads the Thunderbird Mail Start Page. |

## The Message Menu

| COMMAND | DESCRIPTION |
|---|---|
| New Message | Launches a new message screen. |
| Reply | Launches a reply-to screen to the sender only for the selected message. |
| Reply to All | Launches a reply-to screen to all message recipients for the selected message. |

| COMMAND | DESCRIPTION |
| --- | --- |
| Forward | Forwards the selected message to the recipient you specify. |
| Forward As | Allows you to choose whether to forward the message inline (in the message body) or as an attachment. |
| Edit Message as New | Displays a copy of the message that you can edit. |
| Open Message | Opens the message in a new window. |
| Move | Displays a submenu that allows you to the move the selected message(s) to another account. |
| Copy | Displays a submenu that allows you to copy the selected message(s) to another account. |
| Label | Displays a submenu that allows you to label a message in the following categories: Important, Work, Personal, To Do, and Later. |
| Mark | Displays a submenu that allows you to mark a message in the following categories: As Read, Thread as Read, As Read by Date, All Read, Flag, As Junk, As Not Junk, and Run Junk Mail Controls on Marked Messages. |
| Create Filter from Message | Launches a Filter Rules screen that captures the filter information for that message. |

## The Tools Menu

| COMMAND | DESCRIPTION |
| --- | --- |
| Address Book | Opens the Address Book, where you can configure your Personal Address Book and Collected Addresses. You can also create mailing lists here. |
| Extensions | Opens the Extension Manager so you can update, uninstall, and potentially change settings for the extensions you have installed in Thunderbird. |
| Themes | Opens the Theme Manager so you can change your theme or uninstall themes you are no longer using. |
| Message Filters | Displays the Message Filter screen, which allows you to create new filters, manage your existing filters, and enable and view the Filter Log. |

| Command | Description |
|---------|-------------|
| Run Filters on Folder | Applies the existing filters listed in the Message Filter Screen (in order) to the selected folder. |
| Junk Mail Controls | Displays the Junk Mail Control screen, which allows you to configure white lists, handling, and logging. You can also enable the adaptive filter and reset your training data in this area. |
| Run Junk Mail Controls on Folder | Applies the existing Junk Mail Controls listed in the Junk Mail Controls screen to the selected folder. |
| Delete Mail Marked as Junk in Folder | Deletes mail marked as junk in the selected folder. |
| Import | Launches the Import wizard, which allows you to import mail, addresses, and settings from other mail programs. |
| JavaScript Console | Starts the JavaScript console, used for debugging JavaScript code embedded in a web page. |
| Account Settings | Displays the Account Settings screen, the primary place to manage account settings for all your Thunderbird accounts. |
| Options | Displays the Options screen, where you can change the options in Thunderbird. (Mac users use the Thunderbird \| Preferences command; Linux users use Edit \| Preferences.) |

# The Help Menu

| Command | Description |
|---------|-------------|
| Release Notes | Sends you to a web page that contains the Thunderbird Release Notes when you are online. |
| Mozilla Thunderbird Help | Sends you to a web page that has Thunderbird Help Info when you are online. At the time of this writing, Thunderbird does not contain a Help Viewer. |
| About Mozilla Thunderbird | Displays the Thunderbird version number, build ID, and copyright information. You can click **Credits** for a scrolling list of who worked on Thunderbird. |

# Hacking Configuration Files

Both Firefox and Thunderbird contain configuration files that can be edited. Editing these configuration files allows you some flexibility in making changes to both the program itself and its appearance. Hacking these files is relatively simple, but beware—things can sometimes go awry, so before you delve into this area, read this appendix carefully, and be aware that sometimes things might go completely haywire if, for example, you mistype a line. *Remember—you have been sufficiently warned.* Have fun, but be careful!

## Hacking about:config

Firefox and Thunderbird both contain an **about:config** file where you can make changes to your preferences by virtue of a simple right-click. I can't emphasize enough that making changes here may have grave consequences. If you don't know what you are doing, please read all the documentation before proceeding. For a good explanation of what all these **about:config** entries mean and how they function in the context of both products, go to http://kb.mozillazine.org/About:config_Entries.

Another thing to be aware of is that there may be preferences listed in **about:config** that are actually Mozilla legacy preferences, so everything in the **about:config** list may not necessarily apply to Firefox or Thunderbird (as a reminder, Firefox and Thunderbird were both built from Mozilla, so they share the same roots).

To access **about:config** in Firefox, simply type **about:config** in the URL bar.

Accessing **about:config** in Thunderbird is a little harder, but there is an extension you can install to access the settings. (You can get this extension from https://addons.update.mozilla.org/extensions/. It is discussed in Chapter 13, "Customizing the Look and Feel of Mozilla Thunderbird," in the "Configuration" section.) Again, I caution you to make sure that you know what you are doing before you make any changes to your mail client.

When the **about:config** screen launches, you can either add new preferences or edit existing preferences.

## Adding a New Preference

Type **about:config** in the URL bar of Firefox. In Thunderbird, you will need to access **about:config** by using the *AboutConfig* extension. Figure E-1 shows the **about:config** screen.

**Figure E-1**

*about:config in Firefox.*

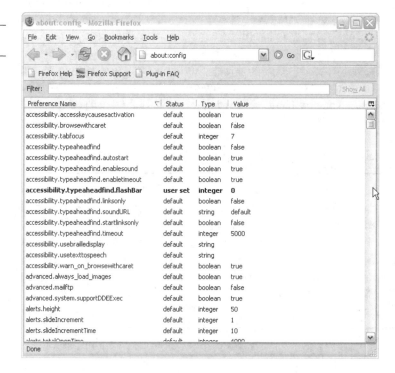

Next, right-click to expose the context menu. As shown in Figure E-2, after selecting **New**, you will need to choose the type of preference you wish to create. The choices are *String, Integer, and Boolean.* Strings are textual values, integers are numerical values, and Boolean values are either "true" or "false."

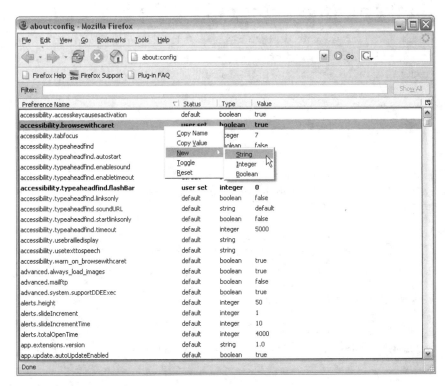

**Figure E-2**

*Creating a new string using the about:config context menu.*

After you make your selection, a dialog box should pop up, as shown in Figure E-3. Type the name of the preference in the first dialog box and the value in the second dialog box.

In most instances, you need to restart Firefox or Thunderbird for the changes to take effect.

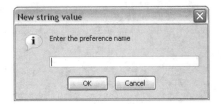

**Figure E-3**

*New string value dialog box.*

## Modifying an Existing Preference

To modify an existing preference in `about:config`, follow the same steps as listed previously, but select Modify from the context menu.

## Where to Go for Some Hacking Ideas

The best place to go to hack **about:config** and **user.js** is
http://www.mozilla.org/support/firefox/tips.

# Hacking Your user.js File

Another way to hack your configuration files is to edit them using a text editor.
For both Firefox and Thunderbird, files can be edited, all of which need to be
created first in the appropriate profile folder:

```
user.js
userChrome.css
userContent.css
```

To create these files, you need to locate your Thunderbird or Firefox Profile
Folder. Tables E-1 and E-2 show profile locations by platform for Firefox and
Thunderbird.

| Table E-1 Firefox Profile Locations by Platform | |
| --- | --- |
| Windows 2000, XP | Documents and Settings\<UserName>\ Application Data\Mozilla\Firefox\ |
| Windows NT | WINNT\Profiles\<UserName>\Application Data\Firefox\ |
| Windows 98, Me | Windows\Application Data\Mozilla\Firefox\ |
| Mac OS X | ~/Library/Mozilla/Firefox/ ~/Library/Application Support/Mozilla/Firefox/ |
| Linux and Unix systems | ~/.mozilla/firefox/ |

| Table E-2 Thunderbird Profile Locations by Platform | |
| --- | --- |
| Windows 2000, XP | Documents and Settings\<UserName>\ Application Data\Mozilla Thunderbird |
| Windows NT | WINNT\Profiles\<UserName>\Application Data\Mozilla Thunderbird |
| Windows 98, Me | Windows\Application Data\Mozilla Thunderbird |
| Mac OS X | ~/Library/Thunderbird |
| Linux and Unix systems | ~/.thunderbird |

Before doing that, you will probably want to go to the Windows Tools | Folder Options | View menu and uncheck the box that says "Hide extensions for known file types" so that it will be easier to see the `.js` extension after you name the file.

Here are the steps to follow to create these files:

1. Create a new document in the appropriate profile directory and name it `user.js`.
2. Create `userChrome.css` and `userContent.css` files by navigating to the Chrome subfolder within the Thunderbird or Firefox profile folder.

After the files have been created, you can edit and save them using your favorite text editor (Wordpad and Notepad are two possibilities if you are using Windows).

If you choose to set preferences by using `user.js` and later change your mind, there is a method that you will have to use to change these preferences back, because the changes are written to `prefs.js` (simply deleting the preferences from `user.js` won't cut it). You have to open a text editor and delete the preferences from `prefs.js`. The other (and easier) option is to edit them using `about:config`, which was explained previously.

Here is an example of a command that you could add to your `user.js` file to change the URL that the *Throbber* takes you to when you click it:

```
// Click on throbber to go to Thunderbird Help:
user_pref("messenger.throbber.url", "http://texturizer.net/thunderbird/");
```

Many more examples of this kind can be found at
http://www.mozilla.org/support/firefox/tips.

# Security, Certificates, and Validation

After dealing with so many IE security patches, I simply can't believe how solid and secure Firefox is. Firefox's default security and privacy options (described in Chapter 2, "Protecting Your Security and Privacy") will work for maybe 95–98% of all users. But if you're the kind of person who wants the maximum in program security, this appendix tells you how to set some additional security options and work with digital certificates.

*Digital certificates* (or *certificates*) are a kind of digital passport used by your browser to uniquely identify web servers. The certificate is usually issued by a *certificate authority* (CA) that is recognized as an independent and trustworthy issuing organization. VeriSign is probably the best-known CA, but there are many others.

Each certificate contains, at a minimum, the owner's name/alias, the certificate's serial number and expiration date, the name of the CA, the digital signature of the CA, and the owner's *public key*, which is a unique encryption key to which anyone can have access (rather like a phone number). The corresponding *private key* is known only to the owner of the certificate. By putting these two keys together, information exchanged by the website and the browser can be encrypted and decrypted.

**FRIDGE**

Certificate files are usually created using a type of encryption known as PKCS12, where "PKCS" is Public Key Cryptography Standards and the "12" refers to a subsection of the standard that deals with private and public key encryption in certificates. It's more than you probably needed to know about the inner workings of certificates.

# Certificates

To set certificate options, start by going to Tools | Options | Advanced and then selecting **Certficates**. The Options screen with the Certificates option is shown in Figure F-1.

**Figure F-1**

*The Options screen with the Certifi- cates option displayed.*

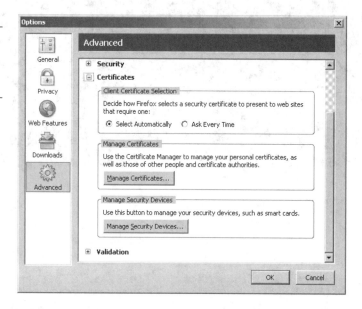

## Getting a Digital Certificate of Your Own

If you're like me and 99% of other web surfers, you won't have bothered getting any certificates of your own. Most of the certificate features described in this appendix won't work unless you've already installed a certificate on your computer that iden- tifies you.

Getting a digital certificate of your own isn't hard or expensive, and it's kinda cool. Stop in at http://www.cacert.org. They're lovely people, and you can get a number of different kinds of certificate for free. For a basic certificate, you need to provide information such as your full name, birthdate, email address, and a pass phrase. It'll take you ten minutes at the most, and you'll have a digital certificate that lets you encrypt emails and show that you're you. Voila!

You can also go to http://www.dekart.com or http://www.thawte.com for digital certificates if you like. (There's no reason you can't have one from each.)

## Client Certificate Selection

As you can see from Figure F-1, the Certificates option has several features. The first, Client Certificate Selection, allows you to specify the certificate to use. By default, when Firefox and a website create a secure connection, Firefox automatically uses the appropriate certificate to identify you, as requested by the website. However, if you check Ask Every Time, you can tell Firefox which certificate to use, which lets you set the security level or use a certificate with specific information.

## Manage Certificates

You can view stored certificates, import new ones, or back up and delete certificates using the Certificate Manager. Click **Manage Certificates** to display the Certificate Manager screen (shown in Figure F-2).

**Figure F-2**

*The Certificate Manager screen showing the Your Certificates tab.*

Firefox lists any certificates you have. You can use this screen to view certificates, back up all or selected certificates, and import or delete certificates. You can adjust the certificate display by clicking the icon at the end of the row of headings. From here, you can select which columns of information you wish to have appear.

You can view certificate information by highlighting the certificate you want to look at and clicking **View**. The Certificate Viewer (shown in Figure F-3) displays information about the selected certificate.

**FRIDGE**

Whenever you're using a secure connection—with an address starting https://—you see a lock icon in the lower-right corner of the Firefox screen. If you hover the mouse pointer over the icon, you'll see who issued the certificate. Double-clicking the lock icon lets you view information about the website's digital certificate if it's using one.

*The Certificate Viewer showing general information about a certificate.*

If you don't feel like you're getting enough information on the General tab, you can display the Details tab. You can select individual elements of the certificate and display just those details on this screen. Figure F-4 shows an example of this.

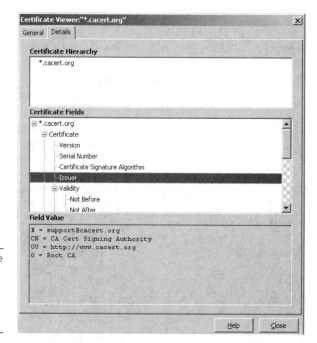

**Figure F-4**

*The Certificate Viewer showing detailed information about a certificate.*

As with any other data, it's a very good idea to back up your certificates as a precaution against disk crashes and data corruption. To back up a certificate, highlight the certificate you want to back up and click **Backup**. In the standard dialog box, enter the filename and directory to back up the certificate to and click OK. The Choose a Certificate Backup Password screen appears. Enter a password for the certificate backup—you don't want just anyone to be able to use this, after all—and then enter it again. As with the master password screen (shown in Chapter 2, Firefox rates the quality of your password on the password quality meter. An example appears in Figure F-5. After you click OK to complete the process, Firefox displays a small alert that tells you you've successfully backed up your certificates and private keys.

*The Choose a Certificate Backup Password screen.*

If you need to restore a certificate that was previously backed up or you just want to install the certificate on another computer, click **Import** and open the certificate file using a standard open dialog box. When you click OK, you need to enter the certificate's backup password. Then Firefox imports the certificate information and updates the certificate list as necessary.

Finally, you can delete a certificate by highlighting the certificate and then clicking **Delete** and confirming the deletion.

If you have specifically requested certificates from other people, they'll show up on the Other People's tab (shown in Figure F-6). As with the preceding tab, you can view, edit, import, or delete certificates from this screen as well as change the column headings that appear in the table. Chances are very good that you'll never need to use this tab.

You can also have certificates for individual websites. These appear on the Web Sites tab, shown in Figure F-7. When you're downloading information from various websites and you encounter certificates, they'll show up in this screen. You won't see any certificates in this screen at first.

**Figure F-6**

*The Certificate Manager screen showing the Other People's tab.*

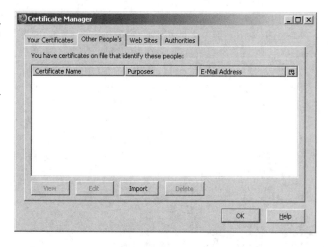

**Figure F-7**

*The Certificate Manager screen showing the Web Sites tab.*

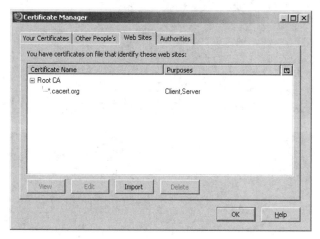

As well as the usual view, import, and delete features, you can edit the certificate's information to tell Firefox if you trust the certificate. Highlight the certificate and click Edit to display the Edit web site certificate trust settings screen, shown in Figure F-8.

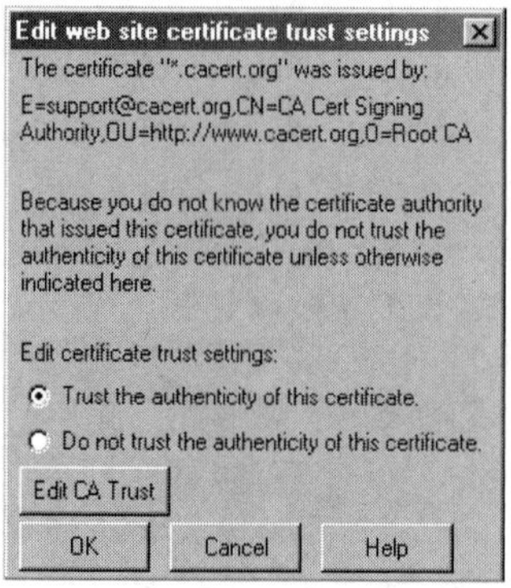

In this screen, you can tell Firefox to trust or not trust the authenticity of the certificate. If you trust the certificate, Firefox will subsequently access the website the certificate is for with no problems. If you do not trust the certificate, Firefox will display warning messages about the website the next time you visit it. If you don't trust the CA itself, you can click Edit CA Trust and edit the trust settings for the CA, as shown in a moment in Figure F-10.

**Figure F-8**

*The Edit web site certificate trust settings screen.*

The other tab on this screen that will have a lot of activity is the Authorities tab, shown in Figure F-9. The Authorities tab shows the CAs from whom you have accepted certificates. As with the other tabs, you can view, edit, import, or delete certificates and tweak the column display.

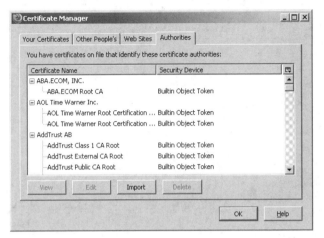

**Figure F-9**

*The Certificate Manager screen showing the Authorities tab.*

> **Caution**
>
> While you can delete a CA from this list, be really sure that you won't have a need for the information again. Once you delete a CA, Firefox won't trust any certificates issued by that CA.

You may also want to edit a certificate's trust settings to tell Firefox what you trust the CA to certify. Highlight the certificate and click Edit. The Edit CA certificate trust settings screen appears, as shown in Figure F-10. (You can also see this screen if you click **Edit CA Trust** on the Edit Website Certificate Trust Settings screen, shown earlier in Figure F-8.)

Although the default is for CAs to have authority to identify websites, mail users, and software makers, you may feel less confident about the authority and can specify that you trust the CA's certificates for websites and software makers, but not for mail users. Click OK to save any edits.

**Figure F-10**

*The Edit CA certificate trust settings screen.*

## Manage Security Devices

The final selection for the Certificates option is for managing security devices. You can have a security device to store certificates and passwords as well as to encrypt and decrypt information. Click **Manage Security Devices** to display the Device Manager, as shown in Figure F-11.

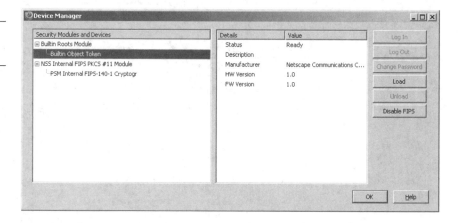

The Device Manager lets you identify *security devices*: any hardware and/or software device that stores information about you and your identity and that uses certificates and private keys to verify access. The security devices that the Device Manager can work with must also use the Public Key Cryptography Standard #11 (similar to the PKCS12 standard for certificate files). Smart cards are the most common type of security device, but there are many others for specialized applications.

### What the heck is a smart card?

A *smart card* is about the size and shape of a credit card, but the resemblance ends there. Instead of being solid plastic and having a magnetic strip, smart cards have an embedded microprocessor that's connected to a gold contact pad on one face of the card. This replaces the magnetic strip that appears on credit cards, a technology that is pretty easy to read or even modify. The microprocessor can store information such as certificates and private keys for encrypting and decrypting information.

You access the smart card through a smart card reader that's connected to your computer. Because of the certificates and private keys, the computer must provide the correct information before it can access any of the smart card's data, which makes smart cards substantially more secure than the magnetic strips on standard credit cards. Smart cards are typically used for credit cards and banking information, security and access systems, and wireless communication. They are still much more popular in Europe than they are in the U.S.

Figure F-11 shows the standard Firefox PKCS#11 module. You can think of modules as security device software drivers that tell Firefox how to interact with a security device. The NSS Internal FIPS module is a general module used for general security device data encryption and decryption and is a place for any software security device certificates.

Any security device you install will have its own software. When the device has been installed, you'll need to install the module in Firefox so that Firefox can communicate with it. Click **Load** to display the Load PCKS#11 Device screen, shown in Figure F-12.

Browse for the module file, and then click OK to install it. When the installation is complete, the module appears in the list of security devices. You can remove a module from the list by highlighting the module and clicking **Unload**.

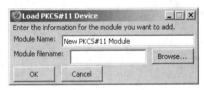

**Figure F-12**
*The Load PKCS#11 Device screen.*

To further configure the security device, you'll probably need to log in to it through the Device Manager. Highlight the module or the device and click **Log In**, and then go through the login procedure. When you're done, be sure to click **Log Out** to prevent unauthorized access to the device.

By default, the standard modules in the Device Manager are already enabled for FIPS: Federal Information Processing Standards 140-1. FIPS is a U.S. government standard for data encryption and decryption. Many, but not all, security devices use FIPS. You can enable or disable FIPS for a module by highlighting the module and clicking Enable FIPS or Disable FIPS.

# Validation

As you've seen in this appendix, certificates use public and private keys and a standardized cryptographic procedure for identification. When you access another person's details or certificate information or a secure website that presents a certificate as his or her identification, you need to be able to validate the information to make sure that the certificate is accurate, that it hasn't expired, and that the CA is one that you trust to issue such a certificate. If there are failures along the way, or if there is reason to believe that the certificate may have been compromised, you can check the CA's *Certificate Revocation List* (CRL) to see if the certificate has been revoked—"disavowed," if you like—by the CA. (This process is almost exactly like phoning a credit card company to see if the card that's being handed to you for payment is in fact authorized for use.)

The Validation options are shown in Figure F-13.

**Figure F-13**

*The Options screen showing the Validation option.*

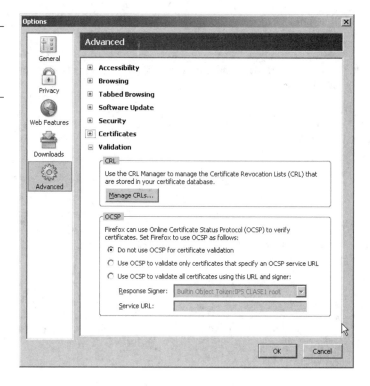

## CRL

Firefox checks CRLs automatically, you have to download and manage them yourself. Click **Manage CRLs** to display the Manage CRLs screen, shown in Figure F-14.

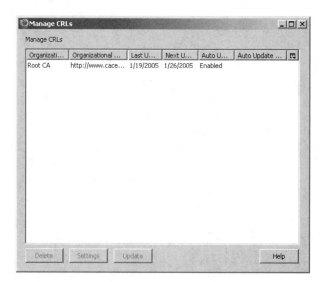

**Figure F-14**

*The Manage CRLs screen.*

Although Figure F-14 shows a CRL already loaded, when you first load Firefox, there are no CRLs in the list. You can get CRLs from the websites for the CAs. When you download a CRL, Firefox displays a CRL Import Status screen like the one shown in Figure F-15.

The CRL Import Status screen shows when the next update will be made to this CA's CRL and also allows you to tell Firefox to update the CRL automatically. When you click Yes, you see the Automatic CRL Update Preferences screen, shown in Figure F-16.

In this screen, you can tell Firefox to update the CRL automatically and when and how often to update the CRL. Click OK to save the information. You need to repeat this process to get CRLs and configure the download options for each one.

You can change a CRL's configuration by highlighting the CRL in the Manage CRLs screen and then clicking **Settings** to display the Automatic CRL Update Preferences screen. Make your changes and then click OK. To force an update, click **Update**. Firefox gets the current CRL and displays the download information on the CRL Import Status screen.

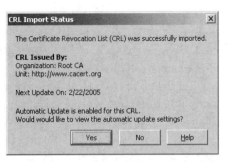

**Figure F-15**

*The CRL Import Status screen.*

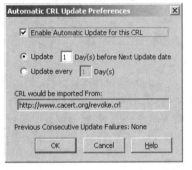

**Figure F-16**

*The Automatic CRL Update Preferences screen.*

## OCSP

Setting up CRLs can be a bit of a pest, particularly if you've got a lot of CAs in your list. You may also not have the very latest data. For example, if the next CRL is due out on Friday but a certificate is revoked on Tuesday, you may want a way to check the certificate directly against the latest information for the tightest validation security. OCSP (Online Certificate Status Protocol) lets you check a certificate's validity *each time* Firefox uses or views the certificate. Instead of checking against a downloaded CRL list, Firefox checks against the CRL list maintained at the CA's website.

The default option is not to use OCSP. The Certificate Manager checks certificates to make sure that they haven't expired and that the issuing CA is recognized by Firefox and is trusted to issue that kind of certificate. If you select **Use OCSP to validate only certificates that specify an OCSP service URL,**

Firefox checks a certificate's validity only if the certificate contains a URL for verification. Firefox again verifies that the certificate hasn't expired and that the CA is trusted to issue this kind of certificate, but it also uses the URL to see if the certificate is listed there as valid.

For the tightest validation, select **Use OCSP to validate all certificates using this URL and signer**. Firefox verifies each certificate online every time. From the dropdown list for Response Signer, choose the appropriate certificate for OCSP. A corresponding URL generally appears in Service URL; if not, you need to enter the URL yourself. This OCSP setting is fairly restrictive: a certificate is validated only if it is recognized with an appropriate OCSP response signed by the Response Signer certificate or by a certificate that chains to it in some way.

---

Digital certicates are a fascinating subject worth exploring if you're interested in security on the Internet. The best place to start is by reading some of the references available at http://www.cacert.org, http://www.dekart.com, and http://www.thawte.com. You can also experiment with different levels of digital certificates to see what effect they have. But if you prefer not to bother with all this, you can always leave things up to Firefox, and you'll be okay.

# Glossary

**about:config**   A file containing a variety of options and variables used by Firefox and Thunderbird when the programs are run. Many of these options are not available except through this file.

**ActiveX**   A powerful technology that is frequently used to exploit security holes in Internet Explorer.

**advanced operator**   A Google word and phrase that lets you refine your search to page titles, URLs, or other criteria.

**adware**   Spyware that can gather information about your system, trigger popup ads, or demonstrate other obnoxious behavior.

**banner ad**   A long, thin graphic, usually at the top of a website, that advertises something, usually another website.

**Bayesian filtering**   A filtering system for trimming the junk mail from your inbox.

**blog**   Short for weB LOG. A blog is an online diary or journal.

**bookmark**   A shortcut to a specific website saved for future reference.

**Bookmarks Manager**   A feature in Firefox that lets you sort, organize, and manipulate your bookmarks.

**bookmarklet**   A small, single-purpose JavaScript program that can be saved like a bookmark. When you click the bookmarklet, it does some small thing, such as centering the current window, hiding the background, or changing the font size.

**Bookmarks toolbar**   A Firefox toolbar that you can add your own bookmarks to for quick access.

**Bugzilla**   The Mozilla project's open bug database, https://bugzilla.mozilla.org.

**cache**   The collection of files, cookies, downloaded web pages, pictures, and other information that is saved on your hard disk to make displaying web pages you've already visited faster.

**certificate authority**   An organization recognized as independent and trustworthy that issues digital certificates.

**chrome**   The parts of the application that surround the content window, such as toolbars, borders, status bars, menus, and so on.

**cookie**   Information saved about you and how you used a website.

**CRL**   Short for Certificate Revocation List. Certificate authorities maintain a CRL for cross-checking certificates against.

**CSS**   Short for Cascading Style Sheet. A cascading style sheet describes how a web page or document is displayed or printed.

**data miner**   Spyware that gathers data about you and your browsing habits with the intention of transmitting this to spammers and marketers so you can be targeted for ads.

**digital certificate**   A kind of digital passport used to uniquely identify web servers and email users. Also known as certificate.

**digital signature**   A technique that lets you "sign" your email with an encrypted key to identify that the email is from you.

**extension**   A mini-program that adds extra features or capabilities to Firefox or Thunderbird.

**favicon**   An icon that appears next to bookmarks in the bookmark list.

**filter**   A set of criteria used to sort email and perform various actions, such as saving email to folders, labeling messages, and so on. Filters are stored in the `msgFilterRules.dat` file.

**FIPS**   Short for Federal Information Processing Standards 140-1. FIPS is a U.S. Government standard for data encryption and decryption.

**Gecko**   The core rendering technology used in the Mozilla suite and Firefox.

**Global Inbox**   An inbox in Thunderbird that you can filter multiple POP accounts into. This is particularly useful if you receive email from several different email accounts but want to handle it all together.

**history**   A record of the web pages you've visited.

**HTML**   Short for HyperText Markup Language. HTML is the language used to code web pages.

**identity**   An identity in Thunderbird is a collection of settings for an individual email account so that you can have a different address in the "From" field. It can be used in conjunction with the Global Inbox to quickly process a large amount of mail without extensive filtering.

**IMAP**   Short for Internet Message Access Protocol. IMAP is a protocol for sending and receiving email. IMAP is most commonly used for corporate email accounts.

**IRC**   Short for Internet Relay Chat. IRC is an Internet-based chat room technology. Individual IRC chat rooms are known as channels. To access IRC, you need an IRC client program. Several extensions for Firefox offer IRC capabilities.

**Jar**   An archive of Java files.

**Java**   A programming language developer for web programming by James Gosling of Sun Microsystems.

**Java applet**   A Java program that is downloaded and run in a web browser.

**JavaScript**   A simple, effective scripting language created by Brendan Eich while he was at Netscape.

**JavaScript Console**   A reporting tool that appears when there are errors with the application's chrome.

**junk mail**   Generally the same as spam, but can also include email from things you've signed up for and haven't gotten around to deleting, professional bulletins you're not interested in at the moment, and so on.

**keystroke logger**   Spyware that logs every keystroke you enter on the computer for transmission to someone. Keystroke loggers are very dangerous!

**live bookmark**   A type of bookmark that updates to reflect changes on the website.

**master password**   The password for the Password Manager that locks and unlocks access to all the other passwords. Master passwords can also protect external hardware devices attached to your computer.

**MIME**   Short for Multipurpose Internet Mail Extensions. MIME is an open standard for sending binary files, such as word processing documents, photos, sound files, video files, and programs, as attachments to email messages.

**Mozilla project**   A project started in 1998 by Netscape to engage a volunteer engineering development community to help Netscape with continued development of the Netscape browser.

**navigation toolbar**   The Firefox toolbar containing the basic navigation icons, the location field (also known as the address field), and the Google search bar.

**newsgroup**   A group of related messages (also known as *posts* or *articles*) on a topic that can be posted and read using a newsreader or a program that offers newsreader capabilities (such as Thunderbird). There are thousands of different newsgroups, each with its own focus.

**OCSP**   Short for Online Certificate Status Protocol. A protocol for checking a digital certificate directly with the certificate authority rather than on a certificate revocation list.

**open source**   Products for which the source code is available for the user to examine and modify.

**phishing**   A bait-and-switch technique using bogus emails that try to get people to enter sensitive information on a website under the illusion that they're solving some kind of account problem.

**PKCS**   Short for Public Key Cryptography Standards. PKCS12 defines public and private key encryption standards for digital certificates.

**plug-in**   Software that adds a specific set of features or capabilities to Firefox or Thunderbird. Plug-ins usually enable the program to open and process a new type of file and are usually from larger software companies.

**POP**   Short for Post Office Protocol. POP is a protocol for sending and receiving email. POP is most commonly used for individual email accounts.

**popup**   A new browser window that appears, usually unrequested and usually with the intention of advertising something.

**private key**   A unique encryption key known only to the owner of the certificate.

**public key**   A unique encryption key that anyone can have access to (rather like a phone number).

**registry cleaner**   A program for Windows systems that remove extraneous entries from the Windows registry.

**RSS**   Originally short for Rich Site Summary but now more commonly used as Really Simple Syndication. (It's a distinction without a difference.)

**saved search**   In Thunderbird, a set of search criteria that you can save and use again later.

**search hijacker**   A spyware program that changes your browser's home page to something you didn't plan on.

**smart card**   A credit-card-sized device that contains a microprocessor and can be used for security access, personal information storage, and the like.

**Smart Keywords**   A feature in Firefox that lets you enter a single keyword in the address field followed by a search word or phrase to access the search engine on a specific website.

**S/MIME**   Short for Secure Multipurpose Internet Mail Extensions. S/MIME is an open standard for authenticating senders and encrypted messages.

**SMTP**   Short for Simple Mail Transfer Protocol. SMTP is used to transfer email for most email accounts.

**spam**   Unwanted email from lowlife advertisers. Not to be confused with Spam, the dandy luncheon meat from Hormel.

**spyware**   Any of a wide variety of programs installed on your system—usually without your knowledge or permission—that can monitor your actions, transmit data back to people without your knowledge, or display ads.

**SSL**   Short for Secure Sockets Layer. SSL is a standardized protocol for sending and receiving encrypted information over the Internet.

**tab**   A separate window you can open in the same instance of Firefox.

**theme**   A package of customized look-and-feel options for Firefox or Thunderbird. You can use themes to change colors, fonts, icon graphics, layouts, and many other things.

**Throbber**   In Firefox and Thunderbird, a small activity indicator in the upper-right portion of the screen.

**TLS**   Short for Transport Layer Security. TLS is an open security protocol for sending and receiving encrypted information over the Internet.

**Trojan horse**   A program that appears to be innocuous but that causes damage to your system when you run it.

**UMO**   Short for update.mozilla.org, the location for Firefox and Thunderbird extensions, themes, and plug-ins.

**URL**   Short for Uniform Resource Locator, more commonly known as a web address.

**USB**   Short for Universal Serial Bus. USB ports are common on most computers these days. They provide a common interface for many pluggable hardware devices.

**validation**   Verifying that a digital certificate is still valid by querying the certificate authority.

**virus**   Programs or scripts that get into your computer, replicate, propagate, and cause damage.

**whitelist**   A user-defined list of websites that identifies which websites can be accessed.

**worm**   A program that replicates independently over a network without any human intervention.

**XML**   Short for eXtensible Markup Language. XML is used to exchange structured data (such as news feeds).

**XML feed**   A type of information feed that can be used to create live bookmarks.

**XPI**   Short for Cross-Platform Installable file format. This format is used to install extensions and other add-on programs to Firefox.

**XUL**   Short for eXtensible User interface Language. Pronounced "zool."

# INDEX

# F

# X

# Y

# Z

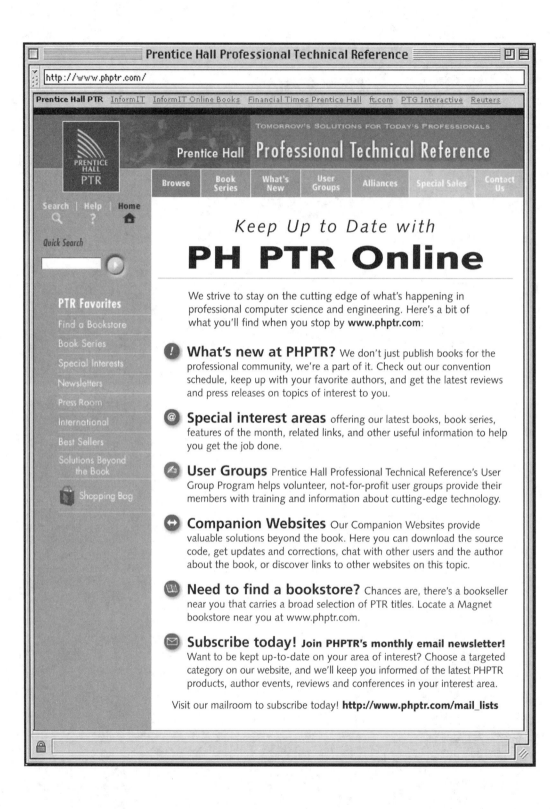

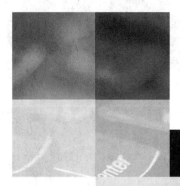